SMARTER BALANCED

GRADE 5

By Taran Escobar-Ausman and Jennifer G.H. Wang, M.A.

About the Authors

Taran Escobar-Ausman is an educator who has six years of experience working with fourth-grade and fifth-grade students in the San Francisco Bay Area. He earned his undergraduate degree in Comparative Religious Studies at Humboldt State University and his multiple-subject credential from San Jose State University. His current focus is bringing a variety of experiences, utilizing PBL and STEAM, into the classroom where students interact with real-world problems while integrating the Common Core Standards. He serves as the Technology Lead for his school and advises educators on the best practices for integrating technology into their curriculum. You can interact with him on Twitter: @taranEDU

Jennifer G.H. Wang, M.A. is an educator who has twelve years of experience working with students from preschool age through eighth grade. Currently, she teaches fifth grade in San Jose, California. She earned her graduate degree in Curriculum and Instruction from San Jose State University and her undergraduate degree in History from the University of Hawaii. She has a passion for combining literacy and writing with inquiry-based activities that engage students in a range of skills. She utilizes a variety of pedagogical methods, including PBL, STEAM integration, Makerspaces, and technology, to inspire her students to be lifelong learners and creators. You can interact with her at: laughingfriends.net/blogpage

Acknowledgments

I would like to express my gratitude and appreciation to my amazing wife for following and supporting my trail of creative endeavors. She is my rock, and I could not do it without her. I extend a big thank you to my two boys for giving Daddy work time and wrestling matches in between for brain breaks. Thank you to my parents and friends for their continued support.

—Taran Escobar-Ausman

A deep gratitude goes to my Mom, Dad, Liz, and Betty for their support, guidance, and encouragement. I thank all my family and friends for their continued support throughout the years. Hugs and kisses go to my niece, Evelyn, for making me laugh and smile after a long day!

—Jennifer G.H. Wang

The Smarter Balanced screenshots, on pages 8, 9, 10, and 68, as well as the Smarter Balanced Performance Task Scoring Rubrics on pages 321–334, are reprinted with permission courtesy of The Regents of the University of California. The publishing of this information does not represent an endorsement of products offered or solicited by Barron's Educational Series, Inc.

Date of Manufacture: October 2016
Manufactured by: B11R11

Printed in the United States of America
9 8 7 6 5 4 3 2 1

All inquiries should be addressed to:
Barron's Educational Series, Inc.
250 Wireless Boulevard
Hauppauge, NY 11788
www.barronseduc.com

ISBN: 978-1-4380-0924-7
Library of Congress Control Number: 2016945095

10%
POST-CONSUMER WASTE
Paper contains a minimum of 10% post-consumer waste (PCW). Paper used in this book was derived from certified, sustainable forestlands.

Contents

PART ONE: ENGLISH LANGUAGE ARTS

PART TWO: MATH

Chapter 8
Number and Operations—Fractions and Decimals   193

Chapter 9
Operations and Algebraic Thinking   209

Chapter 10
Geometry and Graphing　　　　　　　　　　　239

Chapter 11
Measurement and Data　　　　　　　　　　　249

Introduction

Overview for Students

At the end of your fifth-grade year, you will have to take an important test. This test is referred to as the SBAC, which stands for the Smarter Balanced Assessment Consortium. The purpose of the test is to assess what you learned during your fifth-grade year. All the skills you practiced in your class will now be applied to this test.

The SBAC will test both English Language Arts (ELA) and Mathematics. Both the ELA and Math portions of the test will have two parts: a **Computer Adaptive Test** (CAT) and a **Performance Task**. That is a total of four different parts for the SBAC. This may seem overwhelming, but each of these parts will be tested at different times during your school's testing window. The test is set up this way on purpose so that you are able to focus on smaller sections of the test in order to do your best. Table I-1 presents a sample schedule of what a testing week could look like.

Table I-1. Sample Schedule

Monday	Tuesday	Wednesday	Thursday	Friday
ELA: Computer Adaptive Test	Math: Computer Adaptive Test	ELA: Pre-Performance Task Activity	ELA: Performance Task Math: Pre-Performance Task Activity	Math: Performance Task

For each part of the test you take, you will be given an amount of time for the session based on your school's bell and testing schedule. This could be, for example, an hour and a half or a full two hours. No matter the amount of time set aside for each testing session, you are allowed as much time as you need to finish that portion of the test. If you do need more time, there should be some system in place to allow you to continue the test in a quiet area.

The length of both the ELA and Math CAT portions of the test will range anywhere from 30 to 45 questions, or tasks. The amount will change, however, based on the student taking the test. Because the test adapts to the test taker, the number of actual problems each student answers can change.

Let's look at each part of the SBAC and what you will be responsible for.

Computer Adaptive Test Expectations

Why is it called the Computer Adaptive Test? This is because the test has been programmed to change the difficulty of the tasks depending upon the answers given for previous questions. For example, if a student answers a question incorrectly, the test will change the next question to a level that the student could possibly answer correctly. This is not done for the purpose of making the test harder or easier, but it is instead done to assess students at their optimum level within their grade level.

In English Language Arts, you will be expected to

- read and comprehend fiction and nonfiction passages
- answer multiple-choice questions
- respond to multiple-part tasks that require both selective answering and short, written responses
- focus on providing evidence for your answers and responses
- respond to technology-enhanced tasks

In Mathematics, you will be expected to

- answer multiple-choice, basic computation problems
- use technology-enhanced methods to answer math problems
- respond to multiple-part tasks that require both selective answering and short, written responses
- provide short, written responses that explain your answers

Performance Task Expectations

Pre-Performance Task Class Activity

Before you take the Performance Task for both the ELA and Math portions of the test, your teacher will present an activity the day before. The purpose of this activity is to give you background information for the Performance Task the next day. Make sure you are present that day, and pay attention! The information presented by your teacher can be used in your responses on the Performance Task during the following test session.

Performance Task

A Performance Task is a series of complex questions focused on a common topic or theme. These tasks will assess your critical thinking skills as you apply your learning to problems that mirror the real world.

The Performance Task is organized so that the set of questions, or tasks, gradually get more complex. It is important to keep in mind that you can receive partial points for a particular task. For instance, in the Math Performance Task, you could be asked to (1) create an expression for a word problem, (2) solve it, and, finally, (3) explain, in your own words, how you found the rule or expression. Let's say you get the expression incorrect but were able to show your work correctly and explain your reasoning. In that case, you would get 0 points for the answer, but you would still receive points for the last two parts. Examples and more details of this will be given in the ELA and Math Performance Task chapters (Chapters 4 and 12) of this book.

Let's look at what you will be responsible for during the Performance Tasks for both English Language Arts and Mathematics.

English Language Arts

On the English Language Arts Performance Task, you will

- read and comprehend different fiction or nonfiction passages of various lengths
- research by taking notes and/or highlighting
- write an informative essay combining evidence from multiple sources
- respond to multiple-part tasks with technology-enhanced elements

Mathematics

On the Mathematics Performance Task, you will

- respond to different tasks about the same real-world problem
- apply your math skills from different areas of the curriculum to solve increasingly complex problems
- explain your thinking and be able to prove your claims using mathematical vocabulary
- respond to multiple-part tasks with technology-enhanced elements

Technology Expectations

You will notice that all sections of the test are taken on a computer. Make sure to give yourself time to practice your typing skills. This will allow you to use more of your brainpower on the content of the test rather than worry about your typing skills during the test. If you do not have access to typing programs at school, there are many online programs you can search from home.

You should also get used to working with either a trackpad on a laptop computer or a mouse. Your school should make accommodations for what works best for you. Ask your teacher about what device you will be using if you are unsure.

The main goal of the SBAC is to test you on the skills laid out in the Common Core Standards. This book is designed to guide you through these skills with strategies and practice tasks that mirror the SBAC. Each chapter will feature an overview of the skills tested, examples of the type of tasks the SBAC may ask you, and independent practice tests. You should be well prepared for the test after practicing with this guide!

Overview for Parents and Teachers

The SBAC, or Smarter Balanced Assessment Consortium, is a formative assessment given in the spring of the school year and aims to measure not only student learning but also students' critical thinking skills developed during the school year. The Common Core Standards are the guide for how the SBAC is organized and assessed. The standards also bring instructional shifts to the classroom in order to prepare students for 21st-century learning. These shifts, as outlined in Table I-2, are important to understand as they help build how the SBAC is written.

Table I-2. ELA and Math Shifts

ELA Shifts	Math Shifts
1. Focus on Informational Text Students spend more time building knowledge with content-rich nonfiction.	**1. Deeper Focus** Students dive deeper into math concepts to build a stronger understanding of underlying mathematical concepts and patterns.
2. Using Textual Evidence Students show their analytical skills and support their ideas with direct and indirect evidence from the text.	**2. Coherence** Students see math concepts linked across grade levels in a structured way for students to build upon previous learning.
3. Complexity of Texts Students develop their reading comprehension with increasing complexity of texts in preparation for high school and college level readiness.	**3. More Rigor** With teacher guidance, students strive to achieve three areas in mathematical proficiency: procedural skills and fluency, conceptual understanding, and application.

What Does This Mean for How Your Child Learns and Is Assessed?

In ELA, students should focus on reading texts and being able to use evidence from the text to support their claims. Students should get in the habit of reading texts multiple times while highlighting evidence and taking notes by annotating. Whether they are answering a short-answer question or writing an informative essay, students should be able to refer back to the text and support their statements with evidence. On the SBAC, particularly on the Performance Task, partial credit will be given to those responses that correctly integrate textual evidence, even if the statement or claim made is untrue. A good rule of thumb for students is to always support their ideas with strong evidence and evidence written in their own words.

For the ELA portions of the test, this means that your child needs to practice reading and writing for different purposes. Have your child read a variety of texts with an emphasis on informative texts. When writing their responses, students should pay attention to the structure and organization of their responses and make sure that they have provided evidence to back up their responses. In fifth grade, students are assessed on three writing areas: **informative**, **opinion**, and **narrative**. Table I-3 outlines the writing skills for each of these three areas.

Table I-3. ELA Writing Areas—Informative, Opinion, and Narrative

Informative	Opinion	Narrative
> Introduce the topic and purpose of the essay clearly.	> Introduce the topic or issue with a clear purpose for the essay.	> Establish a situation with characters and a setting.
> Provide a clear and appropriate thesis statement that includes the main idea.	> Provide a thesis statement that clearly states an opinion with reasons.	> Use a variety of techniques that include dialogue and descriptions.
> Identify key ideas and develop the topic with concrete details and facts.	> Provide logical reasons for your opinion that can be supported with concrete details or examples.	> Use transitional words and phrases to show the sequence of events.
> Support claims and statements with appropriate evidence from the text.	> Support your opinions with textual evidence.	> Provide a logical and appropriate ending that follows the sequence of events.
> Include a conclusion that restates the thesis statement.	> Include a conclusion that restates the thesis statement.	

In Math, the shifts emphasize more conceptual thinking, which requires the student to write about math. Students will spend more time focusing on one math concept in order to identify various patterns that can be applied to other situations. The SBAC will focus on three areas to assess mathematical proficiency: **skills**, **conceptual understanding**, and **application**. It is no longer sufficient to merely know the right answer to a math problem. Students will now need to know how and why a mathematical concept works in addition to being able to explain, in words, how to prove it. Table I-4 outlines the expectations in these three areas.

Table I-4. Math Areas of Proficiency—Skills, Conceptual Understanding, and Application

Skills	Conceptual Understanding	Application
› Students develop speed and accuracy with simple calculations. › Memorization and repetition support students' ability to complete more complex problems.	› Students develop their ability to explain how they got an answer. › Students manipulate numbers to solve a problem in more ways than one. › Students demonstrate that they can apply mathematical concepts to different scenarios.	› Students are able to identify the appropriate math concepts that should be applied to real-world problems. › Students can recognize that real-world problems can be solved in more ways than one.

The main goal for this study guide is to help fifth-grade students become accustomed to the structure and format of the SBAC exam. It will provide strategies for mastering these new instructional shifts as they are assessed on the SBAC. In addition, students will become familiar with the Common Core Standards being tested, and they will learn strategies for successfully showing proficiency in their grade-level standards. This study guide is written to address each fifth-grade standard for both English Language Arts and Mathematics as they would be tested on the actual SBAC exam.

Task Types

The SBAC was designed as an assessment tool that tests not only the student's ability to recall facts and provide correct responses but also the student's critical thinking skills. Five different types of tasks were created to assess student learning. Students should become familiar with each type of task to be successful on the test.

1. Selected-Response Tasks

Selected-response tasks are the most familiar type of question, more commonly referred to as a multiple-choice question. They consist of a short passage or text, known as a stimulus, followed by a stem, which is a statement or question that the student responds to by selecting a correct answer. This type of task is primarily used to test the student's recall of facts, comprehension, and instructional learning for the tested grade level. A selected-response task can have just one answer, in which a circle precedes all of the answer choices, and students select only one answer. This type of task can also have multiple correct responses, in which square boxes precede all of the answer choices, and students click on more than one answer. Note that if a student selects one wrong square box on a multiple-response question, he or she will receive zero points for the whole question. Figure I-1 shows an example of what a selected-response task with multiple answers would look like.

Select two fractions that can be rewritten with a denominator of 24.

☐ $\frac{1}{6}$

☐ $\frac{1}{5}$

☐ $\frac{5}{7}$

☐ $\frac{9}{10}$

☐ $\frac{1}{9}$

☐ $\frac{7}{8}$

Figure I-1. Example of a selected-response task with multiple answers

2. Constructed-Response Tasks

A constructed-response task aims to test specific claims and standards of greater complexity by requiring students to write short responses instead of selecting from a list of suggested answers. Constructed-response tasks require more analytical thinking and reasoning. Students need to show their thinking, while using key vocabulary, when responding to these tasks. For the ELA constructed-response tasks, it is important for students to always use evidence from the text when responding to questions related to a passage. Figure I-2 shows an example of an ELA constructed-response task.

> What conclusion can be drawn about the author's point of view about litter? Support your answer with details from the text.

Figure I-2. Example of an ELA constructed-response task

3. Extended Constructed-Response Tasks

An extended constructed-response task is the same as a constructed-response task, except that there is a second part of the task that requires students to refer to their first answer in order to successfully answer both questions. Figure I-3 provides an example of a Math extended constructed-response task.

Ms. McCrary wants to make a rabbit pen in a section of her lawn. Her plan for the rabbit pen includes the following:
- It will be in the shape of a rectangle.
- It will take 24 feet of fence material to make.
- Each side will be longer than 1 foot.
- The length and width will measure whole feet.

Part A
Draw 3 different rectangles that can each represent Ms. McCrary's rabbit pen. Be sure to use all 24 feet of fence material for each pen.

Use the grid below. Click the places where you want the corners of your rectangle to be. Draw one rectangle at a time. If you make a mistake, click on your rectangle to delete it. Continue as many times as necessary.

Key
☐ = 1 square foot

Use your keyboard to type the length and width of each rabbit pen you draw. Then type the area of each rabbit pen. Be sure to select the correct unit for each answer.

[Students will input length, width, and area for each rabbit pen. Students will choose unit from drop down menu.]

Pen 1:
Length: ____ (feet, square feet)
Width: ____ (feet, square feet)
Area: ____ (feet, square feet)

Pen 2:
Length: ____ (feet, square feet)
Width: ____ (feet, square feet)
Area: ____ (feet, square feet)

Pen 3:
Length: ____ (feet, square feet)
Width: ____ (feet, square feet)
Area: ____ (feet, square feet)

Part B
Ms. McCrary wants her rabbit to have more than 60 square feet of ground area inside the pen. She finds that if she uses the side of her house as one of the sides of the rabbit pen, she can make the rabbit pen larger.

- Draw another rectangular rabbit pen.
- Use all 24 feet of fencing for 3 sides of the pen.
- Use one side of the house for the other side of the pen.
- Make sure the ground area inside the pen is greater than 60 square feet.

Use the grid below. Click the places where you want the corners of your rectangle to be. If you make a mistake, click on your rectangle to delete it.

Key
☐ = 1 square foot

Use your keyboard to type the length and width of each rabbit pen you draw. Then type the area of each rabbit pen. Be sure to select the correct unit for each answer.

Length: ____ (feet, square feet)
Width: ____ (feet, square feet)
Area: ____ (feet, square feet)

Figure I-3. Example of a two-part math extended constructed-response task

4. Technology-Enhanced Response Tasks

Technology-enhanced items require students to interact with the test in a non-traditional way. Rather than select or type, students may be asked to **drag**, **select**, **highlight**, **input**, or **draw** (Connect Line Tool). "Enhanced" also refers to the use of different ways of delivering information connected to the question, which can include videos, animation, or sound recordings. These items can stand alone or be part of the Performance Task. The tasks will instruct the student on how to answer the question. The teacher, or test administrator, however, will go over how to use these tools prior to the test. Figure I-4 shows an example of a technology-enhanced response task that requires the student to drag the correct answers to an answer space.

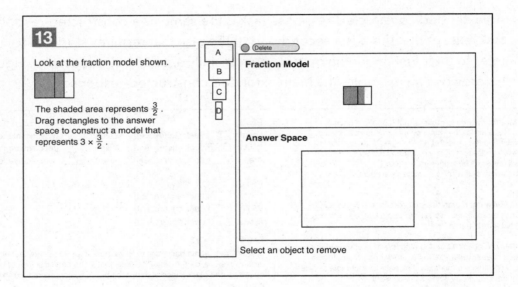

Figure I-4. Example of a technology-enhanced response task

5. Performance Tasks

The Performance Task uses all of the aforementioned types of responses to measure more complex thinking. In addition, the ELA Performance Task will require more writing and typing since students will be asked to type an essay. More space will be provided to accommodate the essay writing.

Scoring

Each question and task on the SBAC is given a score. The total possible score for each question depends on the task. Most questions are worth 1 point, especially any selected-response (multiple-choice) tasks. When a task is technology-enhanced with a single possible answer, it is still worth 1 point.

Constructed-response tasks, however, depend on a tiered point system based on certain criteria for that question. For instance, the question may ask you to write a short answer stating your opinion. The scoring may look something like this:

2 points

The response

- states an opinion that reflects the text as a whole
- provides information to put the opinion in context
- supports the opinion with adequate evidence and/or relatable facts

1 point

The response

- provides a partial or limited opinion
- provides an opinion that partially reflects the body of writing as a whole
- may provide limited evidence and/or relatable facts to put the opinion in context
- may just list supporting reasons—formulaic

0 points

The response

- provides no opinion or provides an opinion that is not appropriate based on the text
- provides irrelevant information or no information to put the opinion into context

In Math, there may be a two-part task, with one part being computation and the other part asking for an explanation in your own words. In this case, the Math portion of the task would be scored 1 point if correct, and the writing portion would be scored according to a tiered point system (0–2) such as that shown in the example above.

Each Performance Task will have its own scoring system based on the content. For ELA, a writing rubric is used to score each student's writing based on a 0–4 score range. (These rubrics are provided in Appendix A.)

On the Math Performance Task, it is important to remember that you can receive partial credit for showing certain skills. For instance, you may have provided the wrong answer but showed the correct way to set up the problem. You would get 1 point for showing the correct equation.

How the SBAC Is Formatted

The SBAC is formatted in a couple of different ways. A selected-response task with a short question or a math problem will be presented by itself on the screen. When there is a text passage with multiple tasks afterwards, both the passage and the tasks will be presented on the same screen. Students will be presented with two columns that are scrollable. The left side of the screen will be the text passage, and the right side will be the tasks that respond to the passage. This is beneficial in three ways. First, the exam was designed this way so that students could refer back to the passage with ease. Second, the split screen makes it easier to preview the questions and tasks before looking for evidence in the passage. Finally, this makes many test-taking strategies, as outlined in this test prep guide, easier to use.

How to Use This Test Prep Guide

This test prep guide is organized to prepare you for taking the SBAC. It takes into account both the demands of the SBAC format and expectations as well as the expectations of the Common Core Standards. Since the SBAC is designed to test your proficiency in the Common Core Standards, both the ELA and Math sections of this book list the standards that chapter focuses on as well as key strategies to meet the SBAC expectations. The types of tasks and prompts have been designed to mirror the vocabulary and format of the actual exam.

Learning and Applying Academic Vocabulary

One of the biggest hurdles that students face when taking the SBAC is understanding what the exam is asking them to do. All too often, students respond to a question or task incorrectly because they did not understand the question. Instead, they just guess what the test is asking of them rather than trying to determine the true meaning of the question. The key to overcoming this hurdle is

understanding the vocabulary used on the SBAC so that you can become
aware of what the test is asking of you.

Pay attention to the academic vocabulary used on the SBAC since it wi
a clue as to what the question is asking of you. For example, rather than asking,
"What is the central idea of the passage?" the question may ask you to "**Determine**
the central idea of the passage and provide details to support your answer."

In the Math section of this study guide, each chapter will include the academic
vocabulary used for that particular skill set. For the ELA section of this book, refer
to Table I-5 below for the most common academic vocabulary words used on the
Grade 5 Smarter Balanced test. Make sure to review these words and/or refer back
to them so you fully understand how to respond to them and how to use them in
your writing.

Table I-5. Common Academic Vocabulary Used
on the Grade 5 Smarter Balanced Test

Word	Definition
Analyze	to examine the problem carefully in detail
Apply	to put to use, especially for a particular purpose
Categorize	to describe by labeling or giving a name to and/or to arrange in categories or classes; to classify
Compose	to make or form by combining things, parts, or elements
Construct	to build or form by putting together parts; to frame; to devise
Demonstrate	to make evident or establish by arguments or reasoning; to prove
Describe	to tell or depict in written words or spoken words; to give an account of
Determine	to conclude or decide after reasoning or observation
Discuss	to consider or examine by argument, comment, etc.; to talk over or write about, especially to explore solutions; to debate
Evaluate	ELA: to give evidence on both sides of an issue; to draw conclusions from this evidence; to make a judgment about the topic in question; Math: to solve

Table I-5. Common Academic Vocabulary Used
on the Grade 5 Smarter Balanced Test (*continued*)

Word	Definition
Examine	to inspect carefully; to explore or study
Explain	to make clear and known in detail
Identify	to give the characteristics by which a thing is recognizable or known
Infer (inference)	to hint or guess, imply by reasoning; suggest
Interpret	to explain the meaning, such as interpreting a dream; to bring out the meaning of a dramatic work, a character, or a musical composition
Justify	to show a satisfactory reason or excuse for something done; to defend
Specify	to name or state as a condition

Helpful Hints

Throughout the chapters in this book, you will see Helpful Hint boxes that will give you important reminders along the way. Here are some examples:

Helpful Hint	On the SBAC, questions or problems are referred to as tasks. Not all the problems on the SBAC are presented as questions to be answered. They will present various tasks for you to complete instead.

or

Helpful Hint	Some tasks have more than one answer. Tasks with more than one answer are marked with squares next to each selection. Tasks with just one answer have circles next to each selection.

Practice Tests

This book is divided into two parts, English Language Arts and Math, and each part concludes with its own practice test. The practice tests will mirror the types of questions and tasks that students will encounter on the actual SBAC. At the conclusion of each practice test, students will find the answers explained for both the practice questions throughout that half of the book as well as the answers for that part's practice test.

PART ONE
English Language Arts

Selected-Response Tasks (Multiple-Choice)

CHAPTER 1

Overview

On the SBAC test, you will be required to answer what the SBAC calls selected-response tasks. These are what you know as multiple-choice questions. Selected-response tasks can include questions that have only one correct answer, questions that can have multiple correct answers, and technology-enhanced tasks, which include an interactive selection format. These questions cover content comprehension, author's purpose, grammar skills, and vocabulary development. You will find these questions in both the Computer Adaptive Test section and the Performance Task section of the test.

In this chapter, you will be guided through and practice the various forms of selected-response tasks. First, let's review some test-taking strategies that will help you be successful with all types of selected-response tasks.

Applying Your Strategies

Strategy 1: Always Refer Back to the Text

This is one of the most important strategies to remember. All too often students want to hurry up and finish the test without taking the time to correctly answer simple comprehension questions.

What to do: Slow down, take your time reading the question carefully, and go back and reread the passage to verify your own thinking. You can often answer your own questions from reading the text a second time.

Strategy 2: Match Key Words/Vocabulary and Ideas

Many times, the same vocabulary or ideas used in certain sentences of the text are repeated in the question and/or possible answer choices. This is especially helpful when answering questions about vocabulary meaning, inferences, and text evidence.

What to do: Choose the main vocabulary words and/or the central idea in the question. Go back to the passage, and scan the text for matching vocabulary and ideas. This will point you in the right direction to confirm your answer.

Strategy 3: Use the Process of Elimination

Sometimes it is easier for your mind to narrow down your options and make sense of fewer possibilities. You can do that by eliminating, or getting rid of, those possible answers that you are sure cannot be the correct answer.

What to do: If the incorrect answer is obvious, eliminate it. Once you narrow down your choices to at least two possibilities, you can use another strategy to make the correct choice.

Practice Exercises

Exercise 1

Common Core Standard RL.5.1
Quote accurately from a text when explaining what the text says explicitly and when drawing inferences from the text.

Common Core Standard RL.5.2
Determine a theme of a story, drama, or poem from details in the text, including how characters in a story or drama respond to challenges or how the speaker in a poem reflects upon a topic; summarize the text.

Common Core Standard L.5.4
Determine or clarify the meaning of unknown and multiple-meaning words and phrases based on grade 5 reading and content, choosing flexibly from a range of strategies.

Common Core Standard RI.5.1
Quote accurately from a text when explaining what the text says explicitly and when drawing inferences from the text.

> Note that, on the actual exam, the format for longer text passages and questions will be different. The text passages, and the questions that accompany them, will be placed in a side-by-side scrollable format. This side-by-side format will allow you to easily refer back to the passage for textual evidence.

Directions: Read the text. Then answer questions 1–3.

The Grasshopper and the Ant

All summer long the Grasshopper could be heard in the fields. He hopped and he leaped and he sang away at the top of his voice. "The sun is warm!" he sang. "The leaves taste good! It is so nice to be alive!"

The summer days passed quickly. It seemed to the Grasshopper he had barely turned around when already it was fall. The cold wind was blowing. All the flowers and grasses in the field were dead. The bushes and the trees had stripped themselves for their winter sleep. And there was nothing to eat—simply nothing.

The Grasshopper no longer sang about how nice it was to be alive. Indeed, how could he live at all if somebody didn't help him?

"Please," he said, stumbling over to an Ant, "Will you give me something to eat?"

The Ant was busy. She was dragging a dead fly into the nest. It was one of a hundred insects she had lugged home. For she had worked, worked, and worked all summer, storing up food for the winter.

She stopped a moment to stare at the beggar. "Something to eat?" she asked sternly. "And what, if you please, were you doing all summer? That is the time when sensible folk provide for the winter."

"I had no time to work," the Grasshopper said. "Please don't be cross with me. All summer long I hopped and leaped and sang."

"What? All you did was sing and prance?" cried the Ant, turning her back on him. "Well, my good fellow, now you can dance!"

1. Read the following sentences from the text. Then, answer the question.

"She was dragging a dead fly into the nest. It was one of a hundred insects she had lugged home."

What is a possible meaning for the word lugged as it is used in the passage?

- O A. to eat
- O B. to hide
- O C. to lift or carry
- O D. to keep warm

2. What is the meaning of the word cross as it is used in this passage?

- O A. lie
- O B. moved
- O C. angry
- O D. canceled

3. This is a fable. All fables teach a lesson. Which sentences from the text best support the lesson to be learned in this fable?

- O A. "She stopped a moment to stare at the beggar. 'Something to eat?' she asked sternly."
- O B. "'And what, if you please, were you doing all summer? That is the time when sensible folk provide for the winter.'"
- O C. "It seemed to the Grasshopper he had barely turned around when already it was fall. The cold wind was blowing."
- O D. "He hopped and he leaped and he sang away at the top of his voice. 'The sun is warm!' he sang. 'The leaves taste good! It is so nice to be alive!'"

(Answers are on page 133.)

Exercise 2

Common Core Standard RL.5.1
Quote accurately from a text when explaining what the text says explicitly and when drawing inferences from the text.

Common Core Standard RL.5.2
Determine a theme of a story, drama, or poem from details in the text, including how characters in a story or drama respond to challenges or how the speaker in a poem reflects upon a topic; summarize the text.

Common Core Standard L.5.4
Determine or clarify the meaning of unknown and multiple-meaning words and phrases based on grade 5 reading and content, choosing flexibly from a range of strategies.

Common Core Standard RI.5.1
Quote accurately from a text when explaining what the text says explicitly and when drawing inferences from the text.

Directions: Read the text. Then answer questions 1–3.

The Hare and the Tortoise

The Hare was showing off before the other animals. "I can run faster than any of you," he boasted. "Nobody can beat me."

"Well, I'm not so sure of that," a low voice said. "I'll race you if you like." It was the Tortoise speaking. Everybody was surprised, for they all knew what a slowpoke he was.

The Hare laughed. "That's a good joke," he said.

"But I mean it," the Tortoise said. "Let's have a race."

So the animals marked out a racecourse. The runners would start here on the dirt road, and they would end there, by the big oak tree.

"It's a good two miles," said the Hare. "Now let's go!" And at the word of command he started lickety-split down the road. In half a minute the Hare was almost out of sight. He looked back. The Tortoise had moved only a couple of yards!

"I've got plenty of time to take a nap," the Hare said to himself with a grin. And just to make fun of the Tortoise, he lay down and made believe he had gone to sleep. But it was a hot day, and before he knew it he really was asleep.

By and by he woke up with a start. Wasn't he supposed to be in a race with somebody? He looked back down the road. Nobody there. He looked the other way. There was the Tortoise—almost at the end of the course!

The Hare laid his ears back close to his body and dashed away at his highest speed. But it was too late. Before he could get to the oak tree, the Tortoise was already there, resting quietly in its shade.

1. Read the following sentence from the text. Then, answer the question.

   "'I can run faster than any of you,' he <u>boasted</u>."

   Identify the antonym of the underlined word.

   O   A.   to brag
   O   B.   to gloat
   ⊙   C.   to be modest
   O   D.   to flaunt

2. Which statement best describes the central idea of this fable?

   O   A.   Slow and steady wins the race.
   O   B.   This fable shows how a person can be determined to prove someone wrong.
   O   C.   This fable shows that hares are faster than tortoises.
   O   D.   This fable is a story about a hare and tortoise racing to prove who is faster.

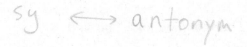

3. **Part A:** What can you infer about the Hare's attitude toward the Tortoise? Check **all** that apply.

☐ A. The Hare enjoys showing off to tease the Tortoise.

☐ B. The Hare thought the Tortoise was slow and that he could easily beat him.

☐ C. The Hare thought highly of the Tortoise and respected him for carrying his home with him.

☐ D. The Hare was jealous of the Tortoise's shiny shell and how popular he was.

Part B: Which evidence from the passage supports your inference from Part A?

O A. "'Well, I'm not so sure of that,' a low voice said. 'I'll race you if you like.' It was the Tortoise speaking."

O B. "And at the word of command he started lickety-split down the road. In half a minute the Hare was almost out of sight."

O C. "He looked back down the road. Nobody there. He looked the other way. There was the Tortoise—almost at the end of the course!"

O D. "'I've got plenty of time to take a nap,'" the Hare said to himself with a grin. And just to make fun of the Tortoise, he lay down and made believe he had gone to sleep."

(Answers are on page 133.)

During the Performance Task, there will also be selected-response tasks to complete. The format, however, can be different. The exam will give you two passages to read before answering any questions. Each question will refer to both passages. When you come across these types of selected-response tasks, it is important to make sure that you refer back to both texts as much as you can. Exercise 3 presents questions that require you to refer back to two passages.

Exercise 3

Common Core Standard RL.5.3
Compare and contrast two or more characters, settings, or events in a story or drama, drawing on specific details in the text (e.g., how characters interact).

Common Core Standard RL.5.6
Describe how a narrator's or speaker's point of view influences how events are described.

Common Core Standard RL.5.9
Compare and contrast stories in the same genre (e.g., mysteries and adventure stories) on their approaches to similar themes and topics.

Common Core Standard RI.5.3
Explain the relationships or interactions between two or more individuals, events, ideas, or concepts in a historical, scientific, or technical text based on specific information in the text.

Common Core Standard RI.5.5
Compare and contrast the overall structure (e.g., chronology, comparison, cause/effect, problem/solution) of events, ideas, concepts, or information in two or more texts.

Common Core Standard RI.5.6
Analyze multiple accounts of the same event or topic, noting important similarities and differences in the point of view they represent.

Common Core Standard RI.5.7
Draw on information from multiple print or digital sources, demonstrating the ability to locate an answer to a question quickly or to solve a problem efficiently.

Common Core Standard RI.5.8
Explain how an author uses reasons and evidence to support particular points in a text, identifying which reasons and evidence support which point(s).

Common Core Standard RI.5.9
Integrate information from several texts on the same topic in order to write or speak about the subject knowledgeably.

Directions: Base your answers to questions 1 and 2 on "The Grasshopper and the Ant" fable (on page 19) and "The Hare and the Tortoise" fable (on pages 21–22). Reread those texts. Then answer questions 1 and 2.

1. Which statement best describes the similarities between the Hare and the Grasshopper?

   ○ A. Both the Hare and the Grasshopper are patient.
   ○ B. The Grasshopper and the Hare both learn from their mistakes.
   ○ C. Both the Hare and the Grasshopper think they know best.
   ○ D. The Hare is a rabbit, whereas the Grasshopper is an insect.

2. What statements show the differences between the two fables? Select **all** that apply.

   ☐ A. Both fables have talking animals.
   ☐ B. The lesson from "The Hare and the Tortoise" is to take it slow and steady, whereas the lesson from "The Grasshopper and the Ant" is to always be prepared.
   ☐ C. Both fables have the same characters.
   ☐ D. The Hare teases the Tortoise unlike the Grasshopper who asks the Ant for help.

   (Answers are on page 134.)

Exercise 4

Common Core Standard RL.5.2
Determine a theme of a story, drama, or poem from details in the text, including how characters in a story or drama respond to challenges or how the speaker in a poem reflects upon a topic; summarize the text.

Common Core Standard RL.5.4
Determine the meaning of words and phrases as they are used in a text, including figurative language such as metaphors and similes.

Common Core Standard RL.5.5
Explain how a series of chapters, scenes, or stanzas fits together to provide the overall structure of a particular story, drama, or poem.

Common Core Standard L.5.4
Determine or clarify the meaning of unknown and multiple-meaning words and phrases based on grade 5 reading and content, choosing flexibly from a range of strategies.

Common Core Standard L.5.5
Demonstrate understanding of figurative language, word relationships, and nuances in word meanings.

Directions: Read the poem. Then answer questions 1–3.

Life's Mirror

There are loyal hearts, there are spirits brave,
There are souls that are pure and true;
Then give to the world the best you have,
And the best will come back to you.

Give love, and love to your life will flow,
A strength in your utmost need;
Have faith, and a score of hearts will show
Their faith in your work and deed.

Give truth, and your fit will be paid in kind;
And honor will honor meet,
And the smile which is sweet will surely find
A smile that is just as sweet.

Give pity and sorrow to those who mourn;
You will gather in flowers again
The scattered seeds from your thought outborne;
Though the sowing seemed in vain.

For life is a mirror of king and slave;
'Tis just what we are and do;
Then give the world the best you have,
And the best will come back to you.

Source: Bridges, Madeline S. *Life's Mirror* from *Poems Teachers Ask For.*
Project Gutenberg, 2006. *www.gutenberg.org/files/18909/18909-h/18909-h.htm.*

1. Which line from the poem is an example of a metaphor?

    O A.   "Their faith in your work and deed."

    O B.   "For life is a mirror of king and slave;"

    O C.   "Have faith, and a score of hearts will show"

    O D.   "Then give to the world the best you have, / And the best will come back to you."

2. Which line from the poem best represents the theme of the poem?

    ○ A. "Give pity and sorrow to those who mourn;"

    ○ B. "The scattered seeds from your thought outbourne;"

    ○ C. "Have faith, and a score of hearts will show / Their faith in your work and deed."

    ○ D. "Then give to the world the best you have, / And the best will come back to you."

3. What does the poet compare seeds to? Select **all** that apply.

    ☐ A. outborne

    ☐ B. flowers

    ☐ C. thoughts

    ☐ D. ideas

(Answers are on page 134.)

Exercise 5

Common Core Standard RL.5.2
Determine a theme of a story, drama, or poem from details in the text, including how characters in a story or drama respond to challenges or how the speaker in a poem reflects upon a topic; summarize the text.

Common Core Standard RL.5.4
Determine the meaning of words and phrases as they are used in a text, including figurative language such as metaphors and similes.

Common Core Standard L.5.4
Determine or clarify the meaning of unknown and multiple-meaning words and phrases based on grade 5 reading and content, choosing flexibly from a range of strategies.

Common Core Standard L.5.5
Demonstrate understanding of figurative language, word relationships, and nuances in word meanings.

Directions: Read the text. Then answer questions 1–3.

Life on Mars?

Fossils are the remains of animals or plants preserved in rock or stone. Fossils can be around for millions of years. Scientists who study fossils, called archeologists, look for these fossils and uncover them to learn about the past.

Once in 1996 these scientists looked closely at a very special type of fossil. This fossil was found inside a rock believed to be from Mars! How did this rock from Mars make it to Earth?

Well, this rock was originally found in 1984 by a team of researchers in Antarctica. It was a one of a kind rock. In fact, it was later found to be a meteorite from Mars. Scientists believe that millions of years ago a large asteroid hit Mars, which sent fragments of rock from Mars into space. These fragments became meteorites that eventually hit Earth in Antarctica.

Inside the meteorite they found a tiny fossil of a worm. This was a big deal because it could mean that Mars once hosted life on its surface! Later, scientists found that the meteorite and fossil came from a time when Mars had water on its surface. Water is needed for life to survive. This explained how the tiny worm could be in the rock. This was an exciting discovery!

The discovery of water once existing on Mars led to more research about Mars and the possibility of life there. Since then, more evidence has been found that there was once water, and therefore life, on Mars. Some scientists in 2015 even went so far as to say that there is enough evidence that supports that there is an ancient Martian ocean the size of our Arctic Ocean.

As we know, you need water to have life, so it could be that we will find more evidence of life from Mars in our lifetime!

1. Determine the main idea of the passage.

    O A.   Scientists found fossils.

    O B.   Scientists continue to study fossils.

    O C.   Scientists may have proof that that there was life on Mars.

    O D.   Scientists continue to study rocks on Mars.

2. Which details support the main idea? Select **all** that apply.

   ☐ A. A rock from Mars contained a tiny worm fossil.

   ☐ B. A rover is a robot car.

   ☐ C. Scientists found a place on Mars that was once filled with water.

   ☐ D. Water is not needed for life.

3. The following sentence from the passage has grammatical errors:

"Once in 1996 these scientists looked closely at a very special type of fossil."

Circle or underline the two parts of the sentence that should have commas after them.

(Answers are on page 134.)

Constructed-Response Tasks

CHAPTER 2

Overview

The short-response section of the SBAC will consist mostly of short passages with either fiction or nonfiction selections. The passages can range from a variety of text types, such as articles, biographies, essays, stories, or even poetry. These passages will be followed by questions that require typed short responses. The short responses place an emphasis on both the Reading and Writing Anchor Standards of the Common Core Standards, which focus on supporting conclusions with specific textual evidence and with logical reasoning. In addition, you will need to successfully identify the main (central) idea and supporting details to successfully determine the correct evidence to cite in your responses.

This section will vary in the types of prompts and questions depending on the different comprehension strategies and text structures. These questions will require you to use any one or more of the following strategies and structures outlined in Table 2-1.

Table 2-1. Comprehension Strategies and Text Structures

Comprehension Strategies	Text Structures
> Predicting > Questioning > Connecting > Visualizing > Summarizing > Inferring > Using Context Clues	> Sequential > Compare and Contrast > Cause and Effect > Problem and Solution

Applying Your Strategies

Strategy 1: Understanding the Question

Before you can successfully answer any questions, you need to make sure you understand what the test is asking you to do for every question or prompt. The SBAC depends heavily on academic vocabulary to convey instructions and directions. For instance, instead of asking you to simply write the main (central) idea of the passage, the SBAC could ask you to **identify**, **determine**, or **analyze** a passage for the main (central) idea. You will need to have an understanding of what these key academic words mean. Understanding these terms will help you save time during the test by narrowing down what is being asked of you and helping you focus your brainpower. Please refer to the Common Academic Vocabulary Used on the Grade 5 Smarter Balanced Test table (Table I-5 on pages 13–14) in the Introduction of this book for an overview of these types of words and their meanings.

Strategy 2: Key Words

Paying attention to key words or ideas (synonyms count!) that are repeated in both the text and the questions makes finding the right response quicker and more precise. Often, there are key words that link the question to the appropriate information in the text. For example, the question and passage below are linked by "counterargument" and the word "although."

Question: What **counterargument** does the author use to make his or her point?

an opposing argument

Although zoos claim that their main purpose is to help prevent animals from becoming extinct and to help educate people about the animals, we think the only thing zoos do is make animals crazy!

"Although" is a key word that you would look for in a "counterargument." In this case, seeing this word in the text would help you answer the question.

Strategy 3: Reading for Different Purposes

We read for different purposes. Sometimes we read to be entertained, and other times we read to gain insight or knowledge about a particular subject. Since this is an end-of-the-year test, you are reading for comprehension in order to answer questions about the text afterwards. You will need to interact with the text more than once to successfully answer the questions in this section. Try following this pattern:

1. First, preview the passage by looking at the title, the text structure, any vocabulary words, the topic sentences, and any visuals, such as picture graphs. Do not read the passage at this point. Previewing the text befo. ...... will prepare your brain for comprehending the text and the questions.

2. Next, read all the questions that accompany that passage. This will give you the key ideas to look for when you read the text all the way through for the first time.

X No note

3. Read the passage for the first time all the way through for general comprehension. Pay attention to any repeated words and ideas that may connect to the questions or prompts. Use the interactive notepad feature provided by the SBAC to take any notes that may help answer the questions. Remember, you will not be able to copy and paste or highlight within the text.

4. Finally, it is time to answer the questions. Use your notes to construct a clear response. Don't forget that you can look back at the text as much as you need to!

Strategy 4: Using A.C.E.

The acronym A.C.E. stands for **A**nswer, **C**ite, and **E**xplain. Using this method will help you create organized and informed responses that communicate your understanding of the prompt or question. Use the simple chart below as a reminder of the A.C.E. strategy.

<u>A</u>nswer	Use part of the question in your answer.
<u>C</u>ite	Support your answer with details (evidence) from the text.
<u>E</u>xplain	Explain how or why the evidence you've cited supports your answer.

Scoring

The scoring for the SBAC short responses are based on a 0- to 2-point system. Below is a general breakdown of how short responses are scored. The questions and prompts can vary in the strategies that they want you to use, but these are the general guidelines for scoring your responses.

2-Point Response

- There is a clear conclusion that correctly answers the question or prompt.
- The conclusion is supported with sufficient evidence or details that make clear references to the text.
- The evidence is clearly explained with relevant information from the text.

1-Point Response

- The conclusion is vague and does not adequately answer the question or prompt.
- The evidence from the text does not sufficiently support the answer.
- The connection between the conclusion and the evidence is unclear.
- The information that is used from the text is not relevant.

0-Point Response

- There is no clear conclusion that answers the question or prompt. The answer simply restates a fact from the passage.
- No evidence is used at all.

Practice Exercises

Exercise 1—Constructed-Response Tasks with One Source

Common Core Standard RL.5.1
Quote accurately from a text when explaining what the text says explicitly and when drawing inferences from the text.

Common Core Standard RL.5.2
Determine a theme of a story, drama, or poem from details in the text, including how characters in a story or drama respond to challenges or how the speaker in a poem reflects upon a topic; summarize the text.

Common Core Standard RI.5.1
Quote accurately from a text when explaining what the text says explicitly and when drawing inferences from the text.

Common Core Standard RI.5.2
Determine two or more main ideas of a text and explain how they are supported by key details; summarize the text.

Common Core Standard RI.5.8
Explain how an author uses reasons and evidence to support particular points in a text, identifying which reasons and evidence support which point(s).

Common Core Standard W.5.2.A
Introduce a topic clearly, provide a general observation and focus, and group related information logically; include formatting (e.g., headings), illustrations, and multimedia when useful to aiding comprehension.

Common Core Standard W.5.2.B
Develop the topic with facts, definitions, concrete details, quotations, or other information and examples related to the topic.

Common Core Standard W.5.2.C
Link ideas within and across categories of information using words, phrases, and clauses (e.g., *in contrast, especially*).

Directions: Read the following passage on Zoochosis while keeping in mind the reading strategies discussed earlier in this chapter. After, you will be asked to respond to a few questions that require you to apply the reading strategies covered.

Zoochosis

Keep animals in zoos! We don't think so. There is documented research that many animals removed from their natural habitat and kept in captivity have developed a kind of mental illness known as zoochosis.

Animals with this disease often pace back and forth, twist their necks, bob their heads up and down, turn in never-ending circles, and even tear holes in their own skin. Can you imagine being so miserable that you would want to inflict harm on yourself?

Once, when we visited a zoo, we noticed that some of the animals kept in cages were grabbing onto the bars and shaking them. If you could have looked into these animals' eyes like we did, you would have seen deep sadness. It is this sadness that continues to haunt us to this day.

It has been documented that Junior, the killer whale, was removed from his natural habitat in Iceland and placed in a tank in Niagara Falls. He died four years later, deprived of outside air, sunlight, and companionship. *Poor Junior* ☹

Humans are mean

Junior is not alone. There are many aquatic animals that are taken from their natural habitats and placed in water tanks in aquariums around the world. These animals are separated from their families and are forced to live in groups that are nothing like their own families. As though that isn't enough, animals like whales and dolphins, who are accustomed to swimming up to 100 miles in one day and diving hundreds of feet, are forced to live in confined space. Do you think they can get this type of exercise in a water tank? We don't think so. *OMG! Pls stop saying "we don't think so!"*

Wait! There's more. Aquatic animals have a special way of talking to one another and finding their prey. They use sound patterns, or echolocation. This natural process is sometimes non-existent in aquariums because of the noise level and the glass enclosures. This type of confinement is unacceptable for any animal, anywhere.

The Born Free Foundation performed a worldwide study of zoos which revealed that zoochosis is rampant in confined animals around the globe. Another study found that elephants in zoos spend 22 percent of their time engaging in abnormal behaviors, such as repeated head bobbing or biting cage bars, and bears spend about 30 percent of their time pacing, a sign of distress.

Although zoos claim that their main purpose is to help prevent animals from becoming extinct and to help educate people about the animals, we think the only thing zoos do is make animals crazy!

Source: Stead, Tony. *Should There Be Zoos?* from *Zoochosis*. Mondo Publishing, n.d.

1. What conclusion can you make about the author's view of zoos? Support your answer with evidence from the text.

Apply Your Strategies

This type of question is asking you to **identify** the author's viewpoint, or how the author feels about the topic being discussed. You will also need to rely on your knowledge of the **author's purpose**. Is the author writing this to persuade, inform, or entertain (P.I.E.)? Knowing the author's purpose will help you answer question 1 correctly.

In order to successfully support your answer with evidence from the text, you should look back at the text and note any sentences that express the author's **opinion**. This will help you recognize the author's viewpoint. This author uses a lot of facts to support his or her viewpoint, but do not confuse these *facts* with how the author *feels* about zoos.

Now, on the next page, answer question 1 using the A.C.E. strategy, and remember to explain why your evidence supports your answer.

Your Answer

Answer (Use part of the question in your answer.) ·	
Cite (Support your answer with details [evidence] from the text.)	
Explain (Explain how or why the evidence you've cited supports your answer.)	

(Answers are on page 135.)

2. Read the following paragraph from the passage.

"Junior is not alone. There are many aquatic animals that are taken from their natural habitats and placed in water tanks in aquariums around the world. These animals are separated from their families and are forced to live in groups that are nothing like their own families. As though that isn't enough, animals like whales and dolphins, who are accustomed to swimming up to 100 miles in one day and diving hundreds of feet, are forced to live in confined space. Do you think they can get this type of exercise in a water tank? We don't think so."

Determine the main (central) idea of the paragraph.

Apply Your Strategies

This type of prompt requires you to **analyze** and **determine** the main (central) idea of one paragraph. Paragraphs are formed around their own main idea that in turn supports the entire text or article. Look for repeated ideas and words that the author uses; these will include synonyms.

Your Answer

Answer (Use part of the question in your answer.)	
Cite (Support your answer with details [evidence] from the text.)	
Explain (Explain how or why the evidence you've cited supports your answer.)	

(Answers are on page 136.)

3. What is the author's purpose for writing this article? Explain how you know using details from the passage.

Apply Your Strategies

This question requires you to both **analyze** and **prove**. You will need to *analyze* the text to determine why the author wrote the article in the first place. Ask yourself, "Is the author trying to persuade, inform, or entertain the audience?" Once you have identified the author's purpose, you will need to *prove* how you know. Use text evidence.

Your Answer

<u>A</u>nswer (Use part of the question in your answer.)	
<u>C</u>ite (Support your answer with details [evidence] from the text.)	
<u>E</u>xplain (Explain how or why the evidence you've cited supports your answer.)	

(Answers are on page 137.)

4. There are many reasons why a person may disagree with keeping animals in zoos. Using at least two details from the text, explain why animals should not be kept in a zoo.

Apply Your Strategies

To answer this question, you will first need to **identify** the main idea. Then, you will need to look for evidence to support this main idea.

Your Answer

Answer (Use part of the question in your answer.)	
Cite (Support your answer with details [evidence] from the text.)	
Explain (Explain how or why the evidence you've cited supports your answer.)	

(Answers are on page 138.)

DON'T FORGET!

- [ ] Always preview the text first.

- [ ] Pay attention to text features, such as bolded, italicized, or underlined words and other key vocabulary words.

- [ ] Don't get confused with *author's purpose* and *purposes of reading*. The *author's purpose* is *why the author wrote the text*, whereas *purpose of reading* is *why you are reading the text.*

- [ ] Use the A.C.E. strategy to construct your responses.

- [ ] Remember not to restate directly from the text without using quotations. Use your own words when drawing your own conclusions.

Exercise 2—Constructed-Response Tasks with Multiple Sources

Common Core Standard RL.5.1
Quote accurately from a text when explaining what the text says explicitly and when drawing inferences from the text.

Common Core Standard RL.5.2
Determine a theme of a story, drama, or poem from details in the text, including how characters in a story or drama respond to challenges or how the speaker in a poem reflects upon a topic; summarize the text.

Common Core Standard RI.5.1
Quote accurately from a text when explaining what the text says explicitly and when drawing inferences from the text.

Common Core Standard RI.5.2
Determine two or more main ideas of a text and explain how they are supported by key details; summarize the text.

Common Core Standard RI.5.8
Explain how an author uses reasons and evidence to support particular points in a text, identifying which reasons and evidence support which point(s).

Common Core Standard W.5.2.A
Introduce a topic clearly, provide a general observation and focus, and group related information logically; include formatting (e.g., headings), illustrations, and multimedia when useful to aiding comprehension.

Common Core Standard W.5.2.B
Develop the topic with facts, definitions, concrete details, quotations, or other information and examples related to the topic.

Common Core Standard W.5.2.C
Link ideas within and across categories of information using words, phrases, and clauses (e.g., *in contrast, especially*).

You may come across sections of the test where you will need to read two different passages before responding to question items. The same strategies used to respond to a single passage can still be used, but now you will need to consider details or evidence from more than one passage or media source. Often, these multiple sources will be linked by a key idea. You may be asked to compare and contrast or bring together details from different sources to support the key idea.

Directions: Read both of the following sources. Afterwards, practice responding to questions that will require you to **analyze** both readings.

Source Number 1

(**Note**: *You may come across an article during your research. The following article, which discusses the current status of the California drought, was published online by a local newspaper.*)

If you live in California, then you have felt the effects of the drought in the last couple of years. Many cities and counties have put restrictions on water use. This includes washing your car or watering your lawn. Some places have even run out of water!

One of the hardest hit areas of California, though, is its agriculture. Why is this so important? The state is one of the top producers of fruits and vegetables. This is a big part of its economy and a source of food for its citizens.

Both 2014 and 2015 were one of the hardest two years for California farmers. Farmers lost about 500,000 acres of land and roughly 17,000 jobs. Farmers have gone into survival mode, simply trying to keep their trees alive while waiting for relief from rains.

California has been in a drought for many years now and this is usually a normal routine for the region. This time, however, the drought is lasting longer than anyone expected. Usually, California winters bring some relief, but even normally wet areas are still dry.

The people of California and farmers rely on getting their water from reservoirs and runoff from the snowpack. These resources, however, are at record lows. Farmers are now looking to get their water from groundwater reservoirs. These are usually a last resort as they are the most difficult to restore.

The more groundwater that is used, the less back-up water we have for future droughts. While the surface reservoirs and snowpack can make a comeback, the groundwater is a precious resource that is hard to get back. The drought has put restrictions on how much groundwater can be used, but these restrictions do not apply to farmers.

An average farmer will use roughly 33 million acre-feet of water in a year with 12 million of that being from groundwater sources. During this recent drought, however, the amount coming from groundwater sources has risen to 25 million acre-feet of total water use by farmers.

Farmers now need to think of different ways to keep their lands profitable and operate in a sustainable way at the same time. Many farmers are doing this by switching to different crops that take less water to grow. Once the drought lets up, they can switch back to their regular crops. This system ensures that the soil does not dry up and is easy to work in the future.

Source Number 2

(**Note**: *This excerpt, taken from a classroom library book, discusses how the Sahara, in northern Africa, is slowly spreading into other ecosystems.*)

Water is one of the most important factors that support life on our planet. The tropical forests of Africa, Asia, and the Americas receive up to four hundred inches of rainfall a year and teem with life. This biodiversity is a stark contrast to parts of the world that receive little or no precipitation. Deserts are areas where the annual rainfall is less than ten inches a year.

The Sahara of northern Africa is the largest of Earth's deserts. It covers an area roughly the size of the United States. While parts of the desert have mountains, the Sahara is primarily a sandy desert. Water is present in the Saharan deserts, but takes the form of ancient underground lakes. The water in these underground lakes can sometimes bubble to the surface in a spring but accessing water in the Sahara usually requires digging wells to reach it. By acquiring water, these areas are transformed into fertile places with rich soil that allows for growing crops and raising animals. The result is an oasis—a respite for travelers making their way across a harsh land.

The Sahel region of Africa, just south of the Sahara, was at one time a lush grassland that provided ample pasture for cattle and good soil for growing food. However, the region has been hit with long dry spells, resulting in the worst droughts in nearly two hundred years. Rivers and lakes are drying up; without sufficient rainfall, grasses are dying and the cattle are starving. Another factor contributing to the problems caused by the epic drought is soil erosion, caused by cutting down too many trees and further depleting fertile agricultural land.

1. Which of the two sources is more likely to be the better source for understanding the effects of drought on grasslands? Explain why this source is more likely to be the better source. Give at least two details from the source to support your answer.

Apply Your Strategies

Pay attention to key words like **more likely**. This means you will need to compare and contrast the two readings. You might identify details or evidence in both sources that would be helpful, but *more likely* means that you will need to determine which source has stronger evidence about the effects of droughts on grasslands. Make sure to refer back to both readings to confirm which one has the stronger evidence.

You are being asked to explain and support your answer with at least two details from the text. Again, using the A.C.E. strategy will ensure you complete this task successfully.

Your Answer

Answer (Use part of the question in your answer.)	
Cite (Support your answer with details [evidence] from the text.)	
Explain (Explain how or why the evidence you've cited supports your answer.)	

(Answers are on page 139.)

2. Both passages discuss the different sources of naturally occurring water. Explain what you have learned about where people get their water from. Use one detail from Source Number 1 and one detail from Source Number 2 to support your explanation. For each detail, include the source title or number.

Apply Your Strategies

Notice that this task is asking you to use details from both sources. This will require you to compare both sources and identify two different details that work together to support your answer. The focus for these two different details is in the question: *sources of naturally occurring water.* Your job will be to find details in both readings about these types of water sources.

Your Answer

Answer (Use part of the question in your answer.)	
Cite (Support your answer with details [evidence] from the text.)	
Explain (Explain how or why the evidence you've cited supports your answer.)	

(Answers are on page 140.)

DON'T FORGET!

- ☐ Always preview the text first.

- ☐ Pay attention to text features, such as bolded, italicized, or underlined words and other key vocabulary words.

- ☐ Don't get confused with *author's purpose* and *purposes of reading*. The author's purpose is *why the author wrote the text*, whereas *purpose of reading* is *why you are reading the text*.

- ☐ Use the A.C.E. strategy to construct your responses.

- ☐ Remember not to restate directly from the text without using quotations. Use your own words when drawing your own conclusions.

Grammar and Conventions

Overview

The language portion of the Common Core Standards focuses on your knowledge of grammar and conventions of the English language. This includes your punctuation, spelling, verb tenses, conjunctions, figurative language, vocabulary development, and ability to build complex sentence structures. Each year, your use and understanding of grammar and conventions grows more complex, and the SBAC will assess this level of complexity in fifth grade.

The exam will test these standards as part of your writing scores for the Performance Task, as shown in the SBAC Writing Rubrics. The convention standards, however, will also be tested directly with individual tasks on both the Computer Adaptive Test and the Performance Task.

Applying Your Strategies

When it comes to grammar and conventions, there are two key strategies you can use to make a more informed and confident selection. Keep in mind that you will not have access to regular classroom resources that you typically depend on when editing and revising your writing. These classroom resources may include a dictionary, a thesaurus, or any other resource for editing needs. Instead, you will have to depend on your understanding of grammar and convention rules.

Strategy 1: Repeat the Text

When looking for mistakes or determining a revision, always repeat the text to yourself multiple times. Check for pauses where commas should be. Think to yourself if each sentence sounds like it is in the right tense. Is the action of the sentence happening in the past, present, or future? Do the verbs show or convey the right time or condition?

Strategy 2: Use Your Editing Skills

In class, you should have learned the writing process and how to edit for grammar and convention mistakes. Do the same to the text that the test gives to you. You can also apply those skills to the exam. Make sure to read sections multiple times, as your brain tends to fill in mistakes that are there.

Conventions of Standard English

Conventions refer to the common way that English grammar is used when writing and speaking. These are the rules for how sentences and words should be arranged. In fifth grade, the standards that will be assessed during the exam focus on the use of conjunctions, prepositions, and verb tenses. In addition, you'll be tested on your spelling and use of punctuation, especially the use of commas and quotation marks to show direct evidence, titles of different works, and sentence structure. Take a look at Table 3-1 to review the different grammar elements being tested.

Table 3-1. Grammar Conventions

Conjunctions	Prepositions
Conjunctions are words that connect two sentences or phrases together. For example:	*Prepositions* are words that show location, time, and space. For example:
and, or, but, because	<u>During</u> the winter, Jennifer and her friends created a snowman <u>near</u> Lake Tahoe.
You may be asked to identify what conjunctions are used in a sentence or paragraph or what sentences can be combined to make a sentence that has the same meaning as the two original sentences.	Some other common prepositions are *in, to, on, into, over, under, before, around, of.*

Perfect Tenses

Perfect tenses are when words such as *have, had,* or *will* are used with an action to show that the action is finished. For instance:

I *have* finished all my homework.
I *had* watched that show before.
I *will* finish my homework after the show.

Table 3-1. Grammar Conventions *(continued)*

Verb Tenses	Irregular Verb Tenses
Verbs are words that show action. There are past, present, and future verbs. Most verb tenses follow a spelling pattern. For example: *Walk* becomes *walked* for past tense and *walking* for present tense. An *-ed* or *-ing* was added to change the tenses.	Verbs are *irregular* when they do not follow the typical spelling patterns for tenses. Some of the most common irregular verbs are *go, get, say, see, think, make, take, come, know.*

Commas and Quotation Marks

Commas are placed at a natural pause when you speak or read. Commas are also used when there's a list in a sentence.

For example: *Many children love watching the movie* Frozen *because of the characters Elsa, Ana, and Olaf.*

Quotation marks are placed at the beginning and at the end of the sentence after the period, exclamation point, or question mark. Quotation marks show when someone is speaking or when evidence is stated. On the SBAC, the appropriate use of quotation marks will be required, and the test makers will ask you to identify the proper placement of the quotation marks. This will also be tested on the Performance Task.

Here are two examples:

Betty and Vinod asked their daughter, "Would you like to go to the park?"

In the school newsletter it states, "The school will be closed for President's Day."

Practice Exercises—Conventions of Standard English

Exercise 1

> **Common Core Standard L.5.1**
> Demonstrate command of the conventions of standard English grammar and usage when writing or speaking.

1. Insert commas in the correct place in the following sentence.

Arjuna and Mekya were sitting on the bench waving hello to the puffy white clouds in the sky.

(Answer is on page 141.)

Exercise 2

> **Common Core Standard L.5.1**
> Demonstrate command of the conventions of standard English grammar and usage when writing or speaking.

1. What interjection would you use to enhance the sentence in Exercise 1?

O A. Ouch, Arjuna and Mekya were sitting on the bench, waving hello to the puffy, white clouds in the sky.

O B. Hey, Arjuna and Mekya were sitting on the bench, waving hello to the puffy, white clouds in the sky.

O C. Ick, Arjuna and Mekya were sitting on the bench, waving hello to the puffy, white clouds in the sky.

O D. Yuck, Arjuna and Mekya were sitting on the bench, waving hello to the puffy, white clouds in the sky.

(Answer is on page 142.)

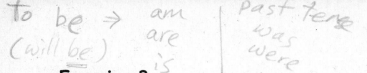

to be → am
(will be)   are
                is

Past tense
was
were
was

Exercise 3

> **Common Core Standard L.5.1**
> Demonstrate command of the conventions of standard English grammar and usage when writing or speaking.

1. Looking at the sentence from Exercise 1, what are the prepositions in the sentence? Select **all** that apply. (Remember, prepositions and prepositional phrases show location, time, and place.)

   direction

   ☑ A. on
   ☑ B. to
   ☐ C. were → past tense verb
   ☑ D. in

   (Answer is on page 142.)

Exercise 4

> **Common Core Standard L.5.1**
> Demonstrate command of the conventions of standard English grammar and usage when writing or speaking.

1. How can the sentence from Exercise 1 be rewritten without changing the content or meaning?

   ○ A. Arjuna and Mekya sitting on the bench, waving hello to the puffy, white clouds in the sky.
   ○ B. Arjuna and Mekya will sit on the bench, waving hello to the puffy, white clouds in the sky.
   ○ C. Arjuna and Mekya sit on the bench, waving hello to the puffy, white clouds in the sky.
   ○ D. Arjuna and Mekya sat on the bench, waving hello to the puffy, white clouds in the sky.

   (Answer is on page 142.)

Knowledge of Applying Language Conventions

If you can successfully use the conventions of English grammar, then you can apply this knowledge to your writing and speaking. The SBAC will test you on how well you can apply this knowledge. The focus of this section is on combining different sentences to make more complex sentences. Why do we want to do this? Combining simple sentences makes your writing flow, and it makes it easier for your audience to understand your thoughts. To do this correctly, you must rely on your knowledge of grammar and conventions.

For example, the following is a list of simple sentences about the same subject:

I like to play at the park.

The park is on Somerset Street.

I play Frisbee at the park.

I go to the park every Tuesday afternoon.

Your job is to now correctly combine these simple sentences and ideas into one sentence that reads smoothly. Using the phrase "the park" four separate times would make your writing choppy and uninteresting. Instead, we can combine all these ideas about the park into one sentence:

Every Tuesday afternoon, I like to play Frisbee at the park on Somerset Street.

Practice Exercises—Knowledge of Applying Language Conventions

Exercise 1

> **Common Core Standard L.5.3.A**
> Expand, combine, and reduce sentences for meaning, reader/listener interest, and style.

1. Michael wrote a paragraph on dinosaurs for his book report. He has too many simple sentences and now needs to revise his paragraph. Read his simple sentences below and choose the best option for combining them.

   Dinosaurs lived a long time ago.

   There were both carnivorous and herbivorous dinosaurs.

   There were not that many omnivorous dinosaurs.

   - ○ A. Both carnivorous and herbivorous dinosaurs lived a long time ago, yet there were not that many omnivorous dinosaurs during that time.
   - ○ B. There were not that many omnivorous dinosaurs. Carnivorous and herbivorous dinosaurs lived a long time ago.
   - ○ C. Dinosaurs lived a long time ago and there were both carnivorous and herbivorous dinosaurs, and not many were omnivorous dinosaurs.
   - ○ D. Dinosaurs can be carnivorous, herbivorous, and omnivorous.

   (Answer is on page 142.)

Vocabulary Meaning and Use

This section will guide you through the three main areas of fifth-grade vocabulary expectations. You will be asked a variety of different types of questions to assess your ability to learn the meaning of new words based on context clues, affixes, and roots, and they will also test you on whether you know how to use reference materials. In addition, you need to be able to identify and interpret figurative language, such as similes and metaphors. Finally, your ability to learn and apply new academic words will also be tested.

Determining the Meaning of New Words

You know you are reading a good book when there are a few words on every other page that you do not know. These unknown words challenge you to use your clues to learn their meaning and make you a better reader. The Common Core Standards aim to test you on your ability to use these clues to correctly determine the meaning of new words. To do this, you will need to depend on the context clues in the text and how the word itself is made.

Using Context Clues

Context clues refer to the other words surrounding the unknown word and the subject being discussed in the text. For instance, read the sentences below:

> He kneeled down with his journal open on his lap, and, taking the stem of the plant in his hands, he started to draw what he observed. Once the botanist finished his drawing of the plant, including the flower, he was then able to label the different parts of the plant.

Now, let's say that the word "botanist" is the unknown word and your job is to determine what the word means using the words around it as clues. Well, you should be able to see that the subject of the paragraph is a person studying a plant. You can infer, then, that a botanist is someone who studies plants. Is there another way to confirm this? Are there other clues we can use? Yes, there are. Those other clues are called affixes and roots, which we will look at next.

Affixes and Roots

Affixes are suffixes and prefixes that change the meaning of words. A **suffix** is a part of a word that goes on the *end* of a root word, and a **prefix** is a part of a word that attaches to the *beginning* of a root word. For instance, take the root word, *honest*. To be honest is to always tell the truth. We can make this the opposite by adding the prefix *dis-*, making it *dishonest*, or always telling a lie. These two words are usually used as adjectives. Now, let's make it a noun by adding the suffix *-y*, making the word *dishonesty*.

How can we use this knowledge to help confirm that a "botanist" is someone who studies plants? If we know that the suffix, *-ist*, means a person who is a specialist or expert in a certain field, then we can be sure that our inference about the word "botanist" is correct.

It is important to familiarize yourself with some of the more common prefixes, suffixes, and root words that you may encounter on the SBAC. Study the prefixes, suffixes, and root words, and their respective definitions and examples, in Tables 3-2, 3-3, and 3-4 to prepare yourself for the SBAC.

Table 3-2. Prefixes

Prefixes	Definition	Example
anti-	against, opposite	antifreeze
auto-	self	autograph, automatic
bi-	two	binocular
centi-	100	centimeter
com-, con-	with, together	combine, conspire
de-	reduce down, away from	decrease
deca-, deci-	10	decade, decimal
dis-	not, opposite of	disagree
em-, en-	to go or put into or onto	employ, encounter
ex, exo-	out of, from	external, exoskeleton
fore-	before, earlier	foreword
il-, im-, in-, ir-	not	illogical, impossible, inactive, irregular
inter-	between	intercept
kilo-	1,000	kilogram, kilowatt
micro-	small	microscope

Table 3-2. Prefixes (continued)

Prefixes	Definition	Example
mid-	middle	midsection
mille-, milli-	1,000	millennium, millimeter
mis-	wrong	mislead
multi-	many, much	multicolor, multipurpose
non-	not	nonsense
oct-	eight	octagon
over-	not much, above	overdone
poly-	many, much	polygon
pre-	before	pretest
pro-	forward	proceed, produce
quad-	four	quadrilateral
re-	again	reread
retro-	back, backwards	retroactive
se-	apart	separate
semi-	half	semicircle
sub-	under, below, secondary	substitute, subway
super-	above, beyond	supersonic
tele-	far, distant	telephone
trans-	across, through, change	transform, transport
tri-	three	triangle
un-	not, opposite of	unlock
under-	too little, below	underfed, underground
uni-	one	uniform

Table 3-3. Suffixes

Suffixes	Definition	Example
-able	can be done	enjoyable
-age	result of an action, collection	acreage, manage
-al, -ial	related to, characterized by	dental, colonial
-an, -ian	one having a certain skill, relating to, belonging to	suburban, electrician, magician
-ation, -ion, -ition, -tion	act of, state of, result of	consideration, tension, condition, action
-en	made of, to make	tighten
-ence, -ance	act or condition of	persistence, clearance
-ent, -ant	an action, a condition, causing a specific action	obedient, student, elegant
-er, -or	person connected with	teacher, conductor
-est	superlative degree	biggest
-ful	full of	beautiful
-fy	to make, to form into	solidify
-hood	state, quality, condition of	neighborhood
-ic	relating to, characterized by	historic
-ice	state of, quality of	service
-ide	chemical	oxide
-ish	like, having the characteristics of	childish
-ity	state of, quality of	clarity, equality
-ive, -ative, -tive	tending toward action	festive, talkative, active
-ize	to make, to cause to become	energize
-less	without	careless, sleepless
-logy, -ology, -ologist	science of, study of, one who studies	biology, chronology, biologist
-ment	act, process	enjoyment
-ness	condition, state of	fairness

Table 3-3. Suffixes (continued)

Suffixes	Definition	Example
-ous, -eous, -ious	full of, characterized by	adventurous, courteous, curious
-some	characterized by a thing, state, quality, or action	awesome
-ward	in the direction of	forward
-ways	in what manner	airways

Table 3-4. Root Words

Roots	Definition	Example
aud	listen, hear	audience, auditory
bene, bon, boun	good, well	benefit, bonus, bounty
chron	time	chronological, synchronize
dict	to say, tell, or speak	contradict, predict
geo	earth, ground, soil	geography, geometry
hydr	water	hydrate
ject	to throw	objection, project
log, logos, logue	word or study	apology, logo, dialogue, prologue
meter	measure	perimeter, thermometer
miss, mit, mitt,	to send	mission, commit, emitted
photo	light	photograph
port	to carry	portable, portfolio
rupt	break, burst	disruptive
scribe, script	to write	describe, manuscript
spec, spect	to see, watch, or observe	spectacular, prospect
struct	to build	construct
terra	land	terrain
therm	heat	thermal, thermos
tract	pull, draw, drag	attract, subtract, tractor
vac	empty	vacate
vid, vis	to see	evidence, vision

Practice Exercises—Vocabulary Meaning and Use

Exercise 1

> **Common Core Standard L.5.6**
> Acquire and use accurately grade-appropriate general academic and domain-specific words and phrases, including those that signal contrast, addition, and other logical relationships (e.g., *however, although, nevertheless, similarly, moreover, in addition*).

1. Read the paragraph below.

   Barrett hated when his older brother, Jim, ignored him. He did everything he could think of to get Jim's attention, but his brother seemed <u>preoccupied</u> *with his homework. Jim had his face in his book and seemed unable to notice his brother's cries.*

   What is the meaning of the word <u>preoccupied</u> as it is used in the paragraph?

   ○ A. thinking about something a lot or too much
   ○ B. being alert and paying attention
   ○ C. to capture or take something
   ○ D. taking up space

   (Answer is on page 142.)

Exercise 2

> **Common Core Standard L.5.6**
> Acquire and use accurately grade-appropriate general academic and domain-specific words and phrases, including those that signal contrast, addition, and other logical relationships (e.g., *however, although, nevertheless, similarly, moreover, in addition*).

1. Read the sentences below.

   While at the airplane convention, she witnessed an airplane do an incredible <u>aerial maneuver</u>. The plane dove down toward the ground, turned the nose back up at the last minute, and then flew circles back up into the sky.

   Which phrase below best states the meaning of <u>aerial maneuver</u> in the text?

   ○ A. a set of movements completed by the airplane while on the ground
   ○ B. a set of movements completed by the mechanic fixing the airplane
   ◉ C. a set of movements completed by the airplane while flying in the air
   ○ D. a set of actions the pilot performs when preparing for flight

   (Answer is on page 143.)

Figurative Language

Figurative language is language that says more than just what the words mean. The opposite of figurative language is the literal meaning. For instance, read the following sentence: *Jennifer ran very fast.* This is very literal. There is only one way to understand it. Now, the author can make it more interesting by using figurative language: *Jennifer ran as fast as the wind.* The use of a simile both explains and paints a better picture for the reader.

   Common figurative language used by authors includes metaphors, similes, personification, and hyperboles.

Metaphors and Similes

For fifth grade, much of the focus in figurative language is on metaphors and similes. Metaphors and similes are literary devices that authors use to make their writing more interesting and rich. They also provide the reader with a deeper understanding of the story or poem. Knowing how to understand these literary devices helps you better comprehend what the author is saying. Table 3-5 illustrates the differences between metaphors and similes.

Table 3-5. Metaphors versus Similes

Metaphors		Similes
When two things that are not alike are compared; replaces the word with another	Definition	When two things that are not alike are compared; replaces the word with another word, but use the words *like* or *as*
To paint a picture for the reader	Purpose	To paint a picture for the reader, but also to give an example
Something *is* the another	Helpful Hint	Something is *like* or *as* another
The classroom is a zoo. Mekya's eyes were fireflies.	Examples	Evelyn is **as** cute as a button. Arjuna sings **like** an angel. Life is **like** a box of chocolates.

Personification

Personification is when an author gives human qualities to an object or animal. The most common examples of this are folktales, such as "The Hare and the Tortoise." In these types of stories, the animals talk and show human emotions, such as jealousy and envy. Personification can also be used to describe interactions with non-living objects.

Some examples of personification include:

Lightning danced across the night sky.

The wind howled in the night.

The car grunted as the key was turned.

Liz heard the last piece of cake calling her name.

My alarm clock screams every morning.

Hyperbole

Hyperbole is a form of exaggeration used for humor and emphasis on a certain feeling. Anytime you exaggerate to make a point, you are most often using hyperbole.

Some examples of hyperbole include:

It was so cold I saw polar bears wearing coats.

I am so hungry I could eat a horse.

I had a million chores to do.

If I can't get the new iPhone, I will die.

Betty told Evie a million times not to tease the dog.

Practice Exercises—Figurative Language

Exercise 1

> **Common Core Standard L.5.5**
> Demonstrate understanding of figurative language, word relationships, and nuances in word meanings.
>
> **Common Core Standard L.5.5.A**
> Interpret figurative language, including similes and metaphors, in context.
>
> **Common Core Standard L.5.5.B**
> Recognize and explain the meaning of common idioms, adages, and proverbs.

1. Match the sentences with the correct figurative language term. Draw a line connecting the two.

Sentence	Figurative Language Term
1. *Her eyes shone like diamonds.*	Metaphor
2. *The tree screamed as the ax hit its trunk.* Poor Tree	Hyperbole
3. *He had worked his fingers to the bone.*	Personification
4. *Books are keys to your imagination.*	Simile

(Answers are on page 143.)

English Language Arts Performance Task

CHAPTER 4

Overview

What Is the English Language Arts Performance Task?

The English Language Arts Performance Task portion of the test is a group of questions and tasks focused on one subject or theme. This set of questions and tasks will be more complex, or demanding, than the Computer Adaptive Test. For the Performance Task, you will be asked to write a multiple-paragraph response to the task.

What Am I Being Tested On?

The ELA Performance Task will test you on how well you can integrate information and research from multiple sources. You will write a response that has one of three goals: to inform, to narrate, or to argue an opinion. Your writing will be assessed for its purpose/organization, evidence/elaboration, and conventions.

The Types of Selections and Media

You will not know the prompt or writing topic you will be given until you sign in to the test. Whatever the task turns out to be, you will be presented with multiple sources of information that will include multiple articles or nonfiction texts. You may also be presented with pictures, videos, and/or audio clips. Using these sources of information, you will be required to construct an essay that uses evidence from each source to support your thinking.

The Classroom Activity

Prior to the ELA Performance Task, you will participate in a classroom activity facilitated by your teacher. The classroom activity is for the whole class and aims to give background information for the theme or topic of the Performance Task. For example, for the ELA Performance Task, the classroom activity could focus on the differences and similarities between spiders and insects. On the actual Performance Task, then, you will be given different sources about spiders and insects. From these sources, you will then be asked to write either an informative essay, an opinion essay, or a narrative that includes facts about spiders and insects.

The classroom activity ensures that all students have the same prior knowledge, or background information, about a certain subject before they have to write about it.

Layout and Interface

One aspect of the Performance Task that can be overwhelming for many students is the layout. There is a lot of information to make sense of in a tight space. The source, or text to be read, is on the left, and the questions, where you will be writing your responses, are on the right. To gather evidence, you may want to use the notepad feature included with the interactive tools. This way, you will save time from having to scroll up and down when referring back to the text.

When you are ready to compose, or write, a multiple-paragraph response, the SBAC will include word processing tools, which would look similar to those in Figure 4-1.

Figure 4-1. Word Processing Tools on the SBAC

If you are not familiar with these tools, ask your teacher or parent to guide you through how to use them before the exam. These tools may be needed to enhance your writing, whether you are bolding text or creating a bulleted list.

Applying Your Strategies

Reading and Researching Strategies

During the Performance Task, you will be asked to read more than one source or text. You will need a note-taking system that works for you to gather the most important information from each source.

First, take notice of the text:

1. Preview the passage by noticing the title, text structure, bolded or underlined vocabulary words, topic sentences, and any visuals, such as pictures or graphs. Do not read the passage at this point. Previewing the text beforehand will prepare your brain for comprehending the text and the questions.
2. Read the passage for the first time all the way through for general comprehension. Pay attention to any repeated words and ideas that may connect to the questions or prompts.
3. Start taking notes on any strong evidence or ideas you may want to use in your writing. You may want to jot down key details, quotes to support details/evidence, and names of experts. Use the interactive notepad feature provided by the SBAC to take any notes for answering the questions. Remember, though, that you will not be able to copy/paste or highlight within the text.

Second, be aware of the Performance Task format. This is very important. The Performance Task is designed with a handful of research questions asked before the writing task to help you analyze the text sources before you start writing. In some cases, your answers to these research questions may be directly used in your essay during the writing task.

Evidence, Evidence, Evidence!

One of the most important elements to always include is your evidence! You want to show that you can refer back to the texts, or sources, to support your own thinking and ideas. Remember the A.C.E. strategy? A.C.E. stands for **A**nswer, **C**ite, **E**xplain and can be applied to writing for the Performance Task. Each of your body paragraphs should include evidence from one of the sources. Use the writing organizers in this chapter to help guide you on how to include evidence.

Constructing Your Response

There are many systems or tools that you can depend on to organize your thoughts and ideas before you begin writing. This could be anything from a Venn diagram to a graphic organizer. These types of systems allow you to take notes on the most important information that you will use from each source. It also gives you a way to organize the structure of your essay.

In this chapter, we will supply you with an essay organizer to fill in and use to organize your thoughts and evidence. This will help you keep track of your evidence, and it will help you plan how you will write your essay.

Planning, drafting, and revising an essay within a testing time frame can seem difficult, especially if you are used to multiple-day essay assignments in class. If you follow a system, however, the overall process won't seem so challenging.

Combining Information from Multiple Sources

All the sources made available during the ELA Performance Task, including articles, videos, and/or audio, will center on a common theme or topic. The SBAC will expect you to take the most important information from each to use in your writing and support your statements.

Identify the main idea and supporting details from each source. This will help you organize the details that support the theme of all the sources. Doing so should help you create a clear and complete thesis statement for your essay.

Make sure to use at least one piece of evidence from each source. The exam is looking for whether you can integrate information from multiple sources.

Revising and Editing

Most writing assignments completed in class are written over the course of a couple of days. This allows you ample time to spend focusing on the writing process. When writing for the SBAC, however, your time will be limited. You will need to use the writing process in a shorter amount of time.

Allow yourself time to revise and edit. Before turning in your essay, make sure to read your writing to yourself. This makes a tremendous difference for many students when they use this simple strategy.

The Performance Task will provide a list of expectations for your writing in the instructions at the beginning of the second part of the Performance Task. You will be given instructions for what you are expected to write. Look back at these instructions, and use them as a checklist. Reread your essay, and mentally check these items off.

As you are reading, also pay attention to your grammar, sentence structure, and punctuation.

Practice Exercises—Research Questions

Common Core Standard W.5.7
Conduct short research projects that use several sources to build knowledge through investigation of different aspects of a topic.

Common Core Standard W.5.8
Recall relevant information from experiences or gather relevant information from print and digital sources; summarize or paraphrase information in notes and finished work, and provide a list of sources.

Common Core Standard W.5.9
Draw evidence from literary or informational texts to support analysis, reflection, and research.

Before you learn how to write the different types of responses, you need to familiarize yourself with the types of research questions you will be asked before the writing task begins. These questions will help you begin to analyze the various sources that you will refer back to in your writing response.

Directions: In this practice exercise, you will read three sources, and then answer three questions based on these sources. Remember, first preview the passage. Pay specific attention to the title, text structure, any bolded or underlined vocabulary words, and the topic sentences. You may also want to briefly scan the questions before reading the sources so that you have an idea of what to keep an eye out for when you're reading. Then, read the passage through for full comprehension. Pay attention to any repeated words or ideas that you may be able to connect to the questions. If necessary, take notes of strong evidence, key details, or quotes that may be helpful to refer back to in your responses.

Source Number 1—Solar Power

Solar, wind, and geothermal energy are a few renewable sources of energy. Renewable sources of energy are an environmentally friendly option to burning fossil fuels.

Solar energy is an endless renewable source of energy. The sun creates an unlimited source of energy that can be used in every single household and every commercial and industrial property.

Solar energy is the transformation of solar radiation into electric power. This is done with the photovoltaic cell.

Photovoltaic cells capture solar energy and transform it into electricity. These cells convert sunlight into electricity by utilizing the energy produced when photons from sunlight push electrons into a greater state of energy. Photovoltaic cells can be used in a variety of applications. Many products use these cells already to replace conventional batteries. These cells can also be used in bigger applications, such as houses and commercial buildings.

When utilizing solar power, you're not only helping reduce air pollution but you are also saving many of the earth's natural resources. The high initial costs of installing solar panels can be one factor that stops people from investing in the technology. The long-term benefits, however, can be great to someone's pocketbook. Some households produce so much energy from solar power that they have some left over to sell back to power companies! Of course, the most important benefit to installing solar panels is knowing that you are not contributing to environmental pollution and damage.

Source Number 2—Save Energy and Money with Home Lighting Techniques

From the kitchen, basement, or even the couch, you can now turn lights on or off remotely, create "zones" of activity, and control every shade of light and color in your home without ever flipping a switch. These benefits—along with the ability to save energy and money—are just a few reasons why consumers are rapidly adopting automated lighting and wireless or cloud-based home management systems.

While these systems aren't new, the ability to combine them with apps and the most energy-efficient lighting technology is. In fact, it's allowing homeowners to use them in ways they never thought possible. One example is matching your family's lifestyle with energy-saving lighting controls. You can use your smartphone or tablet to enhance home security by remotely monitoring and then adjusting lighting status throughout the house while you're away. You can integrate lighting controls with motion sensors to dim or turn off lights automatically when a room is unoccupied. In some cases, you can even have lights flash when the phone or doorbell rings to speed response.

Pairing these systems with Energy Star-certified LED bulb technology will allow for even faster payback. LEDs use 75 to 80 percent less energy than incandescent bulbs which, according to the Environmental Protection Agency, will help you save about $6 per bulb or about $14 a fixture annually on your energy bill. With the addition of lighting controls, you can save even more.

Some LED bulb solutions may look like familiar light bulbs, and some may not. To help you "bulb up" on selecting the right LED light for each area of your home, the New York State Energy Research and Development Authority (NYSERDA) offers all the resources you need. On its website, you'll find instructions on how to read the Lighting Facts label on LED packaging, charts on warm and cool lighting, bulb shapes, and a handy calculator to help you see how much you can save while setting up your specific bulb functions.

Once you get your LEDs and your automated lighting set up, you'll have plenty of time to reap the advantages—especially considering that Energy Star-certified LEDs can last up to 49,000 hours longer than the usual 1,000 hours you get from a standard incandescent bulb. So, have fun using more futuristic apps, well into the future.

Source: *www.newsusa.com*

Source Number 3—Audio Source Transcript: The New World of Light Switches, Controls, and Dimmers

A lighting switch is just a switch, right? As it turns out, not really. Technology is changing the smallest details in your home—switches, controls, and dimmers—to make daily life more beautiful and more functional. The American Lighting Association (ALA) details advances in lighting switches.

New Bulbs Equal New Switches

If you have decided to embrace the energy-smart world that is LED light-bulbs, there is something that might be hindering your use of them: your traditional lighting controls.

"Traditional lighting controls don't work very well with the new bulbs," says Erik Anderson, national sales manager, residential construction for Lutron Electronics Co. The reason is that the physics of the new bulbs is much different than that of incandescent bulbs. "With LEDs and CFLs, the way the light is emitted is driven by a driver or a ballast, and those don't naturally dim."

Say you have a fixture with four bulbs; one burns out, and you decide to replace it with an LED-equivalent version. The old traditional dimmer does not know how to control that mixed load of bulbs, but new specialized dimmers are engineered and designed to work in that situation.

Wireless Lighting Controls

One thing that often stops homeowners from improving the efficiency of lighting controls is wiring. Older systems used to require wires from one control to another. Now, wireless controllers allow control from spots around the room or even another room.

Apps, used on either a tablet or smartphone, are also an integral part of modern-day lighting control systems. The bonus is that they also can control window treatments and in-home temperature. "It's just a matter of swapping out existing controls for wireless versions that can communicate with each other," says Anderson.

The Next Generation of Light Bulbs

Many homeowners still see LED as the wave of the future, and to a certain extent it is. But lightbulbs in development will integrate control technologies in new ways.

"These are smart light bulbs that can fit into any kind of a standard socket," says Terry McGowan, director of engineering and technology for ALA. "They connect to the Internet, and you can adjust them so they dim up and down, come on at appropriate times, change color, even flash in time with music."

As these new bulbs and controls make their way into wider acceptance in the marketplace, consumers are going to have a shift in how they think about lighting.

Source: *www.newsusa.com*

1. Click on the boxes that match the source with the correct idea or ideas that it supports. Some ideas may relate to more than one source.

	Source Number 1— Solar Power	Source Number 2— Save Energy and Money with Home Lighting Techniques (NewsUSA)	Source Number 3— Audio Source Transcript: The New World of Light Switches, Controls, and Dimmers (NewsUSA)
Light bulbs no longer have to be controlled only by a light switch.	☐	☑	☑
Using certain sources of renewable energy can not only save money, but can also help the environment.	☑	☐	☐

2. All three sources discuss different ways to make a home more energy efficient. Explain what you have learned about making a home energy efficient. Use one supporting detail from Source Number 1 and one supporting detail from Source Number 2 to support your reasons. Make sure to refer to which source you used for each detail. Write your answer in the box below.

3. Which of the three sources would most likely be the most helpful in terms of supporting the idea that new lighting technology can help with energy costs? Describe why this source would most likely support this idea. Give at least two details from the source to support your explanation. Write your answer in the box below.

(Answers are on page 144.)

Practice Exercises—Informative Performance Task Essay

Common Core Standard W.5.2
Write informative/explanatory texts to examine a topic and convey ideas and information clearly.

Common Core Standard W.5.2.A
Introduce a topic clearly, provide a general observation and focus, and group related information logically; include formatting (e.g., headings), illustrations, and multimedia when useful to aiding comprehension.

Common Core Standard W.5.2.B
Develop the topic with facts, definitions, concrete details, quotations, or other information and examples related to the topic.

Common Core Standard W.5.2.C
Link ideas within and across categories of information using words, phrases, and clauses (e.g., *in contrast, especially*).

Common Core Standard W.5.2.D
Use precise language and domain-specific vocabulary to inform about or explain the topic.

Common Core Standard W.5.2.E
Provide a concluding statement or section related to the information or explanation presented.

Steps for Constructing an Informative Performance Task Essay

Planning, drafting, and revising an essay within a testing time frame can seem difficult, especially if you are used to multiple-day essay assignments in class. If you follow a system, however, the overall process won't seem so challenging. Let's walk through a possible system for constructing an informative essay within the testing time frame.

Remember, read the directions first! It may seem like a lot, and you may get tired of reading all of it, but the SBAC actually lays out exactly what they want from you. If you simply follow their directions, you should do very well.

Here are some important points to check off to make sure that you have constructed a well-written, informative essay:

- [ ] Has a clear main idea
- [ ] Is well-organized and stays on topic
- [ ] Has an introduction and a conclusion
- [ ] Uses transitions
- [ ] Uses details from the sources to support the main idea
- [ ] Puts the information from the sources in your own words, except when using direct quotations from the sources
- [ ] Gives the title or number of the source when citing the source
- [ ] Develops all ideas clearly
- [ ] Uses clear language throughout the essay
- [ ] Follows the rules of writing (i.e., correct spelling, punctuation, and grammar usage)

Informative Performance Task Essay Prompt

Your school has decided to update its electrical system (solar power, lights, wiring, light switches, etc.) to make the school more environmentally friendly and to save energy. The principal thought it was a good idea to have the students participate in deciding how to make the school more green. Your teacher asked you to complete research in groups. These groups spent time collecting information, and now you have a copy of the three most important sources from your research.

Your teacher now wants you to write an informative essay explaining how to make the school more energy efficient. Reread the three sources from your research, Source Number 1, Source Number 2, and Source Number 3 on pages 72–75, to familiarize yourself with the topic of energy efficiency. Using more than one of these sources, develop a main idea about new technologies for energy efficiency. Choose the most important details from multiple sources to support your main idea. Then, write an informative essay that is multiple paragraphs long. Make sure to organize your essay with the appropriate support for your main idea. Any words that are not your own should be in quotations.

(Before you get started writing your essay, use the essay organizer that follows to organize your thoughts for each paragraph of your essay. Make sure to follow each step carefully. Then use the space that follows to write your essay.)

Informative Performance Task Essay Organizer

Introduction Paragraph

Introduce and Summarize:	
Thesis Statement:	

Body Paragraphs

State the Main Idea:	
Cite Evidence: (Support your answer with details from the text.)	
Explain: (Why or how does your evidence support your answer?)	This means . . . This is an example of . . . This reminds me . . .

State the Main Idea:	
Cite Evidence: (Support your answer with details from the text.)	
Explain: (Why or how does your evidence support your answer?)	This means . . . This is an example of . . . This reminds me . . .

State the Main Idea:	
Cite Evidence: (Support your answer with details from the text.)	
Explain: (Why or how does your evidence support your answer?)	This means . . . This is an example of . . . This reminds me . . .

Conclusion Paragraph

Summarize What You Wrote:	
Restate Your Thesis Statement:	

Informative Performance Task Essay Response

Now, using the information you compiled in your essay organizer, write your essay response in the box on page 83. Once you've finished writing your essay, read the Informative Performance Task Essay Checklist to make sure that your essay meets all of the necessary goals. A Sample Informative Performance Task Essay Organizer and a high-scoring Sample Informative Performance Task Essay Response can be found beginning on page 145.

INFORMATIVE PERFORMANCE TASK ESSAY CHECKLIST

- ☐ Did you identify the main idea?

- ☐ Did you create a clear and concise thesis statement that includes all talking points?

- ☐ Does your thesis statement have supporting evidence, and is your explanation clear?

- ☐ Did you utilize a variety of elaborative techniques effectively (i.e., quotes, experts, explanations, examples, etc.)?

- ☐ Did you give a title for or number the source for your supporting evidence and facts?

- ☐ Do you have an understandable sequence or progression of ideas (i.e., if you disagree with something, your reasons why should be right after, not in a different paragraph)?

- ☐ Do you have transitions?

- ☐ Did you check your grammar, punctuation, and spelling?

- ☐ Do you have an effective conclusion?

Practice Exercises—Opinion Performance Task Essay

Common Core Standard W.5.1
Write opinion pieces on topics or texts, supporting a point of view with reasons and information.

Common Core Standard W.5.1.A
Introduce a topic or text clearly, state an opinion, and create an organizational structure in which ideas are logically grouped to support the writer's purpose.

Common Core Standard W.5.1.B
Provide logically ordered reasons that are supported by facts and details.

Common Core Standard W.5.1.C
Link opinion and reasons using words, phrases, and clauses (e.g., *consequently*, *specifically*).

Common Core Standard W.5.1.D
Provide a concluding statement or section related to the opinion presented.

Steps for Constructing an Opinion Performance Task Essay

Planning, drafting, and revising an essay within a testing time frame can seem difficult, especially if you are used to multiple-day essay assignments in class. If you follow a system, however, the overall process won't seem so challenging. Let's walk through a possible system for constructing an opinion essay within the testing time frame.

Remember, read the directions first! It may seem like a lot, and you may get tired of reading all of it, but the SBAC actually lays out exactly what they want from you. If you simply follow their directions, you should do very well.

Here are some important points to check off to make sure that you have constructed a well-written, opinion essay:

- ☐ Has a clear thesis statement with your opinion
- ☐ Is well-organized and stays on topic
- ☐ Has an introduction and a conclusion
- ☐ Uses transitions
- ☐ Uses details from the sources to support your claims
- ☐ Puts the information from the sources into your own words, except when using direct quotations from the sources
- ☐ Gives the title or number of the source for the details or facts you've included
- ☐ Includes a counterargument
- ☐ Develops all ideas clearly
- ☐ Uses clear language
- ☐ Follows the rules of writing (i.e., spelling, punctuation, and grammar usage)

Opinion Performance Task Essay Prompt

Your school has decided to update its electrical system (solar power, lights, wiring, light switches, etc.) to make the school more environmentally friendly and to save energy. The principal thought it was a good idea to have the students participate in deciding how to make the school more green.

Convince the school district to update and use renewable energy to be more environmentally friendly and energy efficient. Reread the three sources, Source Number 1, Source Number 2, and Source Number 3 on pages 72–75, to familiarize yourself with the topic of energy efficiency. Then, write an opinion essay that is multiple paragraphs long. Make sure to organize your essay with the appropriate support for your opinion. Any words that are not your own should be in quotations.

(Before you get started writing your essay, use the essay organizer that follows to organize your thoughts for each paragraph of your essay. Make sure to follow each step carefully. Then use the space that follows to write your essay.)

Opinion Performance Task Essay Organizer

Introduction Paragraph

Introduce and Summarize:	
Thesis Statement:	

Body Paragraphs

Reason: (Use part of the question in your answer.)	The main reason I think . . . First, I believe that . . . Second, I believe that . . . My final reason for believing . . . In addition, I think . . .
Cite Evidence: (Support your answer with details from the text.)	_____ states "_____."
Explain: (Why or how does your evidence support your answer?)	This shows . . . This means . . . This is an example of . . .

Reason: (Use part of the question in your answer.)	The main reason I think . . . First, I believe that . . . Second, I believe that . . . My final reason for believing . . . In addition, I think . . .
Cite Evidence: (Support your answer with details from the text.)	_____ states "_____."
Explain: (Why or how does your evidence support your answer?)	This shows . . . This means . . . This is an example of . . .

Reason: (Use part of the question in your answer.)	The main reason I think . . . First, I believe that . . . Second, I believe that . . . My final reason for believing . . . In addition, I think . . .
Cite Evidence: (Support your answer with details from the text.)	_____ states "_____."
Explain: (Why or how does your evidence support your answer?)	This shows . . . This means . . . This is an example of . . .

Conclusion Paragraph

Opinion: (State your opinion.)	I believe . . .
Counterargument: (State a sentence of the opposite side and then restate your opinion.)	Some may argue that . . . However . . .
Restate Reasons: (Insert a concluding sentence.)	In conclusion . . .

Opinion Performance Task Essay Response

Now, using the information you compiled in your essay organizer, write your essay response in the box on page 90. Once you've finished writing your essay, read the Opinion Performance Task Essay Checklist to make sure that your essay meets all of the necessary goals. A Sample Opinion Performance Task Essay Organizer and a high-scoring Sample Opinion Performance Task Essay Response can be found beginning on page 148.

OPINION PERFORMANCE TASK
ESSAY CHECKLIST

- [ ] Does your introduction include a strong and clear thesis that states your position or argument?

- [ ] Did you utilize a variety of elaborative techniques effectively (i.e., quotes, experts, explanations, examples, etc.)?

- [ ] Did you give a title for or number the source for your supporting evidence and facts?

- [ ] Do you have an understandable sequence or progression of ideas (i.e., if you disagree with something, your reasons why should be right after, not in a different paragraph)?

- [ ] Does each reason have supporting evidence?

- [ ] Do you have transitions?

- [ ] Did you check your grammar, punctuation, and spelling?

- [ ] Did you state your opinion, introduce a counterargument, and then restate the reasons for your opinion?

- [ ] Does your essay have a clear conclusion that includes your position?

Practice Exercises—Narrative Performance Task Essay

Common Core Standard W.5.3
Write narratives to develop real or imagined experiences or events using effective technique, descriptive details, and clear event sequences.

Common Core Standard W.5.3.A
Orient the reader by establishing a situation and introducing a narrator and/or characters; organize an event sequence that unfolds naturally.

Common Core Standard W.5.3.B
Use narrative techniques, such as dialogue, description, and pacing, to develop experiences and events or show the responses of characters to situations.

Common Core Standard W.5.3.C
Use a variety of transitional words, phrases, and clauses to manage the sequence of events.

Common Core Standard W.5.3.D
Use concrete words and phrases and sensory details to convey experiences and events precisely.

Common Core Standard W.5.3.E
Provide a conclusion that follows from the narrated experiences or events.

Steps for Constructing a Narrative Performance Task Essay

Planning, drafting, and revising an essay within a testing time frame can seem difficult, especially if you are used to multiple-day essay assignments in class. If you follow a system, however, the overall process won't seem so challenging. Let's walk through a possible system for constructing a narrative essay within the testing time frame.

Remember, read the directions first! It may seem like a lot, and you may get tired of reading all of it, but the SBAC actually lays out exactly what they want from you. If you simply follow their directions, you should do very well.

Here are some important points to check off to make sure that you have constructed a well-written, narrative essay:

- [ ] Has a plot with a beginning and an end, using effective transitions
- [ ] Establishes a setting and characters
- [ ] Elaborates details, dialogue, and descriptions to advance the story or illustrate the experience
- [ ] Effectively expresses experiences or events using sensory, concrete, and figurative language that is appropriate for your purpose
- [ ] Follows the rules of writing (i.e. ,spelling, punctuation, and grammar usage)

Narrative Performance Task Essay Prompt

You have done research on how to make your school more energy efficient with new technologies. Now, you are going to write a narrative story from the viewpoint of a student stuck inside an elementary school where the power has gone out. Reread the three sources, Source Number 1, Source Number 2, and Source Number 3 on pages 72–75, to familiarize yourself with the topic of energy efficiency. Then integrate factual details from these sources into your story. Any words that are not your own should be in quotations. Manage your time carefully so that you can:

1. Plan your narrative.
2. Write your narrative.
3. Revise and edit for a final draft.

(Before you get started writing your essay, use the essay organizer that follows to organize your thoughts for each paragraph of your essay. Make sure to follow each step carefully. Then use the space that follows to write your essay.)

Narrative Performance Task Essay Organizer

Beginning

Establish a Setting:	
Introduce the Characters: (Describe the characters.)	

Middle

Event 1: (What's the conflict or problem?)	
Event 2: (How do the characters deal with or try to solve the problem?)	
Event 3: (What is the effect of the characters' actions from Event 2?)	

Ending

What is the Last Effect from the Events? Is the Conflict Solved?	
What Happens to the Characters?	

Narrative Performance Task Essay Response

Now, using the information you compiled in your essay organizer, write your essay response in the boxes on pages 96–97. Once you've finished writing your essay, read the Narrative Performance Task Essay Checklist to make sure that your essay meets all of the necessary goals. A Sample Narrative Performance Task Essay Organizer and a high-scoring Sample Narrative Performance Task Essay Response can be found beginning on page 152.

NARRATIVE PERFORMANCE TASK
ESSAY CHECKLIST

☐ Do you have the main events?

☐ Do you have a beginning, middle, and end?

☐ Did you pay attention to the cause and effect?

☐ Did you develop the characters and setting?

☐ Did you introduce a problem and create a way for the characters to deal with the problem or conflict?

☐ Did you create a hook to gain the reader's interest?

☐ Did you include dialogue?

☐ Did you check your grammar, punctuation, and spelling?

English Language Arts Practice Test

Computer Adaptive Test

Directions: On the actual Grade 5 Smarter Balanced exam, the instructions will inform you about the rules and navigation of the test. These instructions include the fact that you cannot skip questions and that all questions on one page must be answered before moving on to the next page. In addition, you will be able to flag, or mark, a question to review later before submitting your test.

1. Betty is writing an opinion essay on whether or not chocolate milk should be served at school. Read the beginning of her report, her opinion, and the notes that she took from reliable sources. Then, complete the directions that follow.

   Betty's First Paragraph:

   Chocolate milk is popular all over the nation as a school lunch drink choice. Now, there is a debate among nutritionists and educators as to whether or not chocolate milk is a nutritious choice for students. Much of the debate focuses on the balance of sugar and essential nutrients.

   Betty's Opinion:

   Betty decides to take the side that chocolate milk should not be served in schools.

   Betty's Notes from Reliable Sources:

   1. Chocolate milk has more than 30 grams of sugar per serving.
   2. Too much sugar in a child's diet can lead to obesity.
   3. Many other countries have already banned chocolate milk in their schools.
   4. The suggested amount of daily sugar is 37.5 grams for growing children.

Use Betty's notes to compose a paragraph that uses facts and concrete details to support Betty's opinion. Write your answer in the box below.

2. A student wrote the sentence below that includes errors. Circle the two words that should be followed by a comma.

"Yesterday we watched a movie before dinner and had popcorn" said Molly.

3. A student is writing a story for his English class about a nervous soccer player who has to take over for the star player. Read the beginning of the story below, and then answer Parts A, B, and C.

It was a close game. Mekya watched from the sidelines as his team kept their pace with the visiting team. It would be embarrassing for the team to lose on their own field. Their star player, Michael, was working hard to make sure that didn't happen. So far, he had scored the team's three goals. The game was now tied.

The soccer ball went back and forth between the teams as the crowd grew more excited. The fury of the battle made Michael play even harder. Mekya was happy to sit on the sidelines and watch the excitement of the game. It was one of his worst fears to have to be called in to substitute. His heart always pounded faster when he thought of himself being thrown into the game.

Just then, Michael could be heard calling out in pain! Mekya looked across the field and saw Michael lying on the ground. The medics immediately rushed out to the field with a stretcher. In the deep of Mekya's gut, he had a feeling about what was about to happen. Just then, the coach looked over at him.

Part A

What inference can be made about how the character Mekya feels about the soccer game?

- ○ A. Mekya enjoys watching games but would like to be put in the game.
- ○ B. Mekya was confident he would be put in the game by the coach.
- ○ C. Mekya was worried about his team's ability to win the game.
- ◉ D. Mekya felt nervous at the thought of being put in the game.

Part B

Which **two** sentences below support your inference from Part A?

- ☐ A. "Mekya watched from the sidelines as his team kept their pace with the visiting team."
- ☑ B. "Mekya was happy to sit on the sidelines and watch the excitement of the game."
- ☐ C. "Mekya looked across the field and saw Michael lying on the ground."
- ☑ D. "His heart always pounded faster when he thought of himself being thrown into the game."

Part C

Write an ending to this story. Match it to the events and experiences of the previous paragraphs. Write one or two paragraphs in the box below.

Directions: Read the text. Then answer questions 4–8.

compound sentence with ; however,

tenses review

Penguins Are Fascinating!

Birds are fascinating creatures! When we think of birds, however, we tend to think of a creature that flies. Penguins are birds, too, but they cannot fly. How are they still considered a bird, yet they can't fly? Well, scientists hypothesize that penguins could once fly just like other birds.

Penguins cannot fly because the wings they do have are not strong enough to lift them. At one time, though, penguins were birds that could fly. As they migrated to Antarctica and other cold regions, they began to depend on their wings less and less. The landscape of Antarctica is a harsh climate with below zero temperatures and two-mile thick sheets of ice. Here, there are no predators for the penguins to escape from and therefore no reason for them to fly away from anything.

Their wings, though, are not a total loss. Penguins needed to find food in a new way. They became excellent swimmers and started using their shorter, more rigid, wings as flippers to guide them through the icy waters. Their flippers and webbed feet help them dive to depths of seventy feet to catch various foods such as krill, shrimp, fish, lobsters, and crab.

As graceful as they are in the water, many people find penguins to be comical and cute. On land, they tend to waddle and look as if they are wearing tuxedos, with their black and white feathers. Many people might not know that there are several different species of penguins. The one most familiar to people is the Emperor penguin. This penguin can be up to four feet tall and weigh up to ninety pounds. The smallest penguin is simply called Little Penguin and is found on the shores of New Zealand. This penguin grows to a height of 17 in. and weighs about 3 pounds.

One of the most interesting facts about penguins has to be the way they raise their young. Male Emperor penguins in particular keep the eggs warm between their bodies and feet. While the male protects the eggs and keeps them warm, the female penguins are hunting for their families in the frigid waters. As the colder months move along, the male penguins begin to huddle closer and closer together to keep themselves warm. Any male penguin that does not make it into the huddle and is left on his own will usually perish.

It is a sight to see up to half a million birds in one colony huddled together as they fight to keep themselves and their babies alive. Once the female penguins come back, it is about time for the eggs to hatch. For several months, the baby penguins depend on their parents to feed them until they are ready to make it on their own.

There are new dangers now facing penguins who live in Antarctica. Climate change is having a big effect on Emperor penguins in particular. Climate change has brought longer warm seasons to the region, which breaks up the ice that the penguins rely on to raise their young. Baby penguins, who cannot yet swim, can end up being swept away from the colony. Even worse, climate change means lower food supplies for the penguins. Emperor penguins rely heavily on krill for their diet. The warming waters around Antarctica mean less krill for the penguins.

People are often unaware how their everyday lives can impact penguins all the way in Antarctica. Many of our daily routines contribute to the decline in penguin populations. Driving a car to work, using kitchen appliances, or turning on a light all can have an impact on penguins' lives. Every time we turn on one of these things, we are burning fossil fuels. These fossil fuels create climate change, which warms the waters around Antarctica. It may be a big planet, but we can still have a big impact on living things many miles away.

4. Read the statement below. Then, follow the directions.

Penguins began to depend less on their wings as they evolved from birds that needed to fly to escape predators.

Circle the two sentences from the paragraph below that best describe this idea.

"Penguins cannot fly because the wings they do have are not strong enough to lift them. At one time, though, penguins were birds that could fly. As they migrated to Antarctica and other cold regions, they began to depend on their wings less and less. The landscape of Antarctica is a harsh climate with below zero temperatures and two-mile thick sheets of ice. Here, there are no predators for the penguins to escape from and therefore no reason for them to fly away from anything."

5. Read the paragraph below. Then, answer the question.

"As graceful as they are in the water, many people find penguins to be comical and cute. On land, they tend to waddle and look as if they are wearing tuxedos, with their black and white feathers. Many people might not know that there are several different species of penguins. The one most familiar to people is the Emperor penguin. This penguin can be up to four feet tall and weigh up to ninety pounds. The smallest penguin is simply called Little Penguin and is found on the shores of New Zealand. This penguin grows to a height of 17 in. and weighs about 3 pounds."

Which sentence below best describes the central idea of this paragraph?

- A. Penguins look cute.
- B. The Emperor penguin is bigger than the Little Penguin.
- C. There are many different types of penguins that come in varying sizes.
- D. Penguins in New Zealand look as if they are wearing tuxedos.

6. What conclusion can be drawn about the author's viewpoint about penguins? Use details from the text to support your answer. Write your answer in the box below.

7. What conclusion can be drawn about the effects of climate change on penguins? Use details from the text to support your answer. Write your answer in the box below.

8. This question has two parts. First, read the following paragraph from the text. Then, answer Part A and Part B.

"People are often unaware how their everyday lives can impact penguins all the way in Antarctica. Many of our daily routines contribute to the decline in penguin populations. Driving a car to work, using kitchen appliances, or turning on a light all can have an impact on penguins' lives. Every time we turn on one of these things, we are burning fossil fuels. These fossil fuels create climate change, which warms the waters around Antarctica. It may be a big planet, but we can still have a big impact on living things many miles away."

Part A: Which statement below best describes the author's point of view from the information in this paragraph?

- A. The author believes that people should stop turning on lights to help climate change.
- B. The author believes that getting rid of fossil fuels will stop climate change.
- C. The author believes that people can still have a big impact on penguins even though they are many miles away.
- D. The author believes that we cannot help fight the warming waters of Antarctica.

Part B: Which sentences from the paragraph best support your answer to Part A? Choose the **two** that apply.

- A. "It may be a big planet, but we can still have a big impact on living things many miles away."
- B. "These fossil fuels create climate change, which warms the waters around Antarctica."
- C. "Every time we turn on one of these things, we are burning fossil fuels."
- D. "People are often unaware how their everyday lives can impact penguins all the way in Antarctica."

Directions: Read the poem. Then answer question 9.

A Day Well Spent

If you sit down at set of sun
And count the deeds that you have done,
And, counting, find
One self-denying act, one word that eased the heart of him that heard;
One glance most kind, which felt like sunshine where it went,
Then you may count that day well spent.

But if through, all the livelong day
You've eased no heart by yea or nay,
If through it all you've nothing done that you can trace
That brought the sunshine to one face,
No act most small that helped some soul and nothing cost,
Then count that day as worse than lost.

Source: *A Day Well Spent* from *Poems Teachers Ask For.* Project Gutenberg, 2006.
www.gutenberg.org/files/18909/18909-h/18909-h.htm.

9. The central theme of this poem is the importance of doing good deeds for others. Write a paragraph that explains this theme by using key details from the poem to support your answer.

10. Evelyn is writing an opinion letter to her principal trying to convince him to ban soda in the cafeteria due to its bad health effects. Read her draft of her introductory paragraph below and respond to the tasks that follow.

> Dear Mr. Mathew,
>
> I am writing to you today to convince you to stop serving soda in our school cafeteria. Soda is an unhealthy drink that should not be a choice for students. The school has already banned unhealthy junk food from our classroom parties and recess snacks. I believe that soda is also a type of junk food. The amount of sugar in soda can lead to various health problems, such as diabetes and heart disease. In addition, these health risks can add to our obesity epidemic among young people in the country.

Part A

Evelyn still needs to add a thesis statement to her introductory paragraph. Choose which sentence below she should use as her thesis statement.

- ○ A. In my opinion, we should ban soda.
- ○ B. I believe you should ban soda because it is an unhealthy choice.
- ◉ C. In my opinion, we should ban soda because it is a type of junk food, it contains an unhealthy amount of sugar, and it can lead to many health problems.
- ○ D. I hope I convinced you to ban soda.

Part B

Evelyn would like to improve her word choice in her introductory paragraph. Read her sentences below and answer the task that follows.

> I am writing to you today to <u>convince</u> you to stop serving soda in our school cafeteria. Soda is an <u>unhealthy</u> drink that should not be a choice for students. The school has already banned unhealthy junk food from our classroom parties and recess snacks. I believe that soda is also a type of junk food.

She would like to replace the two underlined words with stronger synonyms. Choose the two she should replace them with.

- ○ A. deter, beneficial
- ◉ B. persuade, harmful
- ○ C. understand, bad
- ○ D. tell, another

Directions: Read the text. Then answer questions 11–22.

Modern Farming: Technology Helps Keep Food on the Table

From farm to table, much about food production has changed—for both farmers and consumers. Like any other business, farmers must adapt to a changing world—one that will see its population grow to 9.6 billion by 2050. With finite resources, it will take innovation and a variety of technologies to meet the world's food demand. This includes using new technologies like biotechnology (also referred to as genetic engineering), which can help produce more food on the same amount of land, without having to destroy wildlife habitats.

A 2014 study by the International Food Information Council (IFIC), "Consumer Perceptions of Food Technology," shows that more than seven in 10 consumers agree that modern agriculture—conventional farming using today's modern tools and equipment—can be sustainable and produce high-quality, nutritious foods. The survey also underscored that two-thirds (66 percent) of respondents say it is important that their food be produced in a sustainable way, including producing food affordably with the same or fewer resources, in a way that is better for the environment.

"When consumers understand the potential benefits that technology in food production can have for both people and the planet, they can get behind it," said Marianne Smith Edge, MS, RD, LD, FADA, and senior vice president of Nutrition and Food Safety at IFIC. "People need to know what's in it for them." To this point, of consumers who ranked these factors of sustainability as important, most believe there is a role for biotechnology:

- Ensuring a sufficient food supply for a growing global population
- Producing more food with fewer natural resources
- Conserving the natural habitat
- Reducing carbon footprint

To address increasing interest in how our food is produced, IFIC Foundation provides a glimpse of modern agriculture in its new animated video, "Your Food, Farm to Table," showing how farmers in the U.S. and globally are working to produce our food year-round, including using technology to safely produce more food, while putting less stress on our natural resources. With more "precise" information at their fingertips, farmers can be more selective with supplies and resources such as fertilizers, pesticides, tractors and other fuel-run equipment, and irrigation water. As a result, they can reduce carbon dioxide (CO_2) emissions, pesticide applications, soil erosion, and water run-off—in turn, improving sustainability.

Source: *www.newsusa.com*

11. Circle the two words in the paragraph below that have the same meaning as the word "decrease."

"To address increasing interest in how our food is produced, IFIC Foundation provides a glimpse of modern agriculture in its new animated video, 'Your Food, Farm to Table,' showing how farmers in the U.S. and globally are working to produce our food year-round, including using technology to safely produce more food, while putting less stress on our natural resources. With more "precise" information at their fingertips, farmers can be more selective with supplies and resources such as fertilizers, pesticides, tractors and other fuel-run equipment, and irrigation water. As a result, they can reduce carbon dioxide (CO_2) emissions, pesticide applications, soil erosion, and water run-off—in turn, improving sustainability."

12. Read the following statement. Then, follow the directions.

People must develop new ways to grow food for the planet in a sustainable way due to a growing population.

Circle the sentence in the paragraph below that **best** supports this idea.

"From farm to table, much about food production has changed—for both farmers and consumers. Like any other business, farmers must adapt to a changing world—one that will see its population grow to 9.6 billion by 2050. With finite resources, it will take innovation and a variety of technologies to meet the world's food demand. This includes using new technologies like biotechnology (also referred to as genetic engineering), which can help produce more food on the same amount of land, without having to destroy wildlife habitats."

finite

infinite } antonyms

infinity∞

13. Read the following sentence from the text.

   "With <u>finite</u> resources, it will take innovation and a variety of technologies to meet the world's food demand."

   Why did the author use the word <u>finite</u> to support his or her statement?

   - ○ A. It helps show how important growing food is.
   - ◉ B. It helps support the idea that technology is needed to help with limited food supplies.
   - ○ C. It helps supports the author's view that we need more food.
   - ○ D. It helps support the idea that there are too many people to feed.

14. What is the best reason why the author should include research from different sources?

   - ◉ A. to justify that his or her statements are supported by experts
   - ○ B. to show that modern agriculture uses technology
   - ○ C. to explain how biotechnology reduces pollution
   - ○ D. to persuade readers that they should enjoy the food on their table

15. Read the following sentence from the text.

   "A 2014 study by the International Food Information Council (IFIC), 'Consumer Perceptions of Food Technology,' shows that more than seven in 10 consumers agree that modern agriculture—<u>conventional</u> farming using today's modern tools and equipment—can be sustainable and produce high-quality, nutritious foods."

   Which words are <u>antonyms</u> for the word <u>conventional</u>? Select **all** that apply.

   - ☑ A. untraditional
   - ☑ B. new
   - ☑ C. unusual
   - ☐ D. plain
   - ☐ E. common
   - ☑ F. unconventional

   Convention:
   1. Meeting conference
   2. custom / ways
   3. style / common ways
   4. agreement
   contrast

16. Read the following sentence from the text.

"The survey also underscored that two-thirds (66 percent) of respondents say it is important that their food be produced in a sustainable way, including producing food affordably with the same or fewer resources, in a way that is better for the environment."

Which words are synonyms for the root word affordable? Select **all** that apply.

☑ A. fair
☑ B. cheap
☐ C. premium → exceptional quality or amount
☐ D. exorbitant → too high, too expensive
☑ E. economical
☐ F. expensive

17. Which of the following statements, if added to the text, could be used to support the use of biotechnology in food? Select **all** that apply.

☑ A. "The use of biotechnology ensures enough food supply for the growing population."
☑ B. "The use of biotechnology helps reduce the carbon footprint and helps with the conservation of the natural habitat."
☑ C. "Consumers should support companies that use biotechnology."
☐ D. "Biotechnology still requires some testing so that it can be improved upon."

18. Read the following sentence from the text.

"With more 'precise' information at their fingertips, farmers can be more selective with supplies and resources such as fertilizers, pesticides, tractors and other fuel-run equipment, and irrigation water."

What does the word precise mean?

◉ A. exact
○ B. broad
○ C. correct
○ D. general

19. What is the suggested tone and purpose of the article?

- ◉ A. to inform
- ○ B. to persuade
- ○ C. to entertain
- ○ D. to recall

20. Read the paragraph below and answer the question that follows.

"From farm to table, much about food production has changed—for both farmers and consumers. Like any other business, farmers must adapt to a changing world—one that will see its population grow to 9.6 billion by 2050. With finite resources, it will take innovation and a variety of technologies to meet the world's food demand. This includes using new technologies like biotechnology (also referred to as genetic engineering), which can help produce more food on the same amount of land, without having to destroy wildlife habitats."

Choose the statement that is the best option for showing the author's point of view.

- ○ A. The author believes that food technology is bad for the environment.
- ○ B. The author believes that we have enough resources to meet the world's demand.
- ○ C. The author thinks that there is not enough land for wildlife habitats.
- ◉ D. The author believes that food technology must be used to meet the demands of a growing population.

21. Read the following sentence from the text.

"The survey also underscored that two-thirds (66 percent) of respondents say it is important that their food be produced in a <u>sustainable</u> way, including producing food affordably with the same or fewer resources, in a way that is better for the environment."

Replace the word <u>sustainable</u> with another word that has the same meaning and that doesn't change the original meaning of the sentence.

- ○ A. good
- ○ B. quick
- ○ C. fleeting
- ◉ D. maintainable

22. If you had to rename the title of the article, what would it be and why? Explain your reasoning in the box below.

Directions: Read the text. Then answer questions 23–30.

Drinking Water: An Invaluable Resource Taken for Granted

You turn on the tap, and water comes out. Period. Safe, plentiful, and affordable drinking water is one of our nation's most precious resources and something most of us take for granted. But what if you turned the tap and nothing happened, or if the water you drank made you sick?

While pouring a glass of water may seem simple, before it arrives at your tap there is a complex process of collecting, storing, treating, and distributing that helps ensure its availability and quality. In fact, water utilities implement comprehensive water management plans to ensure that adequate amounts of drinking water are available. These include conservation and reuse, reclamation, and sourcing strategies.

Drinking water supplied by utilities is always treated to remove contaminants and harmful micro-organisms. That treatment process typically consists of clarification (to remove dirt and other particles), filtration (to remove even smaller particles), and disinfection (to kill bacteria and most viruses). The water is then delivered to residential and commercial customers via an extensive pipe network.

Drinking water utilities are committed to protecting public health and constantly monitoring and reassessing their methods for treating water to ensure its quality. In part, this is due to changing government regulations, which periodically alter water quality standards. In addition, they may undertake other forms of treatment not expressly required to comply with regulations in order to ensure that drinking water meets and often exceeds the standards and needs of local communities.

For example, they may seek to remove trace compounds that are not currently regulated, and to enhance the aesthetic quality of the water.

Drinking water utilities carry out these services while also managing costs and minimizing environmental impacts of their processes; they are committed to keeping drinking water affordable. Water utilities and other stakeholders invest more than $12 million each year in the Water Research Foundation to sponsor research that enables water utilities, public health agencies, and other professionals to provide safe and affordable drinking water to the public.

So the next time you pour a glass of water from the tap, take a moment to honor the commitment and significant investment made to ensure the quality of that water.

Source: *www.newsusa.com*

23. Read the following sentences from the passage.

    "While pouring a glass of water may seem simple, before it arrives at your tap there is a complex process of collecting, storing, treating, and distributing that helps ensure its availability and quality. In fact, water utilities implement comprehensive water management plans to ensure that adequate amounts of drinking water are available."

    The author uses a word that means *to make certain*. Circle the word that best represents this meaning.

24. Why are drinking water utilities paying attention to our drinking water? Select **all** that apply.

    ☐ A. to conserve
    ☐ B. to create a marine ecosystem
    ☐ C. to fill water bottles
    ☑ D. to remove harmful contaminants
    ☐ E. to safely distribute water to residential or commercial customers

25. Read the following sentence from the passage.

    "In addition, they may undertake other forms of treatment not expressly required to comply with regulations in order to ensure that drinking water meets and often exceeds the standards and needs of local communities."

    Think about the word comply and what it means. In the box below, write a sentence that uses the word "comply" with the same meaning.

26. Why was this article written? How do you know? Explain and provide evidence in the box below.

27. Read the sentence from the passage.

"For example, they may seek to remove trace compounds that are not currently regulated, and to <u>enhance</u> the aesthetic quality of the water."

Which choice(s) below best states the meaning of <u>enhance</u> in this sentence? Select **all** that apply.

- ☑ A.   make better
- ☑ B.   improve
- ☑ C.   increase
- ☐ D.   boost
- ☐ E.   lessen

28. Read the paragraph below from the passage.

"Drinking water utilities are committed to protecting public health and constantly monitoring and reassessing their methods for treating water to ensure its quality. In part, this is due to changing government regulations, which periodically alter water quality standards. In addition, they may undertake other forms of treatment not expressly required to comply with regulations in order to ensure that drinking water meets and often exceeds the standards and needs of local communities."

Underline the prepositions that were used in this paragraph.

29. Using the information from the article, explain, in your own words, what has to happen to drinking water before you turn on the faucet. Include evidence from the text. Write your answer in the box below.

30. In your opinion, should more people be made aware of the work that goes into producing safe drinking water? Use evidence and details from the text. Write your answer in the box below.

Directions: Read the story below. Then answer questions 31–35.

It was another Friday morning, the last day of school before Winter Break started. Arjuna, a student at BrightMinds Elementary, went inside his classroom. Arjuna saw that nobody was there. He thought to himself, "Where is everybody?"

He looked at his watch. It was 7:10 in the morning. "Well, I can play on the playground," he thought, and he headed off. There, he met up with his friend Mekya and the new student, Evelyn. "Our last day before vacation!" Mekya said excitedly.

"Yeah, but you know Mr. Vinod is going to give us lots of homework over the break." Arjuna said.

Evelyn was surprised, "He will? They never did that at my old school."

"Oh yeah, it's true. Mr. Vinod always gives us packets to do over our breaks," Mekya sighed.

"I know! Don't worry, I will convince him not to give us any homework. Not one bit!" Arjuna said with a sly smile.

"Oh really? How are you going to do that?" asked Evelyn.

"Well, don't worry about it," huffed Arjuna, "I have my ways!"

And with that, the first bell rang. They went to class and took their seats. Mekya and Evelyn were noticeably nervous about what Arjuna was up to. Both of them kept a watchful eye on him as the day went on. Hours went by as they made their way through Math, Language Arts, Science, and PE class. Finally, there was twenty minutes left of school. This was prime time for Arjuna to act on whatever he had up his sleeve.

Every day, Mr. Vinod would give one new quote to his class for them to think about. Then they would discuss it the next day. After that, they would discuss homework before heading home. Today's quote was, *"One boy can be mischievous, but never underestimate the power of two or more."*

"Write the quote in your journal and be ready to share your thoughts about it when we return from break," instructed Mr. Vinod. He continued, "Now class, I will hand out your homework for the two weeks you have off for holiday." He pulled out packets the size of a *Percy Jackson* book and all the students let out an audible moan. Then, Arjuna raised his hand.

"Yes, Arjuna?"

"Why do we even have homework over Winter Break, Mr. Vinod?" Arjuna asked.

"Well, because we need to practice more division and multiplication," Mr. Vinod said, "We have our end-of-the-year test coming!"

Then, Mekya raised his hand.

"Mekya?"

"Can't you teach us multiplication when we get back?" Mekya asked. "Also, maybe you can have us take a pop quiz now to see how we are doing?"

Mr. Vinod's eyes squinted, and he slightly slanted his head back. You could tell that he didn't want to answer Mekya's question. Finally, Mr. Vinod responded, "The homework is to help you study. Without studying, how could you possibly complete the test with a good grade?"

Evelyn the new student slowly raised her hand as she gained the courage to speak up "That's why you can quickly review the lessons now that you taught to us already before we leave for the break. Right?"

"Guys, how can we do anything with fifteen minutes left of school before you go on vacation? I already have your homework all copied and ready to go." After sighing deeply, Mr. Vinod exclaimed, "Fine, you will not have any homework this break and only this break!" Mr. Vinod exclaimed. He had given in.

The whole class cheered. Everybody was so happy to hear that they didn't have any homework. Mekya said, "I won't have homework when I go to Lake Tahoe!"

It had worked. Mekya and Evelyn high fived Arjuna.

"You were right, Arjuna, you did it!" said Evelyn.

"I did it? You two helped, which surprised me!" he replied.

After all the cheering was complete, there was only one minute left before the bell would ring. In that one minute, Mr. Vinod shared what he was doing for his break.

"Class, for my break I am going to Reno with my family to celebrate Christmas. I am going to go skiing . . . ." Mr. Vinod got cut off by the bell.

Everybody rush out the door head out to their parents and left for break . . . homework free.

31. This story is missing descriptive details about the setting. Create a paragraph that uses descriptive elements to give readers a sense of what the setting is like. Write your answer in the box below.

32. Read the following sentence from the story.

"Everybody rush out the door head out to their parents and left for break . . . homework free."

This sentence is grammatically incorrect. Correct the sentence, without changing the content, and write your answer in the box below.

33. Which set of words has the same meaning as the underlined words in the sentence below?

"Mr. Vinod <u>responded</u>, 'The homework is to help you study. Without studying, how could you possibly <u>complete</u> the test with a good grade?'"

⊙ A. replied, finish
○ B. re-joined, admit
○ C. recognized, view
○ D. reciprocated, receive

34. What is the correct position of commas in the sentence below?

"Evelyn the new student slowly raised her hand as she gained the courage to speak up 'That's why you can quickly review the lessons now that you taught to us already before we leave for the break. Right?'"

○ A. "Evelyn, the new student slowly raised her hand as she gained the courage to speak up, 'That's why you can quickly review the lessons now that you taught to us already before we leave for the break. Right?'"

○ B. "Evelyn the new student, slowly raised her hand, as she gained the courage to speak up 'That's why you can quickly review the lessons now that you taught to us already before we leave for the break. Right?'"

⊙ C. "Evelyn, the new student, slowly raised her hand as she gained the courage to speak up, 'That's why you can quickly review the lessons now that you taught to us already before we leave for the break. Right?'"

○ D. "Evelyn, the new student, slowly raised her hand as she gained the courage to speak up 'That's why you can quickly review the lessons now that you taught to us already before we leave for the break. Right?'"

35. In the story, Arjuna can be described as mischievous. Write a paragraph to explain why Arjuna can be considered mischievous. Use details from the story to support your answer. Write your answer in the box below.

Performance Task

Directions: After reviewing the following three sources, you will answer three questions about them and then write an informative essay. Briefly scan the sources and the questions that follow before beginning your close read of the three sources.

Source Number 1—Do More With Less

It's not easy being green. Much of what we purchase to feed our daily habits comes in extraneous packaging better suited to surgery than snacking. While growing eco-consciousness has yielded no shortage of products to help you avoid wastefulness, the simplest solution is to find ways to do it yourself—and the following products are cleverly designed to help you do just that.

Problem: Using too many throw-away cups.

Solution: Canning jar and a Cuppow drinking lid. From the water cooler to the café, bringing your own cup reduces your footprint without sacrificing your favorite routine.

Problem: Taking expensive coffee to go.

Solution: CoffeeSock Pour-Over Coffee Filters. Buying your daily cup can add up to more than $1,000 a year, but brewing it yourself can keep that total under $100. A simple pour-over set-up with a reusable organic cotton filter from CoffeeSock Co. gives you the same great taste with none of the waste.

Problem: Over-packaged junk food snacks.

Solution: Wide-mouth canning jar with a BNTO jar lunchbox adapter. Convenience comes with a hefty cost at the grocery store, and nothing beats making your own snacks for a fraction of the price. Reusable products help you skip the expensive, over-packaged junk and focus on healthy options while saving money and the environment—one treat at a time.

Source: *www.newsusa.com*

Source Number 2—Landfills: An Unexpected Source of Renewable Energy

Did you know that the garbage you throw out every day is a source of green energy? The gas naturally generated by landfills fuels vehicles and powers the electric grid, easing our dependence on fossil fuels and foreign oil.

"Landfill gas is a resource the waste and recycling industry is proud to reliably provide 24 hours a day, seven days a week," said Sharon H. Kneiss, president and CEO of the National Waste & Recycling Association. "It's renewable energy produced in America."

How does it work?

Today's modern landfills are highly engineered facilities run under strict federal and state regulations to ensure protection of human health and the environment.

When trash like grass clippings, banana peels, and coffee grinds get buried beneath a layer of soil in a landfill, it eventually breaks down and produces gas. Landfill operators safely collect this gas by applying a vacuum to collection wells throughout a landfill. The gas is then piped to a compression and filtering unit, where it's prepared for use by power plants and others.

How much energy is generated?

According to the U.S. Department of Energy, waste-based energy is the source of over 5 percent of America's renewable energy—and there's plenty of room to grow. In March 2015, the U.S. Environmental Protection Agency reported that 645 sites had landfill-gas-to-energy programs (in every state except Hawaii and Wyoming). The EPA has identified an additional 440 landfills as expansion candidates.

Landfill operators are also starting to generate energy beyond gas by placing solar panels and windmills on landfills. The power produced can be fed into local electric grids for local homes and businesses.

Stewards of the Land

Today, a landfill is designed from the start to protect the environment and public health. Later, it provides benefits even when it closes. Once a landfill has reached its permitted capacity, it is closed and engineered to keep water out by installing a cap made of clay or a synthetic material. A drainage layer, a protective soil cover and topsoil are then added to support plant growth.

These spaces are transformed into parks, golf courses, wildlife refuges and other places that can be enjoyed by the entire community.

For the Future

Looking ahead, today's landfills provide continued environmental benefits even after they are closed. Engineers and landscape designers transform these sites into parks, golf courses, wildlife refuges, and other spaces that can be enjoyed by the entire community.

Source: *www.newsusa.com*

Source Number 3—Should Food Waste Go Down the Drain?

Americans hoping to live "greener" lives often tackle the kitchen first—after all, separating the recyclables seems easy enough. But proper waste disposal can be more complicated than tossing cans in a blue box.

What's the best way to get rid of table scraps? Should the food waste go in the trash bag? The compost pile? Or down the kitchen sink?

Putting food waste in the trash means it will be trucked to a landfill. Trucking food to landfills generates diesel fumes and emissions. And as food decomposes in landfills, it releases methane, a greenhouse gas.

Composting is a good option but not always practical for people who live in high-rise buildings or in colder climates. Plus, experts advise against composting certain types of food, like meat and dairy.

Numerous independent studies show using a garbage disposer is an environmentally responsible option. More than half of American kitchens have a disposer. On average, they cost less than 50 cents a year in electricity to operate and account for less than one percent of a household's total water consumption. Recent advances in disposer technology make it possible to discard virtually any kind of food waste without concern about clogs or loud noises.

Once food waste enters wastewater treatment plants, it can be recycled into methane and used as a renewable source of power for the plant. Also, many wastewater treatment plants can process food waste into bio-solids, which can be used as fertilizer.

Here are some surprising facts about food waste:

- The average U.S. family of four produces about 2,000 pounds of food waste each year.
- According to the U.S. Environmental Protection Agency, food waste is the third largest category of municipal solid waste (MSW) in the U.S., accounting for about 13 percent of MSW material.
- Americans throw away more than 25 percent of the food we prepare, according to a study by the U.S. Department of Agriculture. Those scraps are 70 percent water, which makes it easy for disposers to pulverize waste and send it through sewage pipes.

Source: *www.newsusa.com*

1. What is one detail about landfills and gas that appears in both Source Number 2 and Source Number 3? Write your answer in the box below.

2. Read the following statement.

Humans are doing all they can to produce less waste.

Do you agree with this statement? Why or why not? Explain your answer using evidence and details from the three sources. Write your answer in the box below.

3. Which sentence below combines the main ideas from all three sources into one thesis statement?

○ A.   Humans produce more garbage and waste than we know what to do with.

◎ B.   There are many ways to create less waste, such as using less packaging, using waste-based energy, and transforming our food waste into useable products.

○ C.   Modern landfills are more environmentally friendly because of the use of waste-based energy and more efficient operations.

○ D.   Food waste and over-packaging are two of the main problems facing over-flowing landfills.

Informative Performance Task Essay Response

In your class, you and a group of students have been working on a project to present information and facts about how much garbage and waste humans produce. Now, your teacher has asked you to write a report on what can be done with the waste and garbage to make a more sustainable waste system.

You have gathered three sources for research. Reread the three sources from your research, Source Number 1, Source Number 2, and Source Number 3 on pages 126–129, to familiarize yourself with the topic of a more sustainable waste system. Using more than one of those sources, develop a main idea about what to do with our waste and garbage. Choose the most important details from multiple sources to support your main idea. Then, write an informative essay that is multiple paragraphs long. Make sure to organize your essay with the appropriate support for your main idea. Any words that are not your own should be in quotations.

Here are some important points to check off to make sure that you have constructed a well-written, informative essay:

- [ ] Has a clear main idea
- [ ] Is well-organized and stays on topic
- [ ] Has an introduction and a conclusion
- [ ] Uses transitions
- [ ] Uses details from the sources to support the main idea
- [ ] Puts the information from the sources in your own words, except when using direct quotations from the sources
- [ ] Gives the title or number of the source when citing the source
- [ ] Develops all ideas clearly
- [ ] Uses clear language throughout the essay
- [ ] Follows the rules of writing (i.e., correct spelling, punctuation, and grammar usage)

Now write your answer in the box below.

(Answers are on page 155.)

English Language Arts Answers Explained

Chapter 1: Selected-Response Tasks (Multiple-Choice)

Exercise 1, page 20

1. **(C)** "Lugged" means to lift or carry something. This type of question tests your ability to determine the meaning of words using context clues. Try replacing each possible answer choice in the sentence to see if that choice would make sense with what is happening in the story.

2. **(C)** This question presents the same type of practice as that of question 1. Keep in mind that the SBAC organizes questions so that some answers will support the next question or task.

3. **(B)** These sentences are evidence that support the lesson of the story, which is to always be prepared for hard times. You must first determine the theme or lesson of the fable. Afterwards, you can look for the clues that would support that lesson. These sentences show that the Grasshopper was unprepared and is now in need of assistance.

Exercise 2, pages 22–23

1. **(C)** "To be modest" is the opposite of people "boasting" about themselves. This question tests your ability to see relationships among grade-level vocabulary that includes both antonyms and synonyms. Using the process of elimination strategy would work well here. Try replacing each possible answer in the sentence to see if it works. The choice that reflects the opposite of what the sentence originally meant is the antonym.

2. **(A)** The Hare became overconfident and acted carelessly. The Tortoise, on the other hand, never stopped and kept a steady pace, winning the race. This question tests whether you can analyze the text and determine the main theme, central idea, and/or lesson of the story. Make sure to refer back to the text and look for clues that will support the lesson in the fable.

3. **Part A: (A)** and **(B)** These are examples of inferences that can be made from the clues in the text. You may be able to think of more, but this type of question tests whether you can distinguish between statements based on evidence and statements without any support from the text. Again, refer back to the text and look for the evidence that would support the right answers.

   Part B: (D) This piece of evidence supports both the inference that the Hare enjoys teasing the Tortoise and the inference that the Tortoise is so slow that the Hare believes that he has time to take a nap and still win the race.

Exercise 3, page 25

1. **(C)** In both fables, the Hare and the Grasshopper don't listen to the other characters in the story because they think they know best.

2. **(B)** and **(D)** If you look at the key words, "whereas" in choice B and "unlike" in choice D, you will notice that these words mean that two things are being contrasted. Note that both question 1 and question 2 aim to test your ability to compare and contrast the structures and ideas in literature.

Exercise 4, pages 27–28

1. **(B)** The line "For life is a mirror of king and slave;" is comparing life to a mirror. It is a mirror, according to the poem, because whatever you put out in life is what you will receive in return. This question tests whether you can identify metaphors and other figurative language.

2. **(D)** The lines, "Then give to the world the best you have, / And the best will come back to you" is in the first stanza of the poem, and it is also the last lines of the poem. The rest of the answer choices are examples of things you can put out in the world and receive in return.

3. **(C)** and **(D)** The author uses the imagery of scattering seeds as a comparison to having lots of thoughts and ideas.

Exercise 5, pages 29–30

1. **(C)** Using the process of elimination, you will notice that choices A, B, and D are general statements and do not provide a specific main idea.

2. **(A)** and **(C)** These two details act as evidence for and support the main idea, that there is scientific proof that there may have been life on Mars.

3. The two parts of the sentence that you should have circled or underlined are "**Once**" and "**1996**." The correct sentence should look like, "Once, in 1996, these scientists looked closely at a very special type of fossil."

Chapter 2: Constructed-Response Tasks

Exercise 1—Constructed-Response Tasks with One Source, pages 36–41

1. Below is a sample of a completed A.C.E. chart, followed by sample 2-point, 1-point, and 0-point answers.

Answer (Use part of the question in your answer.)	I can conclude that the author does not agree with keeping animals in zoos.
Cite (Support your answer with details [evidence] from the text.)	This is evident because the author focuses on facts that show the "sadness" of animals in zoos. Also, the author states, "This type of confinement is unacceptable for any animal, anywhere."
Explain (Explain how or why the evidence you've cited supports your answer.)	This tells me that the author feels strongly that zoos are not good for animals.

Sample Answers

2-point answer

I can conclude that the author does not agree with keeping animals in zoos. This is evident because the author focuses on facts that show the "sadness" of animals in zoos. Also, the author states, "This type of confinement is unacceptable for any animal, anywhere." This tells me that the author feels strongly that zoos are not good for animals.

1-point answer

The author doesn't like keeping animals in zoos because they get sick and sad. "It has been documented that Junior, the killer whale, was removed from his natural habitat in Iceland and placed in a tank in Niagara Falls."

0-point answer

"There are many aquatic animals that are taken from their natural habitats and placed in water tanks in aquariums around the world." This is bad.

2. Below is a sample of a completed A.C.E. chart, followed by sample 2-point, 1-point, and 0-point answers.

Answer (Use part of the question in your answer.)	The central idea of this paragraph is that there are many animals that are separated from their families.
Cite (Support your answer with details [evidence] from the text.)	I know this because the paragraph states that "[t]here are many aquatic animals that are taken from their natural habitats and placed in water tanks in aquariums around the world."
Explain (Explain how or why the evidence you've cited supports your answer.)	The author uses facts about whales and dolphins being separated from their families and then asks the readers how they would feel about that. The author uses words like "taken," "separated," and "forced." These words tell me that the paragraph focuses on animals being separated from their families.

Sample Answers

2-point answer

The central idea of this paragraph is that there are many animals that are separated from their families. I know this because the paragraph states that "[t]here are many aquatic animals that are taken from their natural habitats and placed in water tanks in aquariums around the world." The author uses facts about whales and dolphins being separated from their families and then asks the readers how they would feel about that. The author uses words like "taken," separated," and "forced." These words tell me that the paragraph focuses on animals being separated from their families.

1-point answer

The central idea is that animals are being separated from their families. I don't think they can get exercise in a water tank.

0-point answer

The central idea is about Junior being alone.

3. Below is a sample of a completed A.C.E. chart, followed by sample 2-point, 1-point, and 0-point answers.

Answer (Use part of the question in your answer.)	The author's purpose is to persuade and inform the reader why zoos are terrible for animals. The author does this by using facts about zoos to support his or her opinion about animal confinement. The author focuses on how animals kept in zoos show signs of abnormal behaviors such as head bobbing, pacing, and biting cage bars.
Cite (Support your answer with details [evidence] from the text.)	The text states that, "[a]nother study found that elephants in zoos spend 22 percent of their time engaging in abnormal behaviors, such as repeated head bobbing or biting cage bars, and bears spend about 30 percent of their time pacing, a sign of distress."
Explain (Explain how or why the evidence you've cited supports your answer.)	These abnormal behaviors show that zoos are terrible for animals because they are being removed from their natural habitat and being confined.

Sample Answers

<u>2-point answer</u>

The author's purpose is to persuade and inform the reader why zoos are terrible for animals. The author does this by using facts about zoos to support his or her opinion about animal confinement. The author focuses on how animals kept in zoos show signs of abnormal behaviors such as head bobbing, pacing, and biting cage bars. The text states that, "[a]nother study found that elephants in zoos spend 22 percent of their time engaging in abnormal behaviors, such as repeated head bobbing or biting cage bars, and bears spend about 30 percent of their time pacing, a sign of distress." These abnormal behaviors show that zoos are terrible for animals because they are being removed from their natural habitat and being confined.

<u>1-point answer</u>

The author's purpose is to convince us that zoos are terrible. They make the animals use abnormal behaviors like pacing and biting bars.

<u>0-point answer</u>

The author thinks that zoos are terrible because they are sad and locked up.

4. Below is a sample of a completed A.C.E. chart, followed by sample 2-point, 1-point, and 0-point answers.

Answer (Use part of the question in your answer.)	Animals should not be kept in zoos because they develop an illness called zoochosis. Zoochosis is when animals show abnormal behaviors when they are taken from their natural habitat and kept in zoos.
Cite (Support your answer with details [evidence] from the text.)	The animals end up pacing back and forth, biting cage bars, and tearing at their own skin. Junior the killer whale died after 4 years in a zoo because he was "deprived of outside air, sunlight, and companionship."
Explain (Explain how or why the evidence you've cited supports your answer.)	Junior's and other animals' experiences with zoochosis show why animals should not be kept in zoos.

Sample Answers

2-point answer

Animals should not be kept in zoos because they develop an illness called zoochosis. Zoochosis is when animals show abnormal behaviors when they are taken from their natural habitat and kept in zoos. The animals end up pacing back and forth, biting cage bars, and tearing at their own skin. Junior the killer whale died after 4 years in a zoo because he was "deprived of outside air, sunlight, and companionship." Junior's and other animals' experiences with zoochosis show why animals should not be kept in zoos.

1-point answer

Animals should not be kept in zoos because they get zoochosis. They should be in their natural environment and not be away from family. They will be sad.

0-point answer

Animals should not be kept in zoos because they can get sick and they are separated from their families. No one wants to be separated from their families or get sick.

Exercise 2—Constructed-Response Tasks with Multiple Sources, pages 43–47

1. Below is a sample of a completed A.C.E. chart, followed by sample 2-point, 1-point, and 0-point answers.

Answer (Use part of the question in your answer.)	Source Number 2 would more likely be the better source for understanding the effects of droughts on grasslands.
Cite (Support your answer with details [evidence] from the text.)	This source states that when a drought affects grasslands, rivers and lakes dry up, grass withers, and cattle have no food. This text also says that there are no longer trees around to help keep the soil in place. This leads to erosion.
Explain (Explain how or why the evidence you've cited supports your answer.)	This shows that erosion can make the effect of a drought even worse.

Sample Answers

2-point answer

> Source Number 2 would more likely be the better source for understanding the effects of droughts on grasslands. This source states that when a drought affects grasslands, rivers and lakes dry up, grass withers, and cattle have no food. This shows that droughts have a big impact on the land and livestock. This text also says that there are no longer trees around to help keep the soil in place. This leads to erosion. This shows that erosion can make the effect of a drought even worse.

1-point answer

> Source Number 2 would more likely be the better source for understanding the effects of droughts on grasslands. It states that when a drought affects grasslands, rivers and lakes dry up, grass withers, and cattle have no food. This shows that droughts have a big impact on the land and livestock.

0-point answer

> Source Number 2 is the best one to show the effects of droughts. This is because it says it dries up the grass and makes cows hungry.

2. Below is a sample of a completed A.C.E. chart, followed by sample 2-point, 1-point, and 0-point answers.

Answer (Use part of the question in your answer.)	People rely on sources of naturally occurring water. Some of these sources of naturally occurring water are located underground.
Cite (Support your answer with details [evidence] from the text.)	Source Number 1 says that people in California, farmers especially, are relying more on groundwater reservoirs because of the drought in that state. In Source Number 2, ancient underground lakes form springs in the Sahara of northern Africa. People depend on these ancient underground lakes when the water comes to the surface. The text states, "By acquiring water, these areas are transformed into fertile places with rich soil that allows for growing crops and raising animals."

Explain (Explain how or why the evidence you've cited supports your answer.)	Underground water sources are important for the survival of the people who live there.

Sample Answers

2-point answer

People rely on sources of naturally occurring water. Some of these sources of naturally occurring water are located underground. Source Number 1 says that people in California, farmers especially, are relying more on groundwater reservoirs because of the drought in that state. In Source Number 2, ancient underground lakes form springs in the Sahara of northern Africa. People depend on these ancient underground lakes when the water comes to the surface. The text states, "By acquiring water, these areas are transformed into fertile places with rich soil that allows for growing crops and raising animals." Underground water sources are important for the survival of the people who live there.

1-point answer

People rely on sources of naturally occurring water. Some of these sources of naturally occurring water are located underground. Source Number 1 says that farmers get water from surface reservoirs and snowpack from the mountains. Farmers need this water, but are not getting it because of the drought.

0-point answer

I learned that water comes from rain and the ground. People need it to farm and raise cattle.

Chapter 3: Grammar and Conventions

Practice Exercises—Conventions of Standard English

Exercise 1, page 52

1. The corrected sentence should read as follows: *Arjuna and Mekya were sitting on the bench, waving hello to the puffy, white clouds in the sky.*

Exercise 2, page 52

1. **(B)** The correct interjection for the start of this sentence would be "Hey." This task requires using inference skills to choose the right context for the interjection. It will also be a matter of process of elimination. "Ouch" would not work because no one was hurt in the sentence. "Ick" also does not work because no one is disgusted by something or someone in the sentence. "Yuck" also refers to someone being disgusted, but there is no reference to that in the sentence. This leaves only "Hey," which is a general interjection calling someone's attention to something or someone.

Exercise 3, page 53

1. **(A)**, **(B)**, and **(D)** The words "on," "to," and "in" are all considered prepositions.

Exercise 4, page 53

1. **(D)** This choice rewrites the original sentence without changing its meaning. It replaces "were sitting" with "sat" which both indicate that the action of sitting took place in the past. Choice A is incorrect because it just eliminates the word "were." Choice B is incorrect because it changes the tense of the sentence. The use of "will sit" means that the action will take place in the future, whereas the original sentence clearly indicates past tense. Choice C also changes the tense of the sentence. The use of "sit" indicates present tense, whereas the original sentence clearly indicates past tense.

Practice Exercises—Knowledge of Applying Language Conventions

Exercise 1, page 55

1. **(A)** This choice presents the clearest combination of all three original sentences that retains the meaning of all three sentences. Choice B creates two very disjointed sentences that could be connected better. Choice C is long and wordy. Choice D leaves out key information from the original first and third sentences.

Practice Exercises—Vocabulary Meaning and Use

Exercise 1, page 61

1. **(A)** The context clues hint that the older brother is thinking about his homework. The prefix *pre-* means "before something," and the root word

occupy means "to be busy." Therefore, if a person is *preoccupied*, he is already busy with something.

Exercise 2, page 62

1. **(C)** The context clues hint at the plane completing amazing movements in the air with phrases like "dove down," "turned the nose," and "flew circles." Since this is what she saw, we can infer that an *aerial maneuver* is the set of movements a plane completes in the air.

Practice Exercises—Figurative Language

Exercise 1, page 65

1. You should have matched the sentences with the figurative language terms as follows:

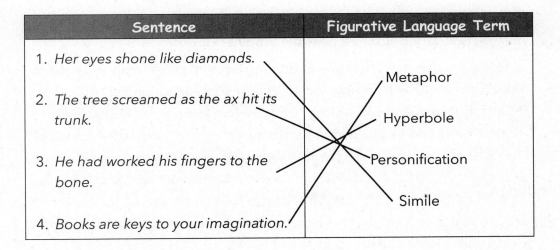

Sentence	Figurative Language Term
1. *Her eyes shone like diamonds.*	Metaphor
2. *The tree screamed as the ax hit its trunk.*	Hyperbole
3. *He had worked his fingers to the bone.*	Personification
4. *Books are keys to your imagination.*	Simile

In the first sentence, the word "like" is a clue that the sentence presents a simile. Her eyes appeared so bright that they were "like" diamonds, a bright object. In the second sentence, the tree "screamed." Giving the human trait of "screaming" to the tree means that the writer of that sentence used personification. In the third sentence, the person in question likely did not literally work his fingers so hard that bone was showing. Instead, the writer of the sentence is using hyperbole, meaning that he has exaggerated how hard the person worked his fingers. The fourth sentence compares "books" to "keys," meaning that books unlock a person's imagination the same way that a key unlocks a lock. Therefore, the writer of the sentence is using a metaphor.

Chapter 4: English Language Arts Performance Task

Practice Exercises—Research Questions, pages 71–77

1. The idea that "light bulbs no longer have to be controlled only by a light switch" is expressed in both Source Number 2 and Source Number 3. You can infer this by looking at the evidence. Source Number 2 states, "From the kitchen, basement, or even the couch, you can now turn lights on or off remotely, create 'zones' of activity, and control every shade of light and color in your home without ever flipping a switch." Source Number 3 states, "Now, wireless controllers allow control from spots around the room or even another room." The idea that "using certain sources of renewable energy can not only save money, but can also help the environment" relates to Source Number 1 specifically. Source Number 1 states, "The long-term benefits, however, can be great to someone's pocketbook. Some households produce so much energy from solar power that they have some left over to sell back to power companies!"

2. Answers will vary. Below is a possible 2-point response:

   I have learned that there are new technologies that can make your home more energy efficient. One way to make your home more energy efficient is to install solar panels. According to Source Number 1, "solar energy is an endless renewable source of energy. The sun creates an unlimited source of energy that can be used in every single household and every commercial and industrial property." Another way to make a home more energy efficient is to use LED lights. Source Number 2 states that "LEDs use 75 to 80 percent less energy than incandescent bulbs which, according to the Environmental Protection Agency, will help you save about $6 per bulb or about $14 a fixture annually on your energy bill." These are just a couple of the ways to make your home more efficient and help the environment at the same time.

3. Answers will vary. Below is a possible 2-point response:

   Source Number 2 would be the most helpful in terms of supporting the idea that new lighting technology can help with energy costs. The central idea of this article is that LED bulbs with new lighting controls are more energy efficient than older technologies. According to the article, "[w]hile these systems aren't new, the ability to combine them with apps and the most energy-efficient lighting technology is." Furthermore, this article states that "LEDs use 75 to 80 percent less energy than incandescent bulbs which, according to the Environmental Protection Agency, will help you save about $6 per bulb or about $14 a fixture annually on your energy bill." Both of these quotes help support the idea that new technologies help with energy costs. The second quote talks about how much money is saved using LED bulbs, while the first quote confirms that using these bulbs with new controls is energy-efficient.

Practice Exercises—Informative Performance Task Essay, pages 78–84

Sample Informative Performance Task Essay Organizer

Below is a sample of how a student could organize his or her thoughts during the prewriting phase of the ELA Performance Task. Keep in mind that your final essay should be longer than this and that this organizer is intended for you to organize the structure of your essay with the most important elements first.

Introduction Paragraph

Introduce and Summarize:	There are many new technologies that not only make life easier but also make our energy use more efficient.
Thesis Statement:	These new efficient technologies involve LED lights, solar panels, and app-controlled lights.

Body Paragraphs

State the Main Idea:	LED lights help us save money and energy.
Cite Evidence: (Support your answer with details from the text.)	Source Number 2 states that "LEDs use 75 to 80 percent less energy than incandescent bulbs which, according to the Environmental Protection Agency, will help you save about $6 per bulb or about $14 a fixture annually on your energy bill."
Explain: (Why or how does your evidence support your answer?)	This means that using LEDs alone is a great way to make a house or building more efficient. You can also be more confident in your choice of using LEDs knowing that they are using less energy that may be polluting our environment.

State the Main Idea:	Solar panels help us take advantage of the sun and use its solar rays to power our devices.
Cite Evidence: (Support your answer with details from the text.)	Source Number 1 states that "[s]olar, wind, and geothermal energy are a few renewable sources of energy. Renewable sources of energy are an environmentally friendly option to burning fossil fuels."
Explain: (Why or how does your evidence support your answer?)	With this kind of new technology in the world, we could not only save our environment but also save the world and our future.

State the Main Idea:	Wirelessly controlled technology paired with LED lights makes them even more efficient.
Cite Evidence: (Support your answer with details from the text.)	In Source Number 3, Terry McGowan, the director of engineering and technology for ALA states that LEDs "connect to the Internet, and you can adjust them so they dim up and down, come on at appropriate times, change color, even flash in time with music."
Explain: (Why or how does your evidence support your answer?)	Being able to turn off and dim your lights from a distance makes the lights even more efficient.

Conclusion Paragraph

Summarize What You Wrote:	Technology is changing how we live.
Restate Your Thesis Statement:	From solar panels, to apps that control all the lights, to LED lights, there are many ways your home can become more efficient.

Sample Informative Performance Task Essay Response

There are many new technologies that not only make life easier but also make our energy use more efficient. Did you know that going green can include technology that makes your home interactive? These new efficient technologies involve LED lights, solar panels, and app-controlled lights.

LED lights help us save money and energy. When people first heard about this product, they thought it was too good to be true, and, when they bought it, the LED lights actually worked! Source Number 2 states that "LEDs use 75 to 80 percent less energy than incandescent bulbs which, according to the Environmental Protection Agency, will help you save about $6 per bulb or about $14 a fixture annually on your energy bill." This means that using LEDs alone is a great way to make a house or building more efficient. You can also be more confident in your choice of using LEDs knowing that they are using less energy that may be polluting our environment.

Solar panels help us take advantage of the sun and use its solar rays to power our devices. Did you also know that solar panels are environmentally friendly? Source Number 1 states that "[s]olar, wind, and geothermal energy are a few renewable sources of energy. Renewable sources of energy are an environmentally friendly option to burning fossil fuels." With this kind of new technology in the world, we could not only save our environment but also save the world and our future.

Wirelessly controlled technology paired with LED lights makes them even more efficient. Wireless, or app-controlled, technology communicates with your smartphone or tablet. App-controlled lights are controlled from a distance by connecting to the Internet. This allows you to have more control over the lights. In Source Number 3, Terry McGowan, the director of engineering and technology for ALA states that LEDs "connect to the Internet, and you can adjust them so they dim up and down, come on at appropriate times, change color, even flash in time with music." Imagine controlling all of the lights in your house, how you want them faded, and the colors, all with a simple tap of a button! Being able to turn off and dim your lights from a distance makes the lights even more efficient.

Technology is changing how we live. From solar panels, to apps that control all the lights, to LED lights, there are many ways your home can become more efficient. The future is bright with the use of these new technologies!

Practice Exercises—Opinion Performance Task Essay, pages 85–91

Sample Opinion Performance Task Essay Organizer

Below is a sample of how a student could organize his or her thoughts during the prewriting phase of the ELA Performance Task. Keep in mind that your final essay should be longer than this and that this organizer is intended for you to organize the structure of the essay with the most important elements first.

Introduction Paragraph

Introduce and Summarize:	Solar energy is a greener, more renewable way to use energy. Updating the school's lights and wiring can have a big effect on saving energy.
Thesis Statement:	I believe that our school can become more energy efficient by using solar energy because it is environmentally friendly, and we can conserve our natural resources, as well as use various lighting technology.

Body Paragraphs

Reason: (Use part of the question in your answer.)	One reason why we should use solar power at our school is because solar energy is an environmental way to get energy.
Cite Evidence: (Support your answer with details from the text.)	In Source Number I, the text states that "[r]enewable sources of energy are an environmentally friendly option to burning fossil fuels."
Explain: (Why or how does your evidence support your answer?)	This shows that using solar energy benefits the ecosystem and is healthier for the earth. By using solar energy, the earth would be more beautiful, and we could prevent the deaths and extinction of beautiful animals because of air pollution that is caused by harmful gases produced from other energy sources.

Reason: (Use part of the question in your answer.)	The second reason why we should use solar energy at our school is because solar energy is also energy efficient!
Cite Evidence: (Support your answer with details from the text.)	In Source Number 2, the text states that "[w]hile these systems aren't new, the ability to combine them with apps and the most energy-efficient lighting technology is." This text also states that LEDs "will help you save about $6 per bulb or about $14 a fixture annually on your energy bill. With the addition of lighting controls, you can save even more."
Explain: (Why or how does your evidence support your answer?)	Any chance to save money and the environment at the same time is a great opportunity.

Reason: (Use part of the question in your answer.)	The third and final reason why our school should use solar energy is because we could use phones and other devices, such as tablets, to control our lighting.
Cite Evidence: (Support your answer with details from the text.)	That would be so convenient especially if you are sick and don't want to move! In Source Number 3, the text states that "wireless controllers allow control from spots around the room or even another room. Apps, used on either a tablet or smartphone, are also an integral part of modern-day lighting control systems."
Explain: (Why or how does your evidence support your answer?)	If you can control the lights in any part of the building, you never have to worry that the lights are left on in an empty classroom!

Conclusion Paragraph

Opinion: (State your opinion.)	Many people have decided to use solar energy, and some may have already started using it. Many schools may also use solar energy to protect what the earth makes every day, beautiful forms of life. Using solar energy can also protect our surroundings every day too! Solar energy can also prevent extinction and make the air cleaner and healthier for us all!
Counterargument: (State a sentence of the opposite side and then restate your opinion.)	Some may say that upgrading to these new technologies, such as solar energy equipment, will be too expensive with money that can be used for other things. However, our school would save more in the long run, and using solar energy is also more energy efficient.
Restate Reasons: (Insert a concluding sentence.)	The reasons why our school should use solar energy are it's an environmental way to get energy, it's energy efficient, and we could use phones and other devices, such as tablets, to control our lighting. In conclusion, our school should use solar energy to be much more green!

Sample Opinion Performance Task Essay Response

Should our school be more energy efficient? The principal and many people at the district office may have thought about this. There are ways to make our schools more energy efficient by using new technology for our energy needs. Solar energy is a greener, more renewable way to use energy. Updating the school's lights and wiring can have a big effect on saving energy. I believe that our school can become more energy efficient by using solar energy because it is environmentally friendly, and we can conserve our natural resources, as well as use various lighting technology.

One reason why we should use solar power at our school is because solar energy is an environmental way to get energy. That means it would be greener and prevent harmful gases from floating everywhere. In Source Number I, the text states that "[r]enewable sources of energy are an environmentally friendly option to burning fossil fuels." This shows that using solar energy benefits the ecosystem and is healthier for the earth. By using solar energy, the earth would be more beautiful, and we could prevent the deaths and extinction of beautiful animals because of air pollution that is caused by harmful gases produced from other energy sources.

The second reason why we should use solar energy at our school is because solar energy is also energy efficient! In Source Number 2, the text states that "[w]hile these systems aren't new, the ability to combine them with apps and the most energy-efficient lighting technology is." This text also states that LEDs "will help you save about $6 per bulb or about $14 a fixture annually on your energy bill. With the addition of lighting controls, you can save even more." Therefore, you're not only saving the environment when you use solar panels, but you're also saving money! Any chance to save money and the environment at the same time is a great opportunity.

The third and final reason why our school should use solar energy is because we could use phones and other devices, such as tablets, to control our lighting. That would be so convenient especially if you are sick and don't want to move! In Source Number 3, the text states that "wireless controllers allow control from spots around the room or even another room. Apps, used on either a tablet or smartphone, are also an integral part of modern-day lighting control systems. If you can control the lights in any part of the building, you never have to worry that the lights are left on in an empty classroom!

Many people have decided to use solar energy, and some may have already started using it. Many schools may also have solar energy to protect what the earth makes every day, beautiful forms of life. Using solar energy can also protect our surroundings every day too! Solar energy can also prevent extinction and make the air cleaner and healthier for us all! Some may say that upgrading these new technologies, such as solar energy equipment, will be too expensive with money that can be used for other things. However, our school would save more in the long run, and using solar energy is also more energy efficient. The reasons why our school should use solar energy are it's an environmental way to get energy, it's energy efficient, and we could use phones and other devices, such as tablets, to control our lighting. In conclusion, our school should use solar energy to be much more green!

Practice Exercises—Narrative Performance Task Essay, pages 92–98

Sample Narrative Performance Task Essay Organizer

Beginning

Establish a Setting:	A classroom with students working on their art projects.
Introduce the Characters: (Describe the characters.)	Victor is a student in the class who is worried because he hasn't finished his art project yet, and he's running out of time.
	Ms. Huang is the teacher in this classroom. She is informative, explaining the new LED technology to her students, but also strict because she tries to keep all of her students in line.
	Daisy is one of Victor's classmates. She gets all of her work done on time.
	Alex is another one of Victor's classmates. He is calmer and doesn't seem to know what's happening around him.

Middle

Event 1: (What's the conflict or problem?)	Victor is running out of time to finish his art project.
Event 2: (How do the characters deal with or try to solve the problem?)	The lights begin to flicker several times, and then the power goes out completely.
Event 3: (What is the effect of the characters' actions from Event 2?)	Victor figures out that Alex sat on the Wi-Fi router cord, knocking it out of its socket. When he plugs it in, though, the power still doesn't come on.

Ending

What is the Last Effect from the Events? Is the Conflict Solved?	Victor eventually realizes that the lights are controlled not only by the Wi-Fi, but also by an app. The conflict is solved when he finds Ms. Huang's smartphone and turns the lights back on using the app.
What Happens to the Characters?	Victor is celebrated for solving the problem, but then he realizes that he still has to finish his art project, and his teacher is not happy that he touched her phone without asking for permission first.

Sample Narrative Performance Task Essay Response

"Daisy, can I borrow your extra crayons for my art project?" asked Victor.

Victor was having trouble finishing his art project on time and saw that Daisy was almost finished. She probably wouldn't mind if he used some of her extra ones, he thought to himself.

"Sure, but you better hurry! We don't have much more time to finish, and you have a long way to go." Daisy answered.

Just then the lights flickered as if they were going to go out. All the students gasped and started talking.

"OK, OK, students . . . it's just a little electric problem." Ms. Huang announced. She then reminded us that the school had been recently upgraded with solar panels for power and special new app-controlled LED lights. She then said, "Please calm down and finish up. You only have 10 minutes left."

Great, that's just what Victor needed. He didn't need for the power to go out so he couldn't finish his project. Victor felt the universe was working against him. Again, the lights flickered on and off, but for a longer interval. Now, the students were a bit more serious. They did not like the idea of sitting in the dark.

The way Victor's school was built, there were no windows in his classroom. If the lights were to go out, there would be absolutely no light to light their way out. This is what all the students must have been thinking when the lights flickered for a third time.

This worried Victor. For one, he was afraid of the dark and would be embarrassed if anyone found out. More importantly, he had to get this art project done in time for the Art Gallery Walk that his parents would be attending.

As he was worrying about this, the lights flickered one more time. But this time they did not turn back on. The lights had gone out.

There was instant chaos, as students did not know what to do or which way to go. Victor was pretty sure that Daisy was hanging on to him, but he couldn't be sure. It was so dark that even giving time to let his eyes adjust was not working for him. Victor could hear students running into desks, chairs, and falling over backpacks. He stayed still, not sure what to do.

"EVERYONE FREEZE!" yelled Ms. Huang at the top of her lungs. It was not only pitch dark; it was also absolutely silent. "Everyone needs to calm down and take a seat on the floor where you are standing."

Victor and the rest of the class sat down. Ms. Huang was testing everything to see if anything would work. Victor was thinking hard. What can be the problem? It didn't make sense for it to be the new solar panels. It was supposed to be sunny all day that day.

Hmm? Victor kept thinking.

Ms. Huang taught the class a lot about how the new technology would work and make the school more energy efficient. Victor thought to himself that maybe he could figure out how to fix it. Once he did, maybe Ms. Huang and his parents would forget that he did not finish his art project. Just maybe . . .

Just then he had an idea! If it wasn't the solar panels, then perhaps it was the lights themselves. Ms. Huang had said these new fancy lights were not only controllable by switches, but over the Internet, too. Maybe the Wi-Fi went out?

Victor ignored his teacher's directions and began to crawl toward the Wi-Fi router. He had to climb over chairs and backpacks. Once he reached the wall, he felt around until he found the router. But wait. There was someone sitting on the wire leading to the router.

"Who is this?"

"It's me, Alex!"

"Oh. Alex, how long have you been sitting here?"

"Well, the whole time."

Victor slapped himself on the forehead, "Oh, Alex. Did you know that you were sitting on the router cord the whole time? I think you made the lights go out!"

Alex got up. Victor plugged the wire back into the router and restarted it. But still no lights.

Victor thought more. Oh, wait! "That's right! The lights are controlled by an app!"

Victor then decided to try to find Ms. Huang's smartphone. She usually left it on her desk. Eventually, Victor reached the desk and felt around until he could clench the smartphone. Good thing, Ms. Huang didn't lock her smartphone. He tapped her phone to turn it on and looked for the lighting app. Bingo! When the lights went out, the app must have reset itself. With the swipe of a finger, Victor slowly turned the lights back on with the app. As the lights came back on and everyone saw Victor standing with Ms. Huang's smartphone, they began to cheer for him!

Victor was so happy . . . that is until he realized that he still needed to finish his artwork and that Ms. Huang was none too happy to see him holding her phone!

Chapter 5: English Language Arts Practice Test

Computer Adaptive Test, pages 99–125

1. **Answers will vary.** Below is a sample response.

   I believe that chocolate milk should not be served with our school lunches. One of the reasons I believe this is because chocolate milk contains a lot of sugar. It contains more than 30 grams of sugar per serving. This might not seem like a lot, but consider that the suggested amount of sugar for a day is only 37.5 grams! That means that one chocolate milk container consumed at lunch contains almost all of the sugar you should consume in one day. Furthermore, all of this extra sugar can lead to obesity and other health problems. These are all reasons why many other countries have already banned chocolate milk in their schools, and why I am convinced that chocolate milk should be banned in ours.

This is an appropriate response because it includes:

- A clear topic sentence
- Research notes as evidence to summarize the writer's opinion
- A clear conclusion sentence that restates the writer's opinion

2. **"Yesterday"** and **"popcorn"** should be circled. The word "yesterday" is being used as a preposition that specifies a time. When a preposition is used in the beginning of a sentence, you need to use a comma afterward. There should also be a comma after the word "popcorn" because you need one before the last quotation mark in dialogue.

3. **Part A: (D)** Mekya is nervous at the thought of being put in the game. The evidence from the text that supports the inference is, "His heart always pounded faster when he thought of himself being thrown into the game." Based on the prior knowledge that the heart can pump at a faster rate when nervous, we can make a guess that Mekya is nervous about being put in the game.

   Part B: (B) and **(D)** Choice B shows that Mekya much prefers to watch the game than to take part in it. Choice D supports the idea that Mekya gets nervous when he even imagines himself being called in to play. Both of these sentences together support the inference that Mekya is nervous about the possibility of filling in for Michael.

   Part C: Answers will vary. Below is a sample response.

   The coach yelled, "You're in, Mekya!"

   Mekya's heart dropped into his stomach. He was scared, but he got up from the bench and ran to his team. Mekya hoped that all he had to do was pass the ball. He would stay away from the goal, he thought, so there wasn't pressure to make a goal.

   Just then, the ball was thrown in. In all the excitement, Mekya didn't realize that there was only one minute on the clock . . . and they were tied! Luckily, his team had the ball. They drove the ball down toward the goal. Mekya was able to pass it back to one of his teammates each time it came to him. Hopefully, he could just keep this up until the game ended. Ten seconds were on the clock now. Mekya found himself in front of the goal, praying the ball didn't come to him.

   But it did! With four seconds on the clock, and the crowd cheering wildly behind him, Mekya took the shot without even thinking. The ball passed through the goalie's legs as he dove to block it. Mekya watched the ball fly into the net. He did it! The crowd went wild and his team hugged all at once.

From then on, Mekya decided that he would rather be in the game than on the bench.

This is an appropriate response because it includes:

- Narrative elements, such as chronological and transitional strategies
- Descriptive elements that continue the story
- A relevant conclusion to the story that supports the audience and the task

4. The following two sentences should be circled: **"As they migrated to Antarctica and other cold regions, they began to depend on their wings less and less."** and **"Here, there are no predators for the penguins to escape from and therefore no reason for them to fly away from anything."**

   This task is assessing your ability to identify evidence that supports a given inference from the text. In this case, the inference is, "Penguins began to depend less on their wings as they evolved from birds that needed to fly to escape predators." The evidence from these two sentences points to the conclusion that penguins evolved to depend less on their wings.

5. **(C)** The paragraph focuses on facts regarding various measurements of penguins. One strategy to use with a question like this is to think of each possible answer as a possible topic sentence for the paragraph. In this case, choice C would work the best as a topic sentence for this paragraph.

6. **Answers will vary.** Below is a sample response.

   The author feels that more people should learn how human actions affect penguins in Antarctica. The author believes that because our everyday activities cause climate change, then the climate change affects the lives of penguins. The author states, "These fossil fuels create climate change, which warms the waters around Antarctica." When the waters around Antarctica are warm, then there is less food for the penguins. The author feels that these changes are because of human activities. The author concludes this passage by writing, "It may be a big planet, but we can still have a big impact on living things many miles away." Therefore, the author believes that people need to recognize the bigger consequences of their actions, and people need to learn ways to reduce the burning of fossil fuels in order to save the lives of these penguins.

This is an appropriate response because it includes:

- A clear topic sentence that states the author's viewpoint
- Details as evidence from the text to support the topic sentence
- Evidence that is relevant and appropriate to support the claim

7. **Answers will vary.** Below is a sample response.

Climate change can have a big effect on the lives of penguins. For one, climate change leads to warmer weather around Antarctica, which means less food for the penguins. The text states that the "warming waters around Antarctica mean less krill for the penguins." This tells me that krill cannot survive in warmer weather. Also, these warmer waters break up the ice that the penguins usually depend on. Many baby penguins get caught on this broken ice and can't survive. The author explains that "baby penguins, who cannot yet swim, can end up being swept away from the colony." This means that climate change negatively affects both baby penguins, who cannot survive these conditions, and adult penguins who can no longer find as much food.

fewer

This is an appropriate response because it includes:

- A conclusion that shows sufficient understanding of the central idea of the passage
- A clear topic sentence that states the conclusion
- Details as evidence from the text to support the topic sentence
- Evidence that is relevant and appropriate to support the claim

8. **Part A: (C)** Using the clues from the text, you can infer that the author believes that human daily activity affects the survival of penguins in Antarctica. This may be inferred because the author gives examples to support his or her claim. These examples include various activities that people do in their everyday lives, such as drive a car or use kitchen appliances, that contribute to the burning of fossil fuels and thus create climate change in Antarctica.

Part B: (A) and **(D)** This question is asking you to determine the evidence from the paragraph that best supports your inference from Part A. Choices A and D show that the author believes that humans can have an impact on other life many miles away.

9. **Answers will vary.** Below is a sample response.

The central idea of this poem is how important it is to do good deeds for others. The author expresses that a day does not matter unless you have brought a smile to someone else. The author writes, "One glance most kind, which felt like sunshine where it went, / Then you may count that day well spent." Therefore, it is a good day if you have helped someone else somehow or if you have shown someone kindness. The author also warns of what will happen if no good deed is done during the day. The author believes that "If through it all you've nothing done that you can trace / That brought the sunshine to one face, / No act most small that helped some soul and nothing cost, / Then count that day as worse than lost." In other words, if you did nothing to make anyone else's day better, then it was a waste of a day.

This is an appropriate response because it includes:

- A clear and precise topic sentence that correctly states the central idea
- Details as evidence from the text to support the topic sentence
- Evidence that is relevant and appropriate to support the claim
- A demonstration of a command of grammar and punctuation when including direct quotes

10. **Part A: (C)** This task is testing if you can identify a thesis statement that introduces the topic clearly and helps organize the structure of the rest of the piece. In this case, choice C is an appropriate thesis statement because it clearly states an opinion by giving three main reasons for not wanting soda served in school.

    Part B: (B) This question tests your ability to identify the meaning of new vocabulary using your knowledge of multiple meanings, synonyms, and context clues. Since this paragraph is taken from an opinion letter, you can infer that "persuade" means the same as "convince." You also know that one of the purposes of the letter is to inform the reader about what the harmful effects of drinking soda are. Therefore, it makes sense to use "harmful" to replace the word "unhealthy."

11. The words **"less"** and **"reduce"** should be circled. This task tests your understanding of synonyms and using context clues to determine meaning.

12. The following sentence should be circled: **"With finite resources, it will take innovation and a variety of technologies to meet the world's food demand."** This task tests you on identifying evidence that will support a given inference from the text. While the whole paragraph had many clues that support this inference, it is this sentence that *best* supports the idea because it states that we have "finite resources," causing the need for "innovations" in technology.

13. **(B)** This task is testing you on identifying and analyzing the author's point of view and word choices that impact meaning. In this case, the author wants to make a point about why new food technology is needed in an effort to persuade the reader to support this view. Using the word "finite" helps give a sense that food supplies are in danger of running out.

14. **(A)** This question is testing your ability to analyze why the author may have organized or structured the piece a certain way to convey meaning. When an author wants to persuade a reader, it helps to include evidence, or facts, supported by experts to justify his or her position.

15. **(A)**, **(B)**, **(C)**, and **(F)** Antonyms are words that mean the opposite. Since the word "conventional" means something that is "plain" (choice D) or "common" (choice E), you need to select all the words that are the opposite of "common."

16. **(A)**, **(B)**, and **(E)** Synonyms are words that mean the same. Since the word "affordable" means something that does not cost a lot, you need to find the words that have the same meaning, that something is inexpensive.

17. **(A)**, **(B)**, and **(C)** This task is testing your ability to identify which statements support the main idea. For this question, these three choices support the main idea that biotechnology should be used in food production.

18. **(A)** This task tests your ability to use context clues to determine the meaning of an unknown vocabulary word. From the context clues, you can see that farmers are able to be "more selective" with "more 'precise' information." You can then infer that the word "precise" means more exact, or the information is more exact, which gives the farmer the ability to make better decisions.

19. **(A)** This task tests identifying the author's purpose for writing the article. The article informs the reader how technology can help produce food.

20. **(D)** This is evident because the author states, "Like any other business, farmers must adapt to a changing world—one that will see its population grow to 9.6 billion by 2050." In addition, the author explains that biotechnology can be used to produce more food on the same amount of land.

21. **(D)** First, you will have to recognize that the root word being used is "sustain," which means to continue. Then, you will have to think of which of the possible words could be used as a synonym in the same sentence. Since something being "sustained" can also be said to be "maintained," or kept the same, the correct answer is choice D.

22. **Answers will vary.** Below is a sample response.

     If I had to rename the title of this article, I would title it, "Producing Food for the Future." I would title it this because the focus of the article is on the sustainability of modern-farming technology. I know that sustainability means to take care of the future environment and our natural resources. The author uses many quotes by experts to support the idea that modern-farming technology will help in becoming more sustainable. For instance, the author uses data from a survey that says "that two-thirds (66 percent) of respondents say it is important that their food be produced in a sustainable way, including producing food affordably with the same or fewer resources, in a way that is better for the environment." This shows that the focus of the article is on using modern technology to help sustain a healthy planet in the future while producing enough food for everyone. This is why I would name the article "Producing Food for the Future."

     This is an appropriate response because it includes:

     - A topic sentence with a clear and precise statement
     - Details from the text as evidence to support the topic sentence
     - Evidence that is relevant and appropriate to support the topic sentence
     - A demonstration of a command of grammar and punctuation when including direct quotes

23. The following word should have been circled: **"ensure."** This task asks you to identify a synonym for a phrase and tests you on using context clues to determine the meaning of a word. In this case, the word "ensure" is used twice, and, in both places, its meaning is "to make certain."

24. **(A)**, **(D)**, and **(E)** This task tests identifying the central idea and supporting details. These three choices support the central idea, that water companies oversee and manage our water for different purposes that benefit us and conserve resources.

25. **Answers will vary.** Below is a sample response.

     The dog had to comply with the owner's command not to cross the street in order to be safe.

     This task tests using context clues and vocabulary knowledge to understand new vocabulary. In this case, the word "comply" means "to act or behave to meet a specific command or expectation." The context clues from the original sentence that should have helped you recognize this meaning are "required" and "regulations," which are two clue words meaning "something must be done."

26. **Answers will vary.** Below is a sample response.

This article was written to inform the public about what happens to their water before it comes out their tap or faucet. It provides information on the different ways the water companies manage the water supplies to provide safe drinking water. The author states, "In fact, water utilities implement comprehensive water management plans to ensure that adequate amounts of drinking water are available." The author also goes on to say that these plans include "clarification (to remove dirt and other particles), filtration (to remove even smaller particles), and disinfection (to kill bacteria and most viruses)." This tells me that the article was written for the purpose of informing readers how their water is made safe to drink.

This is an appropriate response because it includes:

- A topic sentence with a clear and precise statement that states the author's purpose
- Details from the text as evidence to support the topic sentence
- Evidence that is relevant and appropriate to support the topic sentence
- A demonstration of a command of grammar and punctuation when including direct quotes

27. **(A)**, **(B)**, **(C)**, and **(D)** All four of these choices share the same meaning as "enhance." In this case, they all mean that the aesthetic quality of the water was improved upon. Choice E, "lessen," has the opposite meaning of all the other choices.

28. The following words should be underlined: **"with,"** **"to,"** **"of,"** **"for,"** and **"in."** All of these words are prepositions.

29. **Answers will vary.** Below is a sample response.

Drinking water from the faucet seems easy enough, right? Well, you are not thinking about what it takes to make the water drinkable before coming through your faucet. According to the article, "Drinking Water: An Invaluable Resource Taken for Granted," drinking water that is supplied by utilities "is always treated to remove contaminants and harmful micro-organisms." This process requires the removal of dirt, filtration of smaller particles, and disinfection to kill any bacteria and viruses. This shows that it takes a lot of effort to make our water drinkable and safe.

This is an appropriate response because it includes:

- A topic sentence with a clear and precise statement
- Details from the text as evidence to support the topic sentence
- Evidence that is relevant and appropriate to support the topic sentence
- A demonstration of a command of grammar and punctuation when including direct quotes

30. **Answers will vary.** Below is a sample response.

I believe that people should be made aware of the work that goes into creating drinkable water. It takes time to make sure that the water is safe. According to the article, "Drinking Water: An Invaluable Resource Taken for Granted," people need to "take a moment to honor the commitment and significant investment made to ensure the quality" of water that comes from a tap. I agree with this statement and believe that people should feel grateful that they have access to clean and safe water. In a lot of places, they do not have this privilege. There should be a strong effort to make people realize the process it takes to make their water drinkable.

This is an appropriate response because it includes:

- A topic sentence that states a clear opinion
- Details from the text as evidence to support the topic sentence
- Evidence that is relevant and appropriate to support the topic sentence
- Key words and opinions that are elaborated on

31. **Answers will vary.** Below is a sample response.

When the first bell rang, Arjuna and his friends hurried down the long and dark North Hall, so they could arrive to Mr. Vinod's class on time. They all got into their seats just as the second bell rang. Mr. Vinod came in and sat down at his old broken-down desk. The squeaky chair he sat on made its typical high-pitch sound that everyone giggled at.

32. The sentence should read as follows: **"Everybody rushed out the door, headed out to their parents, and left for break . . . homework free."** The tense of "rush" and "head" should be changed to past tense. Also, commas should be placed after "door" and "parents" to make a list of three within the sentence.

33. **(A)** This task tests the multiple meaning of words and using context clues. "Responded" and "replied" both mean "to answer back." "Complete" and "finish" both mean to "reach the end of something."

34. **(C)** This question tests your knowledge of grammar and punctuation. There needs to be commas before and after "the new student" to show that that is a description of Evelyn. There also needs to be a comma before a line of dialogue.

35. **Answers will vary.** Below is a sample response.

Arjuna can be called "mischievous" because he somehow found a way to convince Mr. Vinod not to give out homework. Very few people have that skill. I can tell that Arjuna is persuasive. In the story, there is a quote that states, "One boy can be mischievous, but never underestimate the power of two or more." This proves that, even though Arjuna is mischievous, he could not have accomplished his goal without Evelyn and Mekya, who were also acting a bit mischievously. They were all sly, and they all worked together to achieve a common objective: preventing their teacher from handing out homework for the holiday break.

Performance Task, pages 126–132

1. **Answers will vary.** Below is a sample response.

One detail about landfills and gas that appears in both Source Number 2 and Source Number 3 is that food waste can be used to create energy. I know this because Source Number 2 states, "Did you know that the garbage you throw out every day is a source of green energy?" Also, Source Number 3 talks about how food waste can be turned into a source of energy. It explains that "Once food waste enters wastewater treatment plants, it can be recycled into methane and used as a renewable source of power for the plant." In summary, food waste can become a source of renewable energy in a variety of ways.

2. **Answers will vary.** Below is a sample response.

I agree with this statement because humans are trying to produce less waste. I believe this because Source Number 1 gives advice for the different ways to reduce wasteful packaging. Also, according to Source Number 2, "[l]andfill gas is a resource the waste and recycling industry is proud to reliably provide 24 hours a day, seven days a week." It seems that many people are brainstorming ways to either reduce waste in the first place or to recycle what we have already wasted. Even our food waste is being recycled, according to Source Number 3, which states that "[o]nce food waste enters wastewater treatment plants, it can be recycled into methane and used as a renewable source of power for the plant." This further shows why I believe that humans are indeed trying to produce less waste.

3. **(B)** This is the correct answer because it appropriately combines the main ideas of all three sources into one thesis statement. Notice that this research question sets you up for what your essay for the Performance Task will be about.

Informative Performance Task Essay Response

Answers will vary. Below is a sample response.

Have you ever thought about whether the landfills around the world are overflowing with our waste? Well, humans produce a lot of waste, everything from over-packaging to uneaten food. There are many ways, however, to prevent waste. We can decrease our waste by using less packaging, using landfills as a source for renewable energy, and recycling food waste into other products.

One way that waste can be reduced dramatically is if we use less packaging. There are many inventive ways to do this. In Source Number 1, the text states that "From the water cooler to the café, bringing your own cup reduces your footprint without sacrificing your favorite routine." Reducing the amount of throw-away cups can make a big impact. You can also make your own snacks for less money and conserve resources by using a reusable container. These are a few ways to use less packaging and create less waste.

Surprisingly, landfills can help protect the environment and help produce renewable energy. Landfills can turn the trash they collect into natural gas that can be collected for consumer use. According to Source Number 2, "When trash like grass clippings, banana peels, and coffee grinds get buried beneath a layer of soil in a landfill, it eventually breaks down and produces gas." This gas is then collected and used in power plants. This waste-based energy source has grown to over 5% of America's renewable energy. While landfills can be a source of environmental concern, they can also be a source of positive change toward less pollution and waste.

Finally, the earth's resources can be conserved, without producing a lot of waste, by reusing food waste. A lot of food goes down the drain! Some people don't know whether or not food should go in the trash or in the sink. Reusing food waste, however, is turning food waste into something useful. In Source Number 3, the author states that "Once food waste enters wastewater treatment plants, it can be recycled into methane and used as a renewable source of power for the plant." Furthermore, plant-based foods can be turned into bio-solids, which are then used in fertilizer and other products. This goes to show that even food waste can be turned into something useful, such as a product or another resource.

These are some ways that natural resources can be conserved. Waste can be harmful or useful depending on what you do with it. Since the average U.S. family of four makes close to 2,000 pounds of food waste a year, it's hard to imagine what to do with all that waste. We can think of smarter ways to reduce our waste. In conclusion, these are a few ways people can help protect our natural resources and the environment.

When reviewing this sample response, notice that:

- The response has a clear and effective organizational structure with a progression from beginning to end that makes sense.
- The main idea is stated with a clear and effective thesis statement.
- The introduction contains a brief summary.
- There is an effective use of evidence and direct quotes that support the ideas presented.
- The response uses elaborative techniques that provide more information.
- The response uses grade-level vocabulary with correct grammar and punctuation.

You should have noticed that the three research questions in the Performance Task provided major clues as to how to organize your informative essay. Question 3 in particular asked you to choose the best sentence that combined all three main ideas from each source. If you chose correctly, that answer should have provided you with a thesis statement that helped organize your essay and provide three reasons. From there, you needed to find the evidence and examples from each source to support your thesis statement.

Use the writing rubrics in Appendix A to grade your response.

PART TWO
Math

Number and Operations in Base Ten with Decimals

CHAPTER 7

ACADEMIC VOCABULARY

> **Tenth**—one part of 10 equal parts of a whole

> **Hundredth**—one part of 100 equal parts of a whole

> **Thousandth**—one part of 1,000 equal parts of a whole

> **Round**—the process of replacing a number with the nearest multiple of 10, 100, 1,000, and so on

> **Standard Form**—a common way of writing a number (e.g., 321)

> **Expanded Form**—a way to write a number that shows the place value of each digit (e.g., 300 + 20 + 1)

> **Word Form**—expressing a number with words (e.g., three hundred twenty-one)

Overview

In fifth grade, you are expected to use your understanding of place value in multi-digit whole numbers and apply it to multi-digit decimals. This includes understanding how to round, estimate, compare, and order decimals. You will use this knowledge to add, subtract, multiply, and divide multi-digit decimals as well. To be successful working with decimals, you will need to understand decimal place value and how you can use it to make multiplying and dividing decimals easier.

Whole Numbers Place Value

Our number system is a base-ten system. This means that each digit is 10 times the value to the right of it. Take a look at Table 7-1 for a more detailed explanation.

Table 7-1. Place Value

<100,000	= 10 × 10,000	= 10 × 1,000	= 10 × 100	= 10 × 10	= 10 × 1
Hundred Thousands	Ten Thousands	Thousands	Hundreds	Tens	Ones
100,000	10,000	1,000	100	10	1
100,000 ÷ 10 =	10,000 ÷ 10 =	1,000 ÷ 10 =	100 ÷ 10 =	10 ÷ 10 =	1

What pattern did you notice? Each place value adds a zero as you increase to the next place value to the left. When you move from the left to the right, you take away a zero. For example:

$$100,000 \rightarrow 10,000 \text{ (divided by 10)}$$

$$10,000 \rightarrow 100,000 \text{ (multiplied by 10)}$$

When you multiply, the number increases, and, when you divide, it decreases. This pattern of base-ten numbers allows you to calculate different values quickly and easily.

Practice Exercises—Whole Numbers Place Value

Common Core Standard 5.NBT.A.1
Recognize that in a multi-digit number, a digit in one place represents 10 times as much as it represents in the place to its right and $\frac{1}{10}$ of what it represents in the place to its left.

There are a few ways that the exam could test you on this skill. Questions 1–3 are a few examples, but pay close attention to the bolded vocabulary and phrases used in the questions. These are vocabulary and phrases to use in your written answers during the Math portion of the SBAC:

1. How much **greater** is 7,000 than 70?

    ○ A.   1,000 times greater

    ◉ B.   100 times greater

    ○ C.   10 times greater

    ○ D.   7 times greater

B

2. Which of the following choices describes the **relationship between** 5,000 and 50,000?

    ○ A.   50,000 is $\frac{1}{10}$ of 5,000

    ○ B.   50,000 is 20 times as much as 5,000

    ○ C.   5,000 is $\frac{1}{10}$ of 50,000

    ○ D.   5,000 is $\frac{1}{1,000}$ of 50,000

C

3. How does the value of the 6 in 5,678 compare to the value of the 6 in 24,326? Write your answer in the box below.

(Answers are on page 289.)

In addition to multiple-choice questions, you will be given tasks that require a short response. These are called constructed-response tasks. You will need to make sure to use key vocabulary to describe your thinking. Question 3 above is an example of a constructed-response task.

Other Ways to Talk About Comparing Values
• Different from
• Related to
• Relationship between

Decimal Place Value

What Is a Decimal?

A decimal is a number that shows a part of a whole. This means that decimal place values represent numbers less than one. For example, let's say you have half of a candy bar. You can represent this with a decimal by writing 0.50. It is halfway between 0, or no candy bar, and 1 whole candy bar. Decimals can also be written with a whole number. Let's say you have two candy bars now, but you still have that half of one. You can write this amount of candy bars as 2.50.

1 candy bar:	0.50	0.50

2 candy bars:	0.50	0.50

3 candy bars:	0.50	0.50

To understand how much of a whole a decimal is referring to, you need to understand place value in decimals. Each place value after the decimal tells you how many parts of the whole you have. For example, let's look at the decimal 0.35. If you know that the number 3 is in the tenths place, then you can say that there are 3 tenths. Likewise, the 5 in the hundredths place says that there are 5 hundredths. Or, if we have the decimal 2.35, then we know we have two wholes and thirty-five hundredths of one more whole. It is important to know the value of each decimal place in order to represent decimals in different ways. Table 7-2 shows the value of each decimal place.

Table 7-2. Whole Number and Decimal Place Values

Whole Number Place Values	Decimal Point	Decimal Place Values		
Ones	.	Tenths	Hundredths	Thousandths
1	.	0.1	0.01	0.001
2	.	0.3	0.05	0.007

To master this math standard on the SBAC, you will need to know how to read and write decimals in **standard form**, **expanded form**, and **word form**. Use Table 7-2 as a reference.

Let's use the decimal 2.357 as an example for each:

Standard Form	This is the normal way you would read and use a decimal number: 2.357
Expanded Form	Expanded form breaks down a number into the value of each place. It is written as a number sentence: $$(2 \times 1) + (3 \times \frac{1}{10}) + (5 \times \frac{1}{100}) + (7 \times \frac{1}{1,000})$$
Word Form	Word form is written in the way you would say a decimal number out loud: *Two and three-hundred and fifty-seven thousandths*

Practice Exercises—Decimal Place Value

Common Core Standard 5.NBT.A.3.A
Read and write decimals to thousandths using base-ten numerals, number names, and expanded form, e.g.,
$$347.392 = 3 \times 100 + 4 \times 10 + 7 \times 1 + 3 \times \left(\frac{1}{10}\right) + 9 \times \left(\frac{1}{100}\right) + 2 \times \left(\frac{1}{1,000}\right).$$

The exam will focus on having you change a decimal from one form to another. There are many different tasks they can give you to assess this standard or skill. The following two exercises should help you practice this skill.

1. What is the standard form of the number below?

$$12 + 2 + 0.5 + 0.04 + 0.008$$

- A. 14.548
- B. 1.4548
- C. 145.48
- D. 1454.8

2. Mel has a batting average score of 0.245. What is his batting average score written in expanded form? Enter your answer in the numerical pad below.

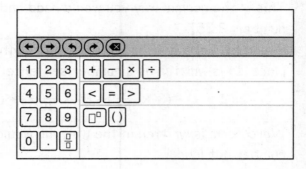

(Answers are on page 289.)

Comparing and Ordering Decimals

To compare decimals is to make a decision about which decimal numbers are **greater**, **less than**, or **equal to** each other. To successfully do this, it is important to understand decimal place value from the previous section.

Let's say you have two decimals: 5.67 and 5.76. When you compare these two numbers, look at the place value of each digit from left to right. Since both decimals have a 5 in the ones place, look to the next place value to the right. The decimal 5.67 has six tenths, whereas the decimal 5.76 has seven tenths. This tells you that 5.67 is less than 5.76, or 5.67 < 5.76. Since there is a difference in value of the tenths place, you do not need to compare the hundredths place of the two decimals.

Let's practice a few basic comparisons:

1. 0.43   ⊘   0.043
2. 22.40   ⊜   22.400
3. 0.233   ⊘   0.23

Another way to compare decimals is to line them up vertically and compare them by place value:

1. 0.43
0.043

You can clearly see, based on the tenths values, that 0.43 > 0.043.

2. 22.40
22.400

You can clearly see that these are the same number. Therefore, 22.40 = 22.400.

3. 0.233

0.23

These two numbers have the same values in the tenths and hundredths place. The first number, however, has a 3 in the thousandths place, whereas the second number has no number, or 0, in the thousandths place. Therefore, 0.233 > 0.23.

Knowing decimal place value and how to compare decimals will also allow you to order decimals correctly. If you are given a list, or a series, of decimals, you will be able to compare all these numbers to determine what the order of each is from least to greatest, or greatest to least.

For instance, let's order the decimals 3.24, 1.04, 3.34, and 5.60 from least to greatest. Right away we can see that 1.04 will be listed first since it has the smallest number in the ones place. Likewise, we can quickly see that the 5 in the ones place of 5.60 is the greatest and therefore will be the greatest decimal. Next, there are two decimals with a 3 in the ones place. You will need to compare more than just the ones place to correctly put these two in order. There are only two tenths in 3.24 and three tenths in 3.34, which means that 3.24 comes before 3.34. The final order, therefore, is: 1.04, 3.24, 3.34, 5.60.

Visualization as a Strategy

Using ten-block visuals helps you to quickly see which decimal is smaller or greater than the other. This is something that you can quickly sketch on scratch paper to compare. Take a look at the visuals for the decimals 3.24 and 3.34 below.

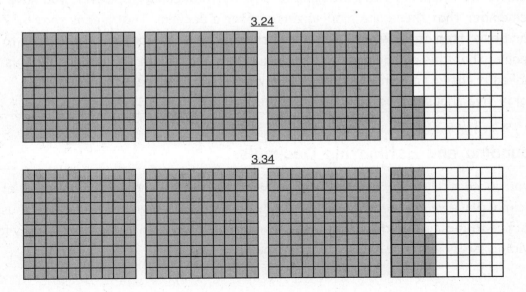

3.24

3.34

Practice Exercises—Comparing and Ordering Decimals

> **Common Core Standard 5.NBT.A.3.B**
> Compare two decimals to thousandths based on meanings of the digits in each place, using >, =, and < symbols to record the results of comparisons.

p. 370

1. Angela and Mekya went on 3 hikes. They hiked 8.2 miles, 8.37 miles, and 8.345 miles. Order the distances from least to greatest. Justify your answer using place value. Write your answer in the box below.

(2)

(Answer is on page 289.)

Common Misunderstanding
A common mistake is to overlook the missing 0 in a decimal. Let's say you are ordering 8.345 and 8.37. You may think that 8.37 is smaller because the number 37 is smaller than the number 345. With decimals, however, you have to remember that there are trailing zeros after a decimal. That means that 8.37 can be written as 8.370. This does not change the value, but it is important to realize that this can be read as three-hundred and seventy thousandths. This makes it easier to compare it to 8.345, which is only three-hundred and forty-five thousandths. This makes 8.345 smaller than 8.37.

Rounding and Estimating Decimals

If you successfully know how to read and write decimals using your knowledge of decimal place value, then you can correctly round decimals to any place. You must practice rounding in order to estimate, which will become an important strategy for dividing larger whole numbers and decimals.

Rounding decimals is the same as rounding whole numbers, which depends on understanding place value. For instance, if you're asked to round 2.45 to the nearest tenth, you would look to the right of that place value. In this case, the 5 to the right of the 4 tells you to round up to 2.50. If the number is less than five, then that digit in the tenths place will stay the same. For example, 2.43 would round down to 2.40 because the 3 is less than 5 and tells you to keep the tenths place the same.

Another way to understand rounding decimals is by using a number line. Look at the number line below:

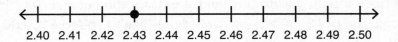

2.40 2.41 2.42 2.43 2.44 2.45 2.46 2.47 2.48 2.49 2.50

As you can see, 2.43 is closer to 2.40.

On the SBAC, you will also be asked to estimate the products of decimals being multiplied or divided. In order to do this, you will need to round first. Let's say you have the number sentence, 2.20 × 14.98. You would first round both factors in the problem, giving you: 2 × 15. These numbers are much easier to work with. Your estimation would be 30.

Practice Exercises—Rounding and Estimating Decimals

> **Common Core Standard 5.NBT.A.4**
> Use place value understanding to round decimals to any place.

1. What is 6.492 rounded to the nearest tenth?

- O A. 6.4
- O B. 6.5
- O C. 6.40
- O D. 6.05

2. Which of these numbers, when rounded to the nearest hundredth, is 0.07? Circle **all** that round to 0.07.

0.67   0.072   0.069   0.066   0.77

3. Taran bought 6.25 pounds of coffee at the supermarket. His coffee machine can only grind 0.26 pounds of coffee at one time. About how many times does he have to grind the total of 6.25 pounds?

○ A.   16   ○ F. 21

○ B.   13.2

○ C.   20

○ D.   24.04

○ E. 25

→ Estimate

4. Evelyn is deciding on gifts to buy her parents for their anniversary. From her piggy bank, she has $250.28. She would only like to spend $100.00 total on as many different items as possible. The possible items that she can buy are as follows:

Book = $22.36

Picture Frame = $12.48

Scarf = $25.35

Tea = $45.07

 How many combinations are there that Evelyn can afford to buy? Explain your answer in the box below.

(Answers are on page 289.)

Adding and Subtracting Decimals

When adding or subtracting decimals, it is important to line up the decimals. Once you line up the decimals, you can add or subtract as you would a regular whole number. Let's look at two examples.

1. 10.22
    + 4.56
    ———   The answer is **14.78**. First, line up the decimals. Then, bring the decimal down before you start adding. Finally, add the values.

2. 10.2
    − 4.03
    ———   The answer is 6.17. First, line up the decimals. Notice the blank spot above the 3. You will need to fill this in with a 0 to subtract. Then, bring the decimal down before you start subtracting. Finally, subtract the values.

Practice Exercises—Adding and Subtracting Decimals

Common Core Standard 5.NBT.B.7
Add, subtract, multiply, and divide decimals to hundredths, using concrete models or drawings and strategies based on place value, properties of operations, and/or the relationship between addition and subtraction; relate the strategy to a written method and explain the reasoning used.

1. The table below shows the ticket prices for the new Star Wars movie, *Star Wars: The Force Awakens*.

Adult	$12.95
Child	$ 6.75
Senior Citizen	$10.25

Part A: The Wang family buys 2 senior citizen tickets and 2 child tickets. What is the total cost of the tickets, not including tax? Enter your answer in the numerical pad below.

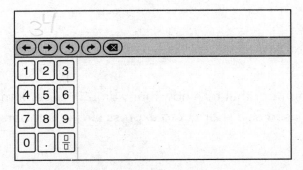

Part B: At the last minute, one of their children cannot make it to the movie. What is the difference in price if one child ticket is not included in the total from Part A? Enter your answer in the numerical pad below.

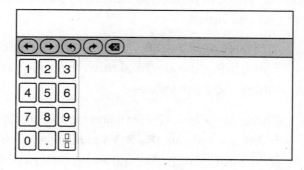

(Answers are on page 290.)

Decimals and the Powers of 10

Remember, our number system is a base-ten system. That means that each place value adds a zero as you increase to the next place value. When you move from the left to the right, you take away a zero. This is true for both whole numbers and decimals. Refer to Table 7-3 to review Decimals and the Powers of 10.

Table 7-3. Decimals and the Powers of 10

0.001 × 10 =	Decimal	0.010 × 10 =	0.10 × 10 =	1.0 × 10
Ones 1.0	.	Tenths 0.1	Hundredths 0.01	Thousandths 0.001

1 ÷ 10 =	Decimal	0.10 ÷ 10 =	0.01 ÷ 10 =	0.001 ÷ 10
Ones 1	.	Tenths 0.1	Hundredths 0.01	Thousandths 0.001

This pattern is used to ease the process of multiplying and dividing decimals by the powers of 10. To do this, however, we must first review what an exponent is and how we use it.

Exponents

An exponent is a number that tells how many times a base number is multiplied. Exponents can be used as a shortcut to express larger numbers that end in zeros.

The base number in this case is 10. The exponent is written as a superscript, or a smaller number set above the base number, and it indicates how many times 10 is multiplied.

Exponential notation is when the exponent is written out in a math sentence showing the repeated multiplication. Look at Table 7-4, and see if you notice any patterns.

Table 7-4. Exponential Notation

Exponential Notation	Exponents	Product
10	10^1	10
10 × 10	10^2	100
10 × 10 × 10	10^3	1,000
10 × 10 × 10 × 10	10^4	10,000
10 × 10 × 10 × 10 × 10	10^5	100,000

You may have noticed the relationship between the number of zeros in the product and the number of the exponent. For instance, based on the pattern in Table 7-4, 10^6 will have six zeros for the product of 1,000,000. You can use this pattern to your advantage to do mental math for large numbers multiplied by exponents. An example math sentence would be $320 \times 10^2 = 32,000$. You can see that you simply needed to add two zeros to the factor 320 to get the right answer.

Multiplying Decimals by 10, 100, and 1,000

Multiplying decimals by a power of 10 follows a particular pattern that makes it easy to mentally calculate. Look at an example of the pattern below:

When you multiply a decimal by 10, the decimal is moved to the right one digit:

$$0.4 \times 10 = 4.0$$

When you multiply a decimal by 100, the decimal is moved to the right two digits:

$$0.4 \times 100 = 40.0$$

When you multiply a decimal by 1,000, the decimal is moved to the right three digits:

$$0.4 \times 1,000 = 400.0$$

Dividing Decimals by 10, 100, and 1,000

Dividing decimals by powers of ten also follows a specific pattern. This time, however, the decimal moves to the left. Let's look at an example using the same decimal as above:

When you divide a decimal by 10, the decimal is moved to the left one digit:

$$0.4 \div 10 = 0.04$$

When you divide a decimal by 100, the decimal is moved to the left two digits:

$$0.4 \div 100 = 0.004$$

When you divide a decimal by 1,000, the decimal is moved to the left three digits:

$$0.4 \div 1,000 = 0.0004$$

Practice Exercises—Decimals and the Powers of 10

Common Core Standard 5.NBT.A.2
Explain patterns in the number of zeros of the product when multiplying a number by powers of 10, and explain patterns in the placement of the decimal point when a decimal is multiplied or divided by a power of 10. Use whole-number exponents to denote powers of 10.

1. Circle all the expressions or numbers below that are equivalent to each other.

8,823,000	$8,823 \times 10^3$
882.3×10^5	88.23×10^5
88.23×10^6	8.823×10^7
$8.823 \div 10^7$	8.823×10^6

2. Match the numbers on the left with an equivalent expression on the right. Some numbers may have more than one equivalent expression. Some numbers may not have an equivalent expression. (Note that this is a technology-enhanced question that, on the actual exam, would require you to use the Connect Line tool to draw a line to the correct digits from the left column to the right column.)

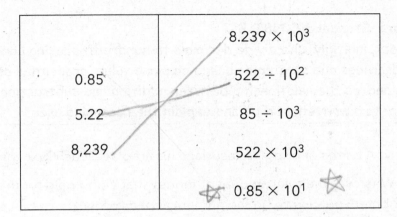

(Answers are on page 290.)

Multiplication with Multi-Digit Whole Numbers and Decimals

Multiplication with Multi-Digit Whole Numbers

When multiplying with whole numbers, it is important to line up the digits. For example, $253 \times 23 =$ should be written as:

$$\begin{array}{r} 253 \\ \times\ \ 23 \\ \hline \end{array}$$

Multiplication with Multi-Digit Decimals

When multiplying with multi-digit decimals, it is important to line up the digits and line up the places to the right of the decimal of both numbers. For example, $2.53 \times 2.3 =$ should be written as:

$$\begin{array}{r} 2.53 \\ \times\ \ 2.3 \\ \hline \end{array}$$

Practice Exercises—Multiplication with Multi-Digit Whole Numbers and Decimals

> **Common Core Standard 5.NBT.B.5**
> Fluently multiply multi-digit whole numbers using the standard algorithm.
>
> **Common Core Standard 5.NBT.B.7**
> Add, subtract, multiply, and divide decimals to hundredths, using concrete models or drawings and strategies based on place value, properties of operations, and/or the relationship between addition and subtraction; relate the strategy to a written method and explain the reasoning used.

1. Vinod buys 4 boxes of bricks to resurface his fireplace. Each box costs $12.52.

Part A: What was the total amount of money that Vinod paid for those 4 boxes? Enter your answer in the numerical pad below.

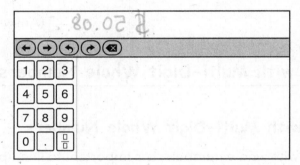

Part B: He needs 232 bricks to resurface the fireplace. Each box has 58 bricks. Does Vinod have enough bricks to resurface the fireplace? Explain and justify your answer in the box below.

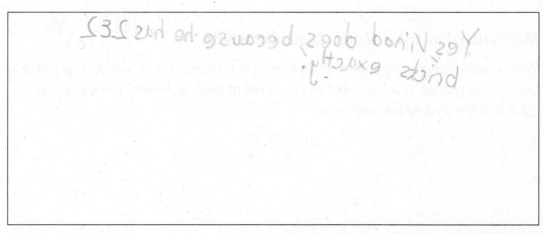

(Answers are on page 291.)

Division with Multi-Digit Whole Numbers

Long division of multi-digit whole numbers is formulaic. This means that you can use a system for dividing step by step. The most common way to remember the steps of long division is with the acronym **D**ivision, **M**ultiply, **S**ubtract, **B**ring Down (DMSB). Make sure to line up the digits with each step. With double-digit divisors, it helps to estimate on scratch paper what number is the closest to the divisor. For example, let's look at the steps for dividing 5,350 by 28:

$$28\overline{)5{,}350}$$

1. Look at the first digit in the dividend. 28 cannot be divided into 5. (Hint: Place a zero or an X, or leave it blank, and look at the next digit.) Can 28 be divided into 53? Yes it can. Using estimation to help you, 28 is close to 30, so the estimate 30 can go into 53 one time. So, 28 can go into 53 one time.

$$
\begin{array}{r}
1 \\
28\overline{)5{,}350} \\
-28 \\
\hline
255
\end{array}
$$

2. Next, on scratch paper, once again use estimation for 255. About how many 30s can fit into 255? By doing this, we know that 255 can be divided by 28 nine times.

$$
\begin{array}{r}
19 \\
28\overline{)5{,}350} \\
-28 \\
\hline
255 \\
-252 \\
\hline
30
\end{array}
$$

3. Finally, we know that 28 can be divided by 30, one time. After subtraction, the remainder would be 2.

$$
\begin{array}{r}
191 \\
28\overline{)5{,}350} \\
-28 \\
\hline
255 \\
-252 \\
\hline
30 \\
-28 \\
\hline
2
\end{array}
$$

Practice Exercises—Division with Multi-Digit Whole Numbers

> **Common Core Standard 5.NBT.B.6**
> Find whole-number quotients of whole numbers with up to four-digit dividends and two-digit divisors, using strategies based on place value, the properties of operations, and/or the relationship between multiplication and division. Illustrate and explain the calculation by using equations, rectangular arrays, and/or area models.
>
> **Common Core Standard 5.NBT.B.7**
> Add, subtract, multiply, and divide decimals to hundredths, using concrete models or drawings and strategies based on place value, properties of operations, and/or the relationship between addition and subtraction; relate the strategy to a written method and explain the reasoning used.

Directions: For questions 1–3, solve the following problems, and enter the quotient in the numerical pad below each question.

1. 6,243 ÷ 32

195 r3

1	2	3
4	5	6
7	8	9
0	.	□/□

2. 2,645 ÷ 21

125 r 20

1	2	3
4	5	6
7	8	9
0	.	□/□

3. 7,362 ÷ 12

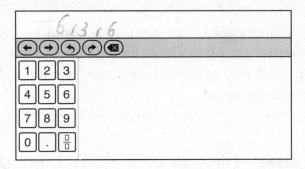

(Answers are on page 291.)

Division with Multi-Digit Decimals

Dividing a Decimal by a Whole Number

If you are dividing a decimal by a whole number, you will start dividing as usual. You do not need to worry about the decimal until you find the answer, or quotient. For instance, if you divide 88.45 by 5, you can ignore the decimal and go through the normal steps of DMSB. Once you get the answer, 1,769, place the decimal right above its location in the quotient. Your final answer will be 17.69.

Dividing a Decimal by a Decimal

To divide a decimal by a decimal, you will use the same skills you do when dividing a decimal by a whole number. First, you will need to add the step of changing the divisor to a whole number to make the process easier. You have to depend on your knowledge of multiplying decimals by powers of ten.

Let's take a look at the steps necessary for 43.2 ÷ 0.6:

1. We want to make the divisor, 0.6, a whole number. We can do that by multiplying 0.6 by 10, which moves the decimal to the right one place, leaving us with the whole number 6.
2. But wait! This means you have to do the same thing to the dividend, 43.2, to get the correct quotient. That means 43.2 becomes 432.0 after multiplying it by 10. You now have the division problem 432.0 ÷ 6.
3. Place the decimal directly above in the quotient and divide as you would when dividing a decimal by a whole number.
4. Your final answer should be 72.0, or just 72.

```
HELPFUL HINT
```

For technology-enhanced questions, you will be asked to drag the correct digits into the missing spaces to make the problem correct. For example, in the number 252, the 5 may be the missing digit, and you will have to drag the number into the missing space.

Practice Exercises—Division with Multi-Digit Decimals

Common Core Standard 5.NBT.B.6
Find whole-number quotients of whole numbers with up to four-digit dividends and two-digit divisors, using strategies based on place value, the properties of operations, and/or the relationship between multiplication and division. Illustrate and explain the calculation by using equations, rectangular arrays, and/or area models.

Common Core Standard 5.NBT.B.7
Add, subtract, multiply, and divide decimals to hundredths, using concrete models or drawings and strategies based on place value, properties of operations, and/or the relationship between addition and subtraction; relate the strategy to a written method and explain the reasoning used.

The division tasks you encounter on the SBAC will be similar to the multiplication tasks reviewed in the previous sections. A few selected-response tasks will be presented, but you should also be prepared for more in-depth tasks, such as constructed-response tasks, extended-response tasks, and technology-enhanced response tasks.

1. Jennifer is planning for a summit conference. Her event planner tells the staff that 256 seats will need to be set up evenly in 16 rows. How many seats are in each row?

Part A: In the box below, draw a picture or table that explains the problem. Then, in the numerical pad that follows, enter an equation that describes your picture or table.

$256 \div 16$

$= 16$

$16 \times 16 = 16^2$

←	→	↶	↷	⌫

1	2	3	+	−	×	÷
4	5	6	<	=	>
7	8	9	□□	( )
0	.	□/□

Part B: In the box below, solve the equation.

16

$256 \div 16 = 16$

2. Liz ran 34.6 miles over 5 days at Stinson Beach. She ran the same number of miles each day.

Part A: How far did she run each day? In the numerical pad, write an equation to solve the problem. Then, in the box below, solve your equation.

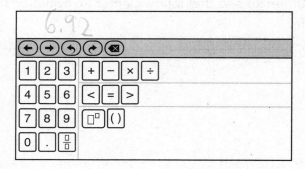

6.92

34.6 ÷ 5 = 6.92

Part B: If Liz keeps running the same number of miles each day, how many miles will Liz run in 7 days? In the numerical pad, write an equation to solve the problem. Then, in the box on the next page, solve your equation.

34.6 ÷ 5   6.92 × 7

Part B (continued)

$$34.6 \div \frac{5}{7} = 34.6 \times \frac{7}{5}$$
$$= 34.6 \times 1.4$$
$$= 48.44$$

don

3. A developer owns 62.5 acres of land. He wants to build an equal number of homes on the land, and each home takes up 2.5 acres. How many homes can he build? In the numerical pad, write an equation to solve the problem. Then, in the box below, solve your equation.

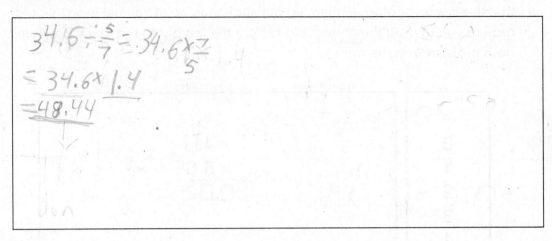

62.5 ÷ 2.5

62.5 ÷ 2.5 = 25

4. Show two different ways to solve the following multiplication problem. (Note that this is a technology-enhanced question that, on the actual exam, would require you to drag the correct digits from the left bar to the blank boxes in both problems on the right.)

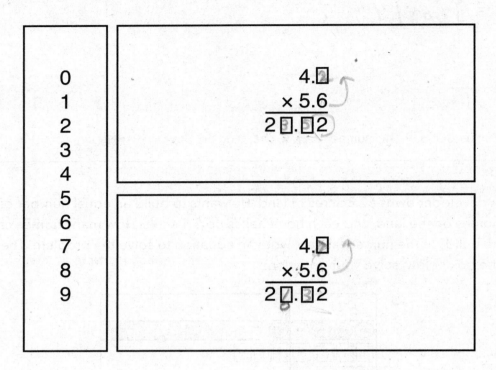

(Answers are on page 292.)

Number and Operations— Fractions and Decimals

CHAPTER 8

ACADEMIC VOCABULARY

> **Denominator**—the number below the fraction bar in a fraction

> **Equivalent Fraction**—a fraction that names the same part of a whole region, length, or set

> **Improper Fraction**—a fraction whose numerator is greater than or equal to its denominator

> **Least Common Denominator (LCD)**—the least common multiple of the denominators of two or more fractions

> **Mixed Number**—a number written with a whole number and a fraction

> **Numerator**—the number above the fraction bar in a fraction

> **Simplest Form**—a fraction in which the greatest common factor of the numerator and the denominator is 1

Overview

You will need to depend on the fraction skills you developed in fourth grade, and apply them to the fifth-grade fraction standards in this section. In fourth grade, you learned how to find equivalent fractions and how to simplify. Also, you should have learned how to add and subtract fractions with like denominators. In case you need a quick refresher, study Table 8-1.

Table 8-1. Review of Fourth-Grade Fraction Standards

The Meaning of Fractions	Equivalent Fractions and Simplifying Fractions
Fractions are related to decimals and division. They represent parts of a whole. These parts are equal and all together add up to a whole.	In fourth grade, you learned about finding fractions that are equal to each other, known as equivalent fractions. You also learned that to find the smallest of these equivalent fractions is called simplifying fractions. You will need to remember how to find equivalent fractions in order to add, subtract, multiply, and divide mixed numbers in this chapter.

Adding and Subtracting Fractions with Like Denominators

Adding and subtracting fractions with like denominators is similar to adding and subtracting whole numbers. Instead, you will be adding or subtracting the numerators while the denominators stay the same. For example:

$$\frac{1}{3} + \frac{1}{3} = \frac{2}{3} \qquad \text{or} \qquad \frac{3}{5} - \frac{1}{5} = \frac{2}{5}$$

With mixed numbers, you would do the same. However, you will also add or subtract the whole number. For example:

$$1\frac{1}{3} + 1\frac{1}{3} = 2\frac{2}{3} \qquad \text{or} \qquad 2\frac{3}{5} - 1\frac{1}{5} = 1\frac{2}{5}$$

Now, you will need to master how to add, subtract, multiply, and divide fractions with unlike denominators.

Adding and Subtracting Fractions with Unlike Denominators

In order to correctly add or subtract fractions with unlike denominators, you must first rewrite the fractions so that each denominator is the same. Once you do this, you can proceed with adding or subtracting the fractions as you would normally.

How do you make the denominators the same? Well, you must first find the Least Common Denominator, or the LCD, to change each fraction to an equivalent fraction. To do this, you must use the Least Common Multiple (LCM) of the two denominators.

For instance, if you were to add $\frac{2}{6}$ and $\frac{2}{8}$, you must first think of the LCM that they share:

Multiples of 6: 12, 18, **24**, 30

Multiples of 8: 16, **24**, 32, 40

As you can see, 6 and 8 share the multiple of 24. This will be the LCD that each equivalent fraction will have. Next, think of the factors you'll need to get the denominator 24. In the first fraction, in order to get a denominator of 24, you have to multiply 6 by 4. Therefore, do the same to the numerator:

$$6 \times 4 = 24$$

$$2 \times 4 = 8$$

In the second fraction, in order to get a denominator of 24, you have to multiply 8 by 3. Therefore, do the same to the numerator:

$$8 \times 3 = 24$$

$$2 \times 3 = 6$$

Now, the denominators are the same, and you can add as normal:

$$\frac{8}{24} + \frac{6}{24} = \frac{14}{24}$$

Based on your calculations, the answer is $\frac{14}{24}$. But wait! Always remember that the SBAC wants you to simplify all fractions if possible! To simplify $\frac{14}{24}$, we can divide each number by 2, resulting in $\frac{7}{12}$. The fraction $\frac{7}{12}$ cannot be simplified any further. Therefore, the final answer is $\frac{7}{12}$.

Let's use the same values, but, this time, let's practice subtraction.

$$\frac{8}{24} - \frac{6}{24} = \frac{2}{24}$$

You may want to say that your answer is $\frac{2}{24}$, but don't forget to simplify! To simplify $\frac{2}{24}$, we can divide each number by 2, resulting in $\frac{1}{12}$. The fraction $\frac{1}{12}$ cannot be simplified any further. Therefore, the final answer is $\frac{1}{12}$.

Practice Exercises—Adding and Subtracting Fractions with Unlike Denominators

> **Common Core Standard 5.NF.A.1**
> Add and subtract fractions with unlike denominators (including mixed numbers) by replacing given fractions with equivalent fractions in such a way as to produce an equivalent sum or difference of fractions with like denominators.

The SBAC may test you in different ways to assess the skills needed to complete this standard proficiently. The tasks will not always be straightforward math problems. Questions 1 and 2 are some examples of these nontraditional question types.

1. Match the solution to each problem. Draw a line from each problem to its corresponding solution.

$\dfrac{3}{6} + \dfrac{4}{8} =$	$\dfrac{1}{8}$
$\dfrac{5}{8} - \dfrac{16}{32} =$	0
$\dfrac{3}{12} - \dfrac{1}{4} =$	1

2. Decide which expressions are true. Select Yes or No for each expression.

$\dfrac{3}{4} - \dfrac{1}{8} = \dfrac{7}{8}$ O Yes ● No

$\dfrac{8}{12} - \dfrac{4}{8} = \dfrac{1}{6}$ ● Yes O No

$\dfrac{3}{5} + \dfrac{2}{6} = \dfrac{14}{15}$ ● Yes O No

$\dfrac{8}{12} + \dfrac{2}{24} = \dfrac{16}{24}$ O Yes ● No

(Answers are on page 294.)

Word Problems Involving Adding and Subtracting Fractions with Unlike Denominators

Solving word problems with fractions requires three steps:

1. **Translate the problem into a solvable equation.** This will require you to look for key words in the problem to tell you whether to add or subtract.
2. Then, **change the denominators** in order to add the fractions.
3. **Solve** and possibly **simplify** or change from an improper fraction to a mixed number.

Practice Exercises—Word Problems Involving Adding and Subtracting Fractions with Unlike Denominators

> **Common Core Standard 5.NF.A.2**
> Solve word problems involving addition and subtraction of fractions referring to the same whole, including cases of unlike denominators, e.g., by using visual fraction models or equations to represent the problem. Use benchmark fractions and number sense of fractions to estimate mentally and assess the reasonableness of answers.

1. Betty and Vinod measured their daughter Evie's height over the course of two months. In the first month, Evie grew $\frac{1}{2}$ an inch. In the second month, Evie grew $\frac{3}{4}$ of an inch. How many inches did Evie grow in all?

   ○ A. 1 inch

   ○ B. $1\frac{1}{2}$ inches

   ○ C. $2\frac{3}{4}$ inches

   ● D. $1\frac{1}{4}$ inches

2. Mekya practices his drums $\frac{3}{8}$ of a day the first week and $\frac{3}{16}$ of a day the next week.

Part A: Write an equation to determine the difference between the amount of days Mekya practiced the first week and the amount of days he practiced the second week. Enter your equation in the numerical pad below.

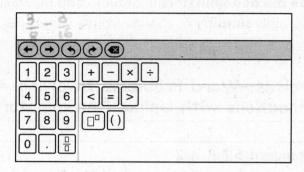

Part B: Solve the equation from Part A. Show your work in the box below.

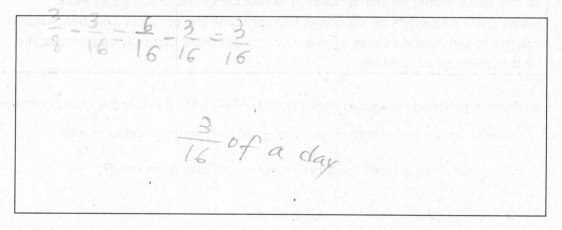

$$\frac{3}{8} - \frac{3}{16} = \frac{6}{16} - \frac{3}{16} = \frac{3}{16}$$

$$\frac{3}{16} \text{ of a day}$$

3. Liz spent $3\frac{1}{8}$ hours at the Farmer's Market, and Taran spent $1\frac{1}{3}$ hours at the supermarket. How much more time did Liz spend at the Farmer's Market than Taran spent at the supermarket?

○ A. $1\frac{17}{24}$ hours

○ B. $1\frac{1}{2}$ hours

◉ C. $1\frac{19}{24}$ hours

○ D. $1\frac{1}{4}$ hours

(Answers are on page 296.)

Interpreting Fractions as Division

For the SBAC, you will need to understand how fractions and division are related. For one, you will be assessed on this concept. Second, this is important to understand as it will support you when you are interpreting word problems.

So, how are fractions and division related? In a fraction, the numerator is the given number of equal parts and the denominator is the total number of parts you are comparing the numerator to. In division, the numerator would be the dividend, and the denominator would become the divisor. For instance, let's look at the fraction $\frac{2}{3}$. The 2 is being divided by 3. A smaller number is being divided by a larger number; this is why we write it as a fraction, $\frac{2}{3}$. It can also be represented as a division problem, $2 \div 3$.

When would you use this knowledge? Well, let's think about a situation when there is not enough of one thing for each person. Let's say there are 2 cookies, but 3 people want to share them. That means 2 cookies have to be divided equally among 3 people. This problem, however, is easy to figure out because the fraction is the answer. Since there are 3 people wanting the same amount of each of the 2 cookies, then each person will get $\frac{2}{3}$ of a cookie. Think about this visually.

Below are two cookies. To divide them evenly among three people (P), we would need to divide each cookie into 3, and each person would get 2 of those pieces.

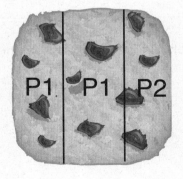 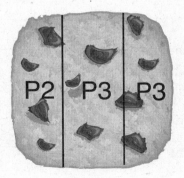

Other examples include:

5 people sharing 3 cans of soda = $\frac{3}{5}$

8 people sharing 1 piece of pie = $\frac{1}{8}$

6 people sharing 2 candy bars = $\frac{2}{6}$ = $\frac{1}{3}$

Practice Exercises—Interpreting Fractions as Division

Common Core Standard 5.NF.B.3
Interpret a fraction as division of the numerator by the denominator ($\frac{a}{b} = a \div b$).
Solve word problems involving division of whole numbers leading to answers in the form of fractions or mixed numbers, e.g., by using visual fraction models or equations to represent the problem.

Common Core Standard 5.NF.B.7
Apply and extend previous understandings of division to divide unit fractions by whole numbers and whole numbers by unit fractions.[1]

[1]Students able to multiply fractions in general can develop strategies to divide fractions in general, by reasoning about the relationship between multiplication and division. But division of a fraction by a fraction is not a requirement at this grade.

Common Core Standard 5.NF.B.7.A
Interpret division of a unit fraction by a non-zero whole number, and compute such quotients.

Common Core Standard 5.NF.B.7.B
Interpret division of a whole number by a unit fraction, and compute such quotients.

---

1. Match the phrases with the correct fraction. Draw a line from the phrase to the fraction that matches it.

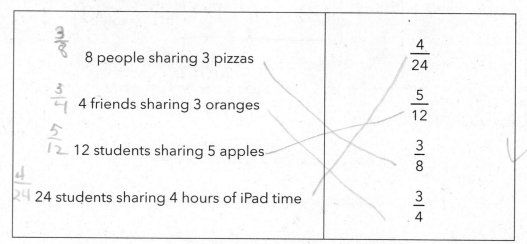

(Answers are on page 298.)

Multiplication of Fractions and Whole Numbers

This section will cover three skills: multiplying fractions by a whole number, multiplying two fractions, and multiplying mixed numbers. It is important to understand the concepts behind these skills, which means you should be able to explain to someone else what you are doing and why you are doing it. You will have to apply this knowledge to different types of questions and problems on the SBAC.

When multiplying two whole numbers, we are used to the product being larger than the factors. Multiplying a whole number by a fraction, however, can result in a smaller product. This can be confusing.

Let's take a look at the concept behind multiplying fractions. Anytime you multiply, you are using a shortcut to repeatedly add a number a certain amount of times. This is no different than when you multiply a whole number by a fraction. The fraction is repeatedly added the number of times based on the whole number. For example, if you have the equation $8 \times \frac{1}{3}$, then you actually have:

$$\frac{1}{3} + \frac{1}{3} + \frac{1}{3} + \frac{1}{3} + \frac{1}{3} + \frac{1}{3} + \frac{1}{3} + \frac{1}{3}$$

Of course, multiplication makes this easier and quicker to solve. To find the answer, simply multiply the whole number by the numerator, $8 \times 1 = 8$. You do not have to do anything to the denominator, which makes your answer $\frac{8}{3}$. This is an improper fraction, and it must be changed to a mixed number. How many 3s go into 8? 3 can go into 8 two times. So, the answer will be $2\frac{2}{3}$.

HELPFUL HINT

Whole numbers can be written as a fraction. For example, $\frac{8}{8} = 1$. Anytime you see that the numerator and the denominator are the same, that fraction equals one whole.

Practice Exercises—Multiplication of Fractions and Whole Numbers

Common Core Standard 5.NF.B.4

Apply and extend previous understandings of multiplication to multiply a fraction or whole number by a fraction.

Common Core Standard 5.NF.B.4.A

Interpret the product $(\frac{a}{b}) \times q$ as a parts of a partition of q into b equal parts; equivalently, as the result of a sequence of operations $a \times q \div b$.

Common Core Standard 5.NF.B.4.B

Find the area of a rectangle with fractional side lengths by tiling it with unit squares of the appropriate unit fraction side lengths, and show that the area is the same as would be found by multiplying the side lengths. Multiply fractional side lengths to find areas of rectangles, and represent fraction products as rectangular areas.

Common Core Standard 5.NF.B.5.A

Interpret multiplication as scaling (resizing), by: Comparing the size of a product to the size of one factor on the basis of the size of the other factor, without performing the indicated multiplication.

Common Core Standard 5.NF.B.5.B

Interpret multiplication as scaling (resizing), by: Explaining why multiplying a given number by a fraction greater than 1 results in a product greater than the given number (recognizing multiplication by whole numbers greater than 1 as a familiar case); explaining why multiplying a given number by a fraction less than 1 results in a product smaller than the given number; and relating the principle of fraction equivalence $\frac{a}{b} = \frac{(n \times a)}{(n \times b)}$ to the effect of multiplying $\frac{a}{b}$ by 1.

1. Select **all** of the expressions that are equivalent to $2\frac{1}{5}$.

☐ A. $\frac{1}{5} \times 3 = \frac{3}{5}$

☒ B. $11 \times \frac{1}{5} = \frac{11}{5} = 2\frac{1}{5}$

☒ C. $22 \times \frac{1}{10} = \frac{22}{10} = 2\frac{2}{10} = 2\frac{1}{5}$

☐ D. $11 \times 5 = 55$

☐ E. $\frac{1}{5} \times 2 = \frac{2}{5}$

2. Which of the following fraction models best represents $4 \times \frac{2}{3}$?

○ A.

○ B.

◉ C.

○ D.

3. Use the following rectangle to solve the problem.

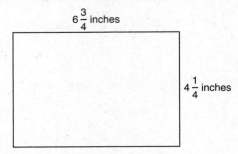

What is the area of the rectangle in square inches?

○ A. $28\frac{1}{4}$ inches

◉ B. $28\frac{11}{16}$ inches

○ C. 22 inches

○ D. $22\frac{11}{16}$ inches

(Answers are on page 298.)

Division of Fractions with a Whole Number

When dividing fractions by a whole number, you must rely on your knowledge of the inverse relationship between multiplication and division. This means that you can use multiplication to undo division. So, if 15 ÷ 3 = 5, then 5 × 3 = 15. This relationship can also be used when dividing fractions by a whole number. To do so, you must first find the **reciprocal** of the divisor. Take for instance, $12 \div \frac{1}{6}$. The problem is easier if you multiply 12 by the reciprocal of $\frac{1}{6}$, which is $\frac{6}{1}$, making the new problem $12 \times \frac{6}{1}$. You can now multiply a whole number by a fraction as you normally would: Multiply the whole number 12 by the numerator 6 to get 72. You do not need to do anything to the denominator, 1. This makes the answer $\frac{72}{1}$, an improper fraction. Anytime the denominator is a 1, then the answer is just the numerator as a whole number. The answer, therefore, is just 72.

Conversely, what is the reciprocal of $\frac{8}{1}$? The reciprocal will be $\frac{1}{8}$.

Practice Exercises—Division of Fractions with a Whole Number

> **Common Core Standard 5.NF.B.7**
>
> Apply and extend previous understandings of division to divide unit fractions by whole numbers and whole numbers by unit fractions.[1]
>
> [1]Students able to multiply fractions in general can develop strategies to divide fractions in general, by reasoning about the relationship between multiplication and division. But division of a fraction by a fraction is not a requirement at this grade.

1. Select **all** of the true statements.

    ☐ A. $3 \div \dfrac{2}{3} = \dfrac{9}{2}$

    ☐ B. $\dfrac{1}{8} \div 2 = \dfrac{2}{8}$

    ☐ C. $\dfrac{6}{8} \div 3 = \dfrac{1}{4}$

    ☐ D. $5 \div \dfrac{2}{5} = \dfrac{10}{25}$

    ☐ E. $2 \div \dfrac{7}{8} = 2\dfrac{2}{7}$

(Answer is on page 299.)

Interpreting and Solving Real-World Problems with Fractions Involving Multiplication and Division

Solving word problems with fractions requires three steps:

1. **Translate the problem into a solvable equation.** This will require you to look for key words in the problem to tell you whether to multiply or divide.

2. **Change the denominators** in order to add the fractions.

3. **Solve** and possibly **simplify** or change from an improper fraction to a mixed number.

Practice Exercises—Interpreting and Solving Real-World Problems with Fractions Involving Multiplication and Division

Common Core Standard 5.NF.B.3

Interpret a fraction as division of the numerator by the denominator ($\frac{a}{b} = a \div b$). Solve word problems involving division of whole numbers leading to answers in the form of fractions or mixed numbers, e.g., by using visual fraction models or equations to represent the problem.

Common Core Standard 5.NF.B.6

Solve real-world problems involving multiplication of fractions and mixed numbers, e.g., by using visual fraction models or equations to represent the problem.

Common Core Standard 5.NF.B.7.C

Solve real-world problems involving division of unit fractions by non-zero whole numbers and division of whole numbers by unit fractions, e.g., by using visual fraction models and equations to represent the problem.

1. Liz works out at the gym for $3\frac{1}{4}$ hours every Monday, Tuesday, and Wednesday.

On each Thursday and Friday, she works out for $2\frac{3}{4}$ hours. Liz believes that she works out for more than 20 hours from Monday to Friday. Is her statement correct? Support your answer visually or with an equation in the box below.

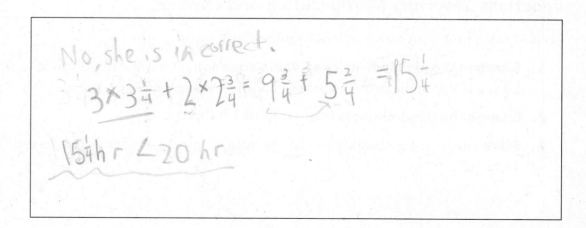

No, she is incorrect.

$3 \times 3\frac{1}{4} + 2 \times 2\frac{3}{4} = 9\frac{3}{4} + 5\frac{2}{4} = 15\frac{1}{4}$

$15\frac{1}{4}$ hr < 20 hr

2. Arjuna buys 4 whole cakes. Each slice of cake is $\frac{1}{8}$ of one cake. How many slices of cake are in all 4 cakes?

○ A. $\frac{1}{32}$

○ B. 8

○ C. $\frac{2}{16}$

◉ D. 32

3. Betty is planning a birthday party for her daughter Evelyn. She needs to have 5 gallons of milk for the party guests. For each gallon that Evelyn helped open for her birthday, she accidentally spilled $\frac{1}{5}$ of the gallon. Betty bought 6 gallons of milk and claims that she still has enough milk for all the guests. Is Betty's claim correct? Explain your answer in the box below.

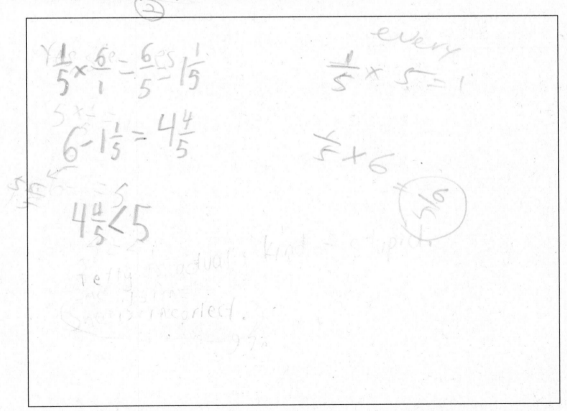

(Answers are on page 299.)

ACADEMIC VOCABULARY

> **Algebraic Expression**—an algebraic expression is a mathematical phrase that includes variables, numbers, and operations

An expression is a written representation of a relationship between two things that includes a variable, or an unknown. Let's use this scenario as an example:

There is a relationship between the number of friends (5 in total) and the number of candy bars in a package that they get to share. This relationship can be translated into an expression, $p \div 5$. Since the number of candy bars in a package is unknown, you can represent that with the variable p.

> **Composite Number**—any number that is not a prime number

> **Coordinate Grid**—a grid that makes it easy to locate points in a plane using an ordered pair of numbers

> **Distributive Property**—multiplying a sum (or difference) by a number is the same as multiplying each number in the sum (or difference) by that number and adding (or subtracting) the products

> **Divisible**—a whole number is divisible by another number when the quotient is a whole number and the remainder is zero

> **Evaluate**—to determine the value of an expression with given variables

> **Factor Pair**—a pair of whole numbers whose product equals a given whole number

> **Factors**—numbers that are multiplied to get a product

> **Line Graph**—a graph that connects points to show how data changes over time

> **Ordered Pair**—a pair of numbers used to locate a point on a coordinate grid

> **Origin**—the point at which the x-axis and the y-axis of the coordinate plane intersect. The origin is represented by the ordered pair (0, 0).

> **Prime Number**—a number greater than 1 that has no other factors other than 1 and itself

ACADEMIC VOCABULARY (continued)

> **Variable**—a variable is a letter or symbol that represents an unknown amount or number

It is important to review what a variable stands for in math. Most often, it is a letter that stands in for an unknown number or amount and can change depending on the unknown in the word problem. An unknown can be anything that you do not know the number for yet. For instance, read the scenario below:

You and five of your friends are going to share a package of candy bars.

This statement does not tell you how many candy bars are in a package. The unknown in this scenario, therefore, would be how many candy bars are in a package. This unknown can be represented by the variable p.

> **x-coordinate**—the first number in an ordered pair. It names the distance to the right or left of the origin along the x-axis.

> **y-coordinate**—the second number in an ordered pair. It names the distance up or down from the origin along the y-axis.

Overview

Algebraic thinking is when you use math sentences to represent math patterns. A very basic example of this is when you use numerical expressions, such as $3 \times 4 = 12$. This is a way to represent the repeated addition pattern of $3 + 3 + 3 + 3 = 12$. These type of patterns become algebraic when you add a **variable**, or symbol, to a math sentence. When a math sentence includes a variable, it is called an **algebraic expression**. Algebraic expressions are used to show patterns, or rules, that are used over and over again in different situations.

In this chapter, you will focus on both identifying the expressions to apply to different patterns and solving different expressions depending on the pattern given.

Table 9-1 highlights the key words that give you clues as to what operation is needed to create and identify expressions. Review these, as you will need to apply your knowledge of them to the word problems in this chapter.

Table 9-1. Operation Key Words

Addition +	Subtraction −	Multiplication ×	Division ÷
Plus	Minus	Each	Quotient
More	Less	Product	Shared
Increased by	Decreased by	Times	Divided by
Together	Take away	Multiple	Ratio
Combined	Subtract	Twice	Decimal
Add	Difference	Of	Per
Sum			
And			

The first six subsections of this chapter (Understanding Fractions, Using Arrays to Find Factors, Using Divisibility Rules to Find Factors, Prime Numbers and Composite Numbers, Prime Factors, and Common Factors and Greatest Common Factors) are an overview of fourth-grade standards that you should review before you begin practicing the fifth-grade Operations and Algebraic Thinking standards. These skills are often rusty by the time fifth grade comes along, but knowing them will provide you with strategies for solving more complex tasks found in the fifth-grade standards.

Why are these skills from fourth grade so important to review? The reason is that these review sections focus on factors and divisibility rules. Knowing these rules will help you better understand the meaning of multiplication and division. Multiplication, for example, can be better understood when you know how to break apart equations into known facts. This will help you when interpreting expressions and understanding the order of operations.

Understanding Fractions

Factors are whole numbers that are multiplied to get a product (the answer of a multiplication problem). A **factor pair** is a pair of two whole numbers that equals a product. For example,

$$2 \times 3 = 6$$

$$\begin{array}{ccc} / & \backslash & \backslash \\ \text{factor} & \text{factor} & \text{product} \\ & \backslash \quad / & \\ & \text{factor pair} & \end{array}$$

Arrays and divisibility rules can help with understanding how to find factors. Arrays can help you find all the factors of a number. An array is a visual arrangement of rows and columns to show the total number of a multiplication sentence. You can count the items in each row and column. Remember though that all numbers also have 1 and themselves as factors.

Reviewing divisibility rules, as outlined in Table 9-2, can also help find the factors for a number.

Table 9-2. Divisibility Rules

A number is divisible by:	If:
2	The number is even
3	The sum of the digits of the number is divisible by 3
4	The last two digits are divisible by 4
5	The last digit is 0 or 5
6	The number is divisible by *both* 2 and 3
8	The number is divisible by 2, 4, and 8
9	The sum of the digits is divisible by 9
10	The last digit is 0

Using Arrays to Find Factors

Below are the 3 steps necessary for using arrays to find all the factors of 6.

STEP 1 To find factors using arrays, you need to draw 6 items. In this case, we are using circles.

STEP 2 Then, think about how many ways 6 can be divided equally. For example:

o o o   *or*   o o
o o o   o o
               o o

o o o o o o   *or*   o
                     o
                     o
                     o
                     o
                     o

In these arrays, there are 2 rows and 3 columns *or* 3 rows and 2 columns.

In these arrays, there is 1 row and 1 column *or* 1 column and 1 row.

STEP 3

This is a factor pair.   This is a factor pair.

$2 \times 3 = 6$ $1 \times 6 = 6$

$3 \times 2 = 6$ $6 \times 1 = 6$

By looking at the arrays and writing down the factor pairs, we know that the factors of 6 are 1, 2, 3, and 6.

Using Divisibility Rules to Find Factors

Below are the 6 steps necessary for using divisibility rules to find all the factors of 6.

STEP 1   Determine if 6 is divisible. Can 6 be divided by another number equally? Yes.

STEP 2   6 is an even number, so it can be divided by 2.

$$6 \div 2 = 3$$

STEP 3   Can 6 be divisible by any other number? 6 can also be divided by 3.

$$6 \div 3 = 2$$

STEP 4   So 6 is divisible by *both* 2 and 3. Refer to the Divisibility Rules (Table 9-2).

STEP 5   1 and 6 are already a factor pair. Remember, any number that is multiplied by 1 is equal to that number. 1 and 6 are also factors.

STEP 6   State that the factors of 6 are 1, 2, 3, and 6.

HELPFUL QUESTIONS TO ASK YOURSELF WHEN FINDING FACTOR PAIRS

1. Can the number be divided by another number equally?
2. If the number can be divided by another number equally, then what is that number?
3. Can the original number be divided by another number(s)?

Prime Numbers and Composite Numbers

Every whole number greater than 1 is either a prime number or a composite number.

A **prime number** has only two factors: 1 and itself. A **composite number** has more than two factors.

For example, is 6 a prime number, or is 7 a prime number?

```
o o o          o o o o o o        or        o o o o o o o
o o o
2 × 3 = 6      1 × 6 = 6                     1 × 7 = 7
```

6 *is not* a prime number because it has factors of 1, 2, 3, and 6. 7 *is* a prime number because it only has factors of 1 and 7. It is not divisible by any other number, such as 2.

HELPFUL HINT

All even numbers are composite except for 2, which is a prime number. But, not all odd numbers are prime numbers. Some odd numbers have more than two factors, so be careful!

Prime Factors

In this section, you will work on finding the prime factors of a number. Remember the following rule from the previous section: A prime number only has factors of 1 and itself. For example, $1 \times 3 = 3$. When you do this, it is called prime factorization. This is when you break down a number to all its smallest factors that are prime as well.

Often, you will see the use of factor tree diagrams to help reinforce your understanding that every number can be written as a product of prime numbers. This means that when you multiply all the prime factors of a number, it should equal the original number.

Let's try some examples:

To find the prime factorization of 8, complete the following 5 steps:

STEP 1 8 is not a prime number, so it can be broken down into smaller numbers. Ask yourself: What factor pairs equal 8?

$$2 \times 4 = 8 \qquad 1 \times 8 = 8$$

Now, choose the factor pairs that are not 1 and that number. The goal is to break down the 8 into smaller numbers that equal 8. In this example, we will use the factor pair of 2 and 4.

```
    8
   / \
  2   4
```

STEP 2 Since 2 is a prime factor already, there are no other factors to list below it. 4 is not a prime factor yet, so find another factor pair that is equal to 4.

$$2 \times 2 = 4$$

STEP 3 2 is now a prime factor. We have found the prime factors. Now, we need to write it.

```
      8
     / \
    2   4
       / \
      2   2
```

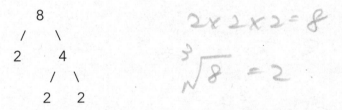

STEP 4 After completing the factor tree, the prime numbers at the end of each "stem" are written with multiplication signs between each number.

$$2 \times 2 \times 2 = 8$$

STEP 5 The answer is $2 \times 2 \times 2 = 2^3$. Note that an **exponent** is a number multiplied by that same number, but the exponent is written as a superscript (a number placed on top of another number). For example, $3 \times 3 = 3^2$.

To find the prime factorization of 12, complete the following 5 steps:

STEP 1 12 is not a prime number, so it can be broken down into smaller numbers. What factor pairs equal 12?

$$3 \times 4 = 12 \qquad 6 \times 2 = 12 \qquad 1 \times 12 = 12$$

STEP 2 Choose any of the factor pairs that are not 1 and that number. The goal is to break down the 12 into smaller numbers that equal 12. In this example, we used the factor pairs 3×4 and 6×2.

```
      12                          12
     /  \                        /  \
    4    3                      6    2
```

STEP 3 Since 3 is a prime number already, there are no other factors to list below it.

STEP 3 Since 2 is a prime number already, there are no other factors to list below it.

STEP 4 4 is not a prime number yet, so find another factor pair that is equal to 4. Another factor pair is $2 \times 2 = 4$.

```
      12
     /  \
    4    3
   / \
  2   2
```

STEP 4 6 is not a prime number yet, so find another factor pair that is equal to 6. Another factor pair is $2 \times 3 = 6$.

```
      12
     /  \
    6    2
   / \
  3   2
```

STEP 5 After completing the factor tree, the prime numbers at the end of each "stem" are written with multiplication signs between each number.

$$2 \times 2 \times 3$$

STEP 5 After completing the factor tree, the prime numbers at the end of each "stem" are written with multiplication signs between each number.

$$3 \times 2 \times 2$$

Notice that both have the same prime factors. Thus, the answer is $2 \times 2 \times 3 = 2^2 \times 3$.

HELPFUL HINT

It does not matter which factor pair you choose, just as long as it's not the factor pair of 1 and the number itself.

Common Factors and Greatest Common Factors   *LCM*

In this section, you will compare two numbers and find the **G**reatest **C**ommon **F**actor (GCF). The GCF of two numbers is the greatest number that is a factor of both numbers. The use of factors, or finding the prime factorization (using factor trees), will help in finding the greatest common factor.

Let's try an example:

To find the greatest common factor of 4 and 12, complete the following 3 steps:

STEP 1   Find the factors for each number.

STEP 2   Compare the common factors of each number and find the greatest one that they share. The greatest one is the greatest common factor. Below are 3 ways to find the greatest common factors of 4 and 12.

The factors of 4:

Using Factor Pairs	Listing factors	Factor Tree
$1 \times \mathbf{4} = 4$ $2 \times 2 = 4$	1, 2, **4**	4 / \ 2 2

The factors of 12:

Using Factor Pairs	Listing factors	Factor Tree

$1 \times 12 = 12$
 $2 \times 6 = 12$
 $3 \times \mathbf{4} = 12$
	1, 2, 3, **4**, 6, 12	12 12
		 / \ / \
		 3 4 6 2
		    / \ / \
		    2 2 3 2

STEP 3   *Using factor pairs:* Look for numbers that are the same in the factor pairs of 4 and 12. The numbers would be 2 and 4. 4 is the greatest of these common factors. 4 is the GCF.

Listing factors: Find the greatest "common" number, which in this case is 4.

Factor tree: Write the prime numbers out with multiplication for each one. Notice that 2 is in the factor of 4, and it is also in the factor of 12.

$$4 = \mathbf{2} \times 2$$

$$12 = \mathbf{2} \times 2 \times 3$$

Also notice, that there is another 2 in the factor of 4 and 12.

$$4 = 2 \times \mathbf{2}$$

$$12 = 2 \times \mathbf{2} \times 3$$

The numbers 4 and 12 share the prime factors of 2, two times. If 2 is shared two times, it means $2 \times 2 = 4$. Therefore, the greatest common factor is 4. It will not be 2 because 2 is the smallest number that is shared. In order to find the largest, you need to **multiply all the shared common factors.** Therefore, the **greatest common factor** of these two numbers is **4**.

Interpreting Simple Expressions

This section will review important skills in algebraic thinking, and it will prepare you for the different types of questions on the SBAC exam. You will need to apply your knowledge of interpreting simple expressions to harder test items that are examples of real-world situations. Practicing these skills now will set you up for success on those harder items on the SBAC.

You will have to change key words or phrases found in math word problems into mathematical expressions using variables. To do this, you will need to be able to identify what is in the word problem. You will also need to find what should be represented by the variable. In other words, what is the unknown quantity in the problem?

For example, a word problem may have a phrase such as, *"twice the number of people."* You would change this to the expression $2 \times p$. The number of people is the unknown. The variable can be the symbol p. The keyword *twice* is represented by $2 \times$.

> ### HELPFUL HINT
>
> Multiplying a number by a variable can be expressed, or written, in three different ways. The number and variable can be written next to each other, $5n$. The multiplication symbol can be replaced with a dot, $5 \cdot n$. And, of course, there is the standard way with the multiplication symbol, $5 \times n$.

Practice Exercises—Interpreting Simple Expressions

Common Core Standard 5.OA.A.2
Write simple expressions that record calculations with numbers, and interpret numerical expressions without evaluating them. *For example, express the calculation "add 8 and 7, then multiply by 2" as 2 × (8 + 7). Recognize that 3 × (18,932 + 921) is three times as large as 18,932 + 921, without having to calculate the indicated sum or product.*

Directions: For questions 1–4, create an expression with a variable that represents the word phrase. Pay attention to the different ways phrases can be worded. Write your expressions in the boxes below each question.

1. Three more than a number

2. Five less than a number

3. The product of eight and a certain number of people

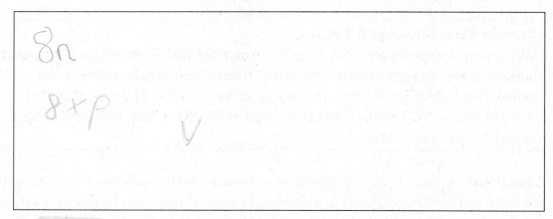

4. The quotient of a number and twelve

(Answers are on page 300.)

Evaluating Simple Expressions

In the previous section, you practiced changing phrases into expressions. The next step is to practice evaluating, or solving, expressions. To do this successfully, remember that expressions are like "if" statements.

For example, if you have the expression, $t \times 6$, then you can say to yourself:

$$\text{if } t = 5, \text{ then } t \times 6 = 30$$

Another example is, if you have the expression, $t \times 2$, then you can say to yourself:

$$\text{if } t = 2, \text{ then } t \times 2 = 4$$

Evaluating expressions is when you replace the variable with an actual number and then solve the expression.

On the Smarter Balanced test, questions will ask you to evaluate expressions by using the word *let*. For example, let *t* equal 5. This means that anytime you see the variable *t*, then you need to replace it with the number 5. That means, $40 \div t$ becomes $40 \div 5$, which equals 8.

Practice Exercises—Evaluating Simple Expressions

Common Core Standard 5.OA.A.1
Use parentheses, brackets, or braces in numerical expressions, and evaluate expressions with these symbols.

Directions: Evaluate the following two expressions. Let $x = 10$. Enter your answer in the numerical pad below each question.

1. $x - 2$

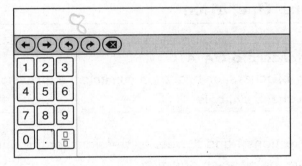

2. $100 \div x$

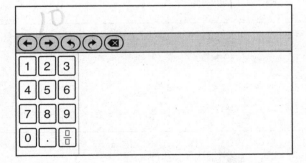

(Answers are on page 301.)

Evaluating Expressions with More Than One Operation

Algebraic expressions can become more difficult by including more than one operation. In this section, you will again practice changing word phrases into expressions, but this time they will need more than one operation performed in order to be solved.

Remember to pay attention to the mathematical key words that tell you which operations need to be used in the expression. For example, a simple expression may be changed from the phrase, *five times a number* to $5 \times n$. The expression can be made longer by adding *plus two*. Now the phrase *five times a number, plus two* becomes: $5n + 2$.

Let's try another one. If you read the phrase, *eight less than a number times three*, you'll notice that you can separate the phrase into two parts. The first part is *eight less than a number*, which you can write as $n - 8$. The second part is *a number times three*, which you can change to $3n$. You can put these two parts together as $3n - 8$.

Practice Exercises—Evaluating Expressions with More Than One Operation

---

Common Core Standard 5.OA.A.1
Use parentheses, brackets, or braces in numerical expressions, and evaluate expressions with these symbols.

Directions: For questions 1 and 2, write expressions for the phrases. Enter your answers in the boxes below each question.

1. Nine plus five times a number

$9 + 5n$ ✓

2. Ten times a number, minus seven

> $10n - 7$ ✓

3. Several expressions are shown in the box below. Decide if the value of the expression is less than, equal to, or greater than 20. Write the expressions in the correct category of the chart.

Less than 20	Equal to 20	Greater than 20
$(4 \times 5) \div 4$ $(4 \times 5) \div 5 \times 4$ $\frac{1}{4} \times (4 \times 5)$	$(5 \times 4) \times 1$ $(9 - 8) \times (5 \times 4)$	$10 + (4 \times 5)$ $(5 \times 4) + 7$ $4 \times \frac{1}{2} \times (5 \times 4)$
$10 + (4 \times 5)$ G	$4 \times \dfrac{1}{2} \times (5 \times 4)$ G	$\dfrac{1}{4} \times (4 \times 5)$
$(5 \times 4) + 7$ G	$(4 \times 5) \div 4$ L	$(9 - 8) \times (5 \times 4)$
$(5 \times 4) \times 1$ E	$(4 \times 5) \div 5 \times 4$	

(Answers are on page 301.)

✓

Using Expressions to Show Patterns and Relationships

You have now practiced evaluating both algebraic and numerical expressions. On the SBAC, you will use these skills to represent mathematical patterns in order to solve real-world problems.

What is a mathematical pattern? A pattern is a rule that repeats itself. These patterns, or rules, are everywhere in math. For example, if you list the sequence of numbers, 1, 4, 7, 10, 13, 16, 19, 22, and so on, you'll notice that the numbers jump by 3. The pattern, therefore, can be simply stated as +3. This means that you are counting by 3s. You can use an expression to represent this rule, or pattern. This rule would be written as $n + 3$.

Being able to identify these rules in word problems is needed to solve word problems on the SBAC test. Your job on the test will be to write an expression for a rule that you identified in a word problem. You will also need to solve them.

Writing Expressions for Real-World Problems

Let's first look at how to write an expression for a rule or pattern.

Read the scenario below. As you read, think about what key words give clues to what operations are needed. Also, try to identify the unknown, which will be the variable.

You run for 20 minutes each day at the track. You also do a number of stretches. You do each stretch for 2 minutes.

STEP 1 Your job now is to write an expression for the number of minutes you spend exercising each day. This will include both the running and stretching. It **does not state** how many different stretches you did. The amount of stretches will be the **unknown**, or **variable**, in the problem. Let s represent the number of stretches.

STEP 2 Did you notice any key words that gave you a clue as to what operations to use? The word **each** tells you that you need to use multiplication. Since the stretches lasted for 2 minutes each day, the expression should be **2s**.

STEP 3 But don't forget that you also ran for 20 minutes each day. Now our expression becomes, **2s + 20**. This expression will tell you the total number of minutes you exercised each day, even if the number of different stretches you do changes each time.

Practice Exercises—Writing Expressions for Real-World Problems

Common Core Standard 5.OA.A.2
Write simple expressions that record calculations with numbers, and interpret numerical expressions without evaluating them. *For example, express the calculation "add 8 and 7, then multiply by 2" as 2 × (8 + 7). Recognize that 3 × (18,932 + 921) is three times as large as 18,932 + 921, without having to calculate the indicated sum or product.*

Common Core Standard 5.OA.B.3
Generate two numerical patterns using two given rules. Identify apparent relationships between corresponding terms. Form ordered pairs consisting of corresponding terms from the two patterns, and graph the ordered pairs on a coordinate plane. *For example, given the rule "Add 3" and the starting number 0, and given the rule "Add 6" and the starting number 0, generate terms in the resulting sequences, and observe that the terms in one sequence are twice the corresponding terms in the other sequence. Explain informally why this is so.*

1. Mekya works in a musical instrument store. He earns $20 per day, plus a $5 commission for each sale. Write an expression for the amount of money Mekya earns each day. Let *s* represent the number of sales he makes. Write your answer in the box below.

20 + 5s

2. At Jennifer's school, 5 classes are going to the Academy of Sciences for their field trip. Each class has 29 students plus 1 teacher. Each bus holds 75 people. The school requests 2 buses.

Part A: Find the total number of people going on the field trip. Enter your answer in the numerical pad below.

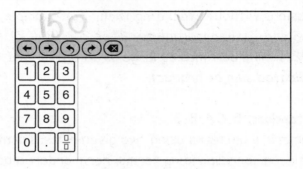

Part B: Select the correct statement that makes Jennifer's argument true.

- ○ A. Jennifer says that only 1 bus is needed.
- ○ B. Jennifer argues that all the classes can fit on 1 normal size bus and one smaller bus that only holds 29 people.
- ● C. Jennifer decides that there are enough buses for the total number of students and teachers.
- ○ D. Jennifer says that there are not enough buses for 150 students.

(Answers are on page 302.)

Evaluating Expressions to Show a Pattern or a Rule

Mathematical rules can be represented by algebraic expressions. These rules are based on patterns. For example, a nickel is 5¢, or 0.05, and for every nickel you add, you simply count by fives. But, let's say you want to know how much money you have if you have a large number of nickels. Let's say you have 1,552 nickels, but don't want to count by fives that many times. You can make this easier by creating a rule. The expression, $n \times 0.05$ can be used based on the pattern of counting by fives. This rule states, that if $n = 1,552$, then you have $77.60.

On the SBAC, you will be asked to **identify** the correct expression that represents the rule shown. The question will usually provide you with a data table. Data tables are organized by input and output. This means that for whatever you put into it, which is represented by the variable x, you get out a certain value, y, based on the pattern or expression.

Practice Exercises—Evaluating Expressions to Show a Pattern or a Rule

> **Common Core Standard 5.OA.A.2**
> Write simple expressions that record calculations with numbers, and interpret numerical expressions without evaluating them. *For example, express the calculation "add 8 and 7, then multiply by 2" as 2 × (8 + 7). Recognize that 3 × (18,932 + 921) is three times as large as 18,932 + 921, without having to calculate the indicated sum or product.*
>
> **Common Core Standard 5.OA.B.3**
> Generate two numerical patterns using two given rules. Identify apparent relationships between corresponding terms. Form ordered pairs consisting of corresponding terms from the two patterns, and graph the ordered pairs on a coordinate plane. *For example, given the rule "Add 3" and the starting number 0, and given the rule "Add 6" and the starting number 0, generate terms in the resulting sequences, and observe that the terms in one sequence are twice the corresponding terms in the other sequence. Explain informally why this is so.*

1. Look at the table below. Find the pattern, and determine the rule. Choose the correct expression that represents the rule.

x	12	16	18	20	22
y	6	8	9	10	11

○ A. $y = x + 2$
◉ B. $y = x \div 2$
○ C. $y = 2x - 4$
○ D. $y = 22 - 2$

2. Consider the table below.

x	y = x + 5
2	7
4	9
6	11
8	13

Use the expression to figure out the missing values. Write in the missing values in the table above.

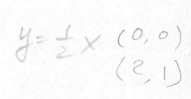

(Answers are on page 302.)

Distributive Property

The **distributive property** is an algebraic property that can be used to remove the parentheses when evaluating an expression. This property is used when you must multiply a value by an equation inside parentheses. It can be a quicker way to solve numerical or algebraic expressions.

For example, look at the expression, $3(2 + 7)$. Instead of working inside the parentheses first, you can multiply the outside number by the two numbers inside the parentheses. The 3 is multiplied by all the values inside the parentheses. Then, add the two products. It would look like this:

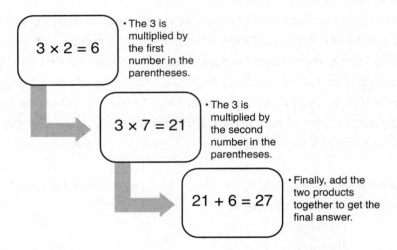

$3 \times 2 = 6$
- The 3 is multiplied by the first number in the parentheses.

$3 \times 7 = 21$
- The 3 is multiplied by the second number in the parentheses.

$21 + 6 = 27$
- Finally, add the two products together to get the final answer.

The distributive property can also be used with variables to simplify an algebraic expression. For example, if you have the expression $2(4n + 8)$, since you cannot add inside the parentheses, you must multiply the outside number by the two numbers inside the parentheses. Then, you would add the products. It would look like this:

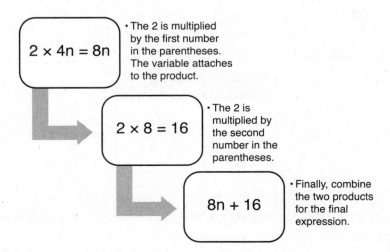

$2 \times 4n = 8n$
- The 2 is multiplied by the first number in the parentheses. The variable attaches to the product.

$2 \times 8 = 16$
- The 2 is multiplied by the second number in the parentheses.

$8n + 16$
- Finally, combine the two products for the final expression.

Practice Exercises—Distributive Property

Common Core Standard 5.OA.A.1
Use parentheses, brackets, or braces in numerical expressions, and evaluate expressions with these symbols.

Directions: Use the distributive property to evaluate the expressions in questions 1–3. Write your answers in the boxes below each question.

1. $6(2 + 5n)$

2. $2 \times (7n - 5)$

3. $12(8 + 6n)$

(Answers are on page 303.)

Order Of Operations

Now, you need to practice longer and more difficult expressions that include different operations and parentheses. To do this correctly, you need to review and practice the Order of Operations. The most common way to remember and apply the order of operations is to use the acronym **P.E.M.D.A.S.**, which stands for **P**arentheses, **E**xponents, (**M**ultiplication and **D**ivision), (**A**ddition and **S**ubtraction).

This is the order to follow when evaluating, or solving, expressions for their value. These are always completed from left to right. Another way to look at it is vertically.

Parentheses

Exponents

Multiplication

Division

Addition

Subtraction

HELPFUL HINT

Also, think of multiplication and division as a group, and think of addition and subtraction as a group. This means that to solve any multiplication or division operations, move from left to right (a division operation can come before a multiplication operation if it is further to the left). The same applies to addition and subtraction.

In the examples that follow, notice how the steps form an upside down pyramid shape. When working these questions out on your scratch paper during the SBAC, you should always write out your work in this shape. This will help you keep track of each operation.

Why Do We Need Parentheses?

Parentheses in algebraic expressions are used to represent a total within a word problem. This total must be calculated on its own before any other operation is completed.

Take a look at the numerical expression below. It needs one more set of parentheses to make it true. Can you find where they go?

$$5 \times (2 + 3) - 2 + 6 \times 3 = 1$$

Without the parentheses around the 2 + 6, the expression would equal a value other than 1. On the SBAC, you will have items that will ask you to identify the correct placement of parentheses to get the correct answer. Also, you will need to apply this to word problems that will ask you to write an algebraic expression to help solve the problem. You will have to first identify what parts of the word problem should be calculated on their own, inside parentheses.

An Example with Variables

What is the value of $6x + 3y - 2$, if $x = 2$ and $y = 4$?

STEP 1 Always replace all the variables with the given values and rewrite the expression.

$$6 \times 2 + 3 \times 4 - 2$$

STEP 2 Notice that there are no parentheses or exponents, so now you will multiply or divide from left to right.

$$6 \times 2 + 3 \times 4 - 2$$
$$\diagup \quad\quad \diagdown \quad\quad \diagdown$$
$$12 \ + \ 12 \ - \ 2$$

STEP 3 Add or subtract from left to right.

$$12 + 12 - 2$$
$$| \quad\quad |$$
$$24 \ - \ 2$$
$$|$$
$$22$$

The answer is 22.

An Example with Parentheses

What is the value of $(5j + e) \div 2 - 3$, if $j = 7$ and $e = 9$?

STEP 1   Always replace your variables with the given values and rewrite the expression.

$$(5 \times 7 + 9) \div 2 - 3$$

STEP 2   Take care of the operations within the parentheses first. The order of operations applies inside of the parentheses, so solve any multiplication or division first before solving any addition or subtraction.

$$(5 \times 7 + 9)$$

$$(35 + 9)$$

$$44$$

STEP 3   Solve any multiplication or division, from left to right.

$$44 \div 2 - 3$$

$$44 \div 2 = 22$$

STEP 4   Solve any addition or subtraction from left to right.

$$22 - 3$$

$$19$$

The answer is 19.

Practice Exercises—Order of Operations

Common Core Standard 5.OA.A.1

Use parentheses, brackets, or braces in numerical expressions, and evaluate expressions with these symbols.

Directions: Use your knowledge of P.E.M.D.A.S. to answer the following questions.

1. Which expression has a value of 13?

○   A. $5 + 4 \times 3 - 1$
○   B. $(5 + 4) \times 3 - 1$
○   C. $5 + 4 \times (3 - 1)$
○   D. $(5 + 4) \times (3 - 1)$

2. Mrs. Mathew ordered 8 small notepads and 4 large notepads for each of the 5 teachers in her grade level. Which expression represents the total number of notepads Mrs. Mathew ordered?

   O A. $8 \times 5 \times 4$
   O B. $(8 + 4) \times 5$
   O C. $8 + (4 \times 5)$
   O D. $(8 + 5) \times 4$

3. Arjuna is solving the following problem on the board during math class:

   $$21 \div (7 - 4) + 2 \times 2$$

   What operation should Arjuna perform first?

   O A. addition
   O B. subtraction
   O C. multiplication
   O D. division

For question 4, use the following picture to answer the question.

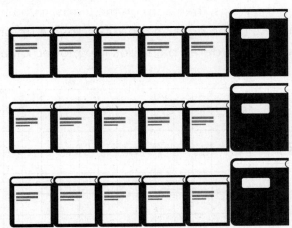

4. Mr. E has 5 small books on each of his 3 shelves, as depicted above. In addition to that, his wife decided that he needed big books on his shelves as well. For his birthday, he received 3 big books. Mr. E placed 1 big book on each shelf. Which expression shows the total amount of books?

   O A. $(5 \times 3) + 3$
   O B. $(3 + 5) \times 3$
   O C. $3 \times (3 \times 5)$
   O D. $5 + 3 \times 3$

(Answers are on page 304.)

Ordered Pairs

An ordered pair is two numbers that represent a location on a coordinate grid. Ordered pairs are written in parentheses, such as (3, 2).

The first number is the x-coordinate, and the second is the y-coordinate. Ordered pairs are coordinates that tell you where to plot a point on a grid. The x-coordinate refers to the x-axis on the coordinate grid, which runs horizontal. The y-coordinate refers to the y-axis on the coordinate grid, which runs vertical.

Ordered pairs are created by using an expression to create both x-values and y-values. These values are listed within a table that makes it easier to identify patterns and keep the values organized. In this section, you will focus on both plotting ordered pairs and using expressions to create ordered pairs.

Plotting Ordered Pairs

First, let's practice plotting ordered pairs. When plotting ordered pairs, always start with the origin. The origin is where the x-axis and the y-axis intersect. The ordered pair of the origin is (0, 0). For instance, if you have the ordered pair, (3, 2), you will move 3 to the right on the x-axis, then 2 up on the y-axis. If you have the ordered pair, (5, 4), you will move 5 to the right on the x-axis, then 4 up on the y-axis. Figure 9-1 shows what these ordered pairs look like plotted on a coordinate grid.

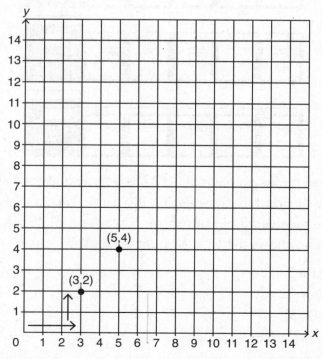

Figure 9-1. Plotting ordered pairs on a coordinate grid

Using Expressions to Create Ordered Pairs

You can use your knowledge of evaluating algebraic expressions to create ordered pairs. Making a list of ordered pairs helps you identify and determine patterns that can be plotted on a graph. These plotted points show the relationships between the different values of an expression. Knowing these patterns and relationships will help you predict outcomes correctly in word problems.

Remember that variables create "if" statements. Look at the expression and table below.

$$y = x + 2$$

x	y
0	2
2	4
4	6
6	8

The expression shows the pattern: 2 is always added to the value of x to get the value of y. The table shows the "if" statements and reveals the pattern: If $x = 2$, then $y = 4$. Likewise, if $x = 6$, then $y = 8$.

Let's try another example. Take a look at the table below.

Day	Height (cm)
1	3
3	6
5	9
7	12

$$y = 1\tfrac{1}{2}x + 1\tfrac{1}{2}$$

Elizabeth is working on her science fair project. She created the table on page 235 to show the growth of a plant over a period of several days. Her data can also be displayed on a coordinate grid, like the one below.

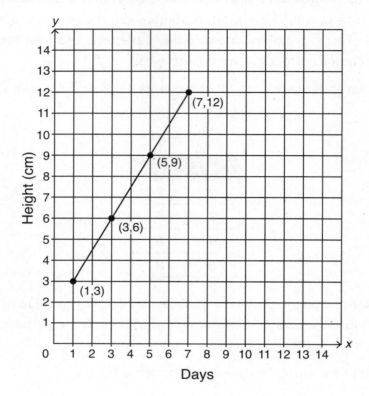

4/16/2018

Practice Exercises—Ordered Pairs

Common Core Standard 5.OA.B.3
Generate two numerical patterns using two given rules. Identify apparent relationships between corresponding terms. Form ordered pairs consisting of corresponding terms from the two patterns, and graph the ordered pairs on a coordinate plane. *For example, given the rule "Add 3" and the starting number 0, and given the rule "Add 6" and the starting number 0, generate terms in the resulting sequences, and observe that the terms in one sequence are twice the corresponding terms in the other sequence. Explain informally why this is so.*

1. Mr. Mathew predicts that his daughter, Evelyn, will grow 4 centimeters each month. He would like to plot her growth on the coordinate grid. Plot her growth on the grid using the table below.

Month	Centimeters (cm)
1	4
2	8
3	12
4	16

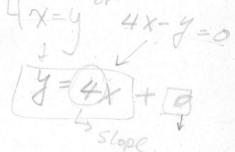

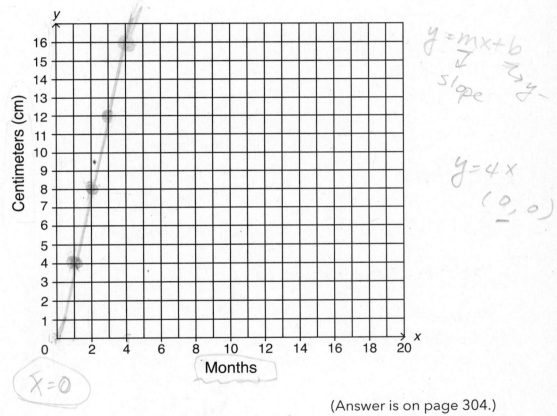

(Answer is on page 304.)

Geometry and Graphing

ACADEMIC VOCABULARY

> **Average**—the number found by adding all of the data and dividing by the number of data

> **Axis (Axes)**—either of two lines drawn perpendicular to each other in a graph

> **Bar Graph**—a graph that uses bars (rectangles) to show and compare data that tells how many or how much

> **Base of a Polygon**—the side of a polygon to which the height is perpendicular

> **Congruent Figures**—figures that have the same size and shape

> **Coordinate Grid**—a grid that makes it easy to locate points in a plane using an ordered pair of numbers

> **Coordinate Plane**—a coordinate grid that extends to include both positive and negative numbers

> **Coordinates**—two numbers in an ordered pair

> **Equilateral Triangle**—a triangle in which all three sides are the same length

> **Hexagon**—a polygon with six sides

> **Histogram**—a bar graph that groups data into equal intervals shown on a horizontal axis. There is no space between the bars.

> **Intersecting Lines**—lines that pass through the same point

> **Interval (on a graph)**—the difference between adjoining numbers on an axis of a graph

> **Isosceles Triangle**—a triangle with two sides of the same length

> **Line Graph**—a graph that connects points to show how data changes over time

> **Line of Symmetry**—the fold line in a symmetric figure

> **Line Plot**—a display of responses along a number line with x's recorded above the response to indicate the number of times the response occurred

> **Line Segment**—part of a line with two endpoints

ACADEMIC VOCABULARY (continued)

> **Mean**—the number found by adding all of the data and dividing by the number of data

> **Median**—the middle data value in an ordered set of data

> **Mode**—the data value that occurs most often in a set of data

> **Net**—a plane figure, when folded, gives a solid figure

> **Obtuse Angle**—an angle that measures between 91 degrees and 179 degrees

> **Obtuse Triangle**—a triangle in which one angle is an obtuse angle

> **Octagon**—a polygon with eight sides

> **Ordered Pair**—a pair of numbers used to locate a point on a coordinate grid

> **Origin**—the point at which the x-axis and the y-axis of the coordinate plane intersect. The origin is represented by the ordered pair (0, 0).

> **Parallel Lines**—in a plane, lines that never cross and stay the same distance apart

> **Parallelogram**—a quadrilateral in which both pairs of opposite sides are parallel and equal in length

> **Pentagon**—a polygon with five sides

> **Perpendicular Lines**—two lines that intersect to form right angles

> **Point**—an exact location in space

> **Polygon**—a closed plane figure made up of line segments

> **Quadrilateral**—a polygon with four sides

> **Range**—the difference between the greatest value and the least value in a data set

> **Ray**—part of a line that has one endpoint and extends forever in only one direction

> **Rectangle**—a parallelogram with four right angles

> **Regular Polygon**—a polygon that has sides of equal length and angles of equal measure

> **Rhombus**—a parallelogram with all sides that are the same length

> **Right Angle**—an angle that measures 90 degrees

> **Right Triangle**—a triangle that has one right angle

> **Scale (in a bar graph)**—a series of numbers at equal distances along an axis on a graph

> **Sides (of an angle)**—the two rays that form an angle

> **Similar Figures**—figures that have the same shape, but may or may not be the same size

---

ACADEMIC VOCABULARY *(continued)*

> **Straight Angle**—an angle that measures 180 degrees

> **Symmetric Figure**—a figure that can be folded into two congruent parts that fit on top of each other

> **Trapezoid**—a quadrilateral that has exactly one pair of parallel sides

> **Triangle**—a polygon with three sides

> **Vertex (in an angle)**—common endpoint of the two rays in an angle

> **x-axis**—a horizontal line that has both positive and negative numbers. It is used to locate points in a coordinate plane.

> **x-coordinate**—the first number in an ordered pair. It names the distance to the right or left of the origin along the x-axis.

> **y-axis**—a vertical line that has both positive and negative numbers. It is used to locate points in a coordinate plane.

> **y-coordinate**—the second number in an ordered pair. It names the distance up or down from the origin along the y-axis.

Overview

In fifth grade, geometry focuses on using coordinate planes and classifying two-dimensional figures. Coordinate planes involve using ordered pairs, and the tasks on the SBAC will involve using interactive elements to successfully complete them. Classifying two-dimensional figures will also involve interactive elements, such as dragging and dropping and using line tools. When classifying figures, knowing definitions is important. You may also be asked to write a response to prove certain figures are classified as you say they are. Let's get started.

Graphing Points to Solve Real-World Problems

A coordinate plane is a grid that acts like a map. It can be used to plot points that have a specific location. These locations on the plane are named with ordered pairs, a pair of numbers that looks like: (x, y). To find the location of the ordered pairs, there are a set of perpendicular lines, one running horizontally called the x-axis and another running vertically called the y-axis. Where they meet is called the origin, located at the ordered pair: $(0, 0)$. To find the location of a point, you first follow the number along the x-axis (since the first number will always be the point along the x-axis), and then you follow the number up along the y-axis (since the second number will always be the point along the y-axis).

Let's look at an example. To locate and plot point A, at (8, 10), we move to 8 along the x-axis first, and then move 10 up from that point to follow the y-axis:

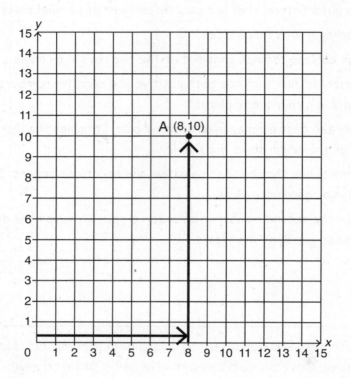

Practice Exercises—Graphing Points to Solve Real-World Problems

Common Core Standard 5.G.A.1
Use a pair of perpendicular number lines, called axes, to define a coordinate system, with the intersection of the lines (the origin) arranged to coincide with the 0 on each line and a given point in the plane located by using an ordered pair of numbers, called its coordinates. Understand that the first number indicates how far to travel from the origin in the direction of one axis, and the second number indicates how far to travel in the direction of the second axis, with the convention that the names of the two axes and the coordinates correspond (e.g., x-axis and x-coordinate, y-axis and y-coordinate).

1. Use the coordinate plane below to find *x*- and *y*-coordinates of the points. Write each set of coordinates next to the appropriate letter in the table that follows.

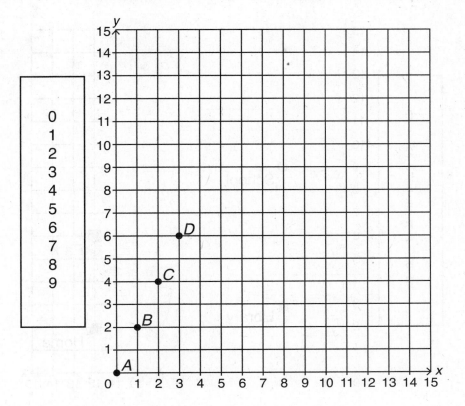

Points	x-coordinate	y-coordinate
A		
B		
C		
D		

2. Based on the coordinate plane below, write the (*x, y*) coordinates of each location in the table that follows.

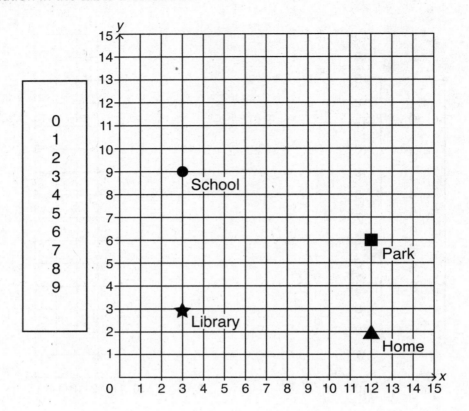

Points	x-coordinate	y-coordinate
School		
Park		
Home		
Library		

(Answers are on page 305.)

Coordinate Systems

Plotting points on a coordinate grid allows you to see patterns and relationships between data. The coordinate grid makes these patterns and relationships into a visual. This visual graph can be analyzed, and more answers can be revealed. Let's look at an example.

Let's say that you want to measure the growth rate of a houseplant. You first create a table that has the days and the height, in centimeters, that the houseplant grew each day.

Days (x)	1	3	5	7
Height (y)	2 cm	3 cm	6 cm	8 cm

Now graph it. Let the number of days be the x-axis, and let the height be the y-axis. Let's plot these points.

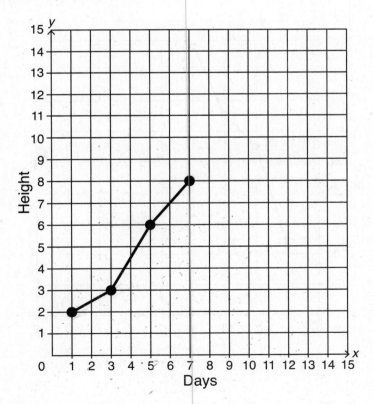

On the SBAC, you will be asked to analyze and come to a conclusion based on these plotted points and the graph. For instance, we can visually see when the plant grew the most: between day 3 and day 5.

Practice Exercises—Coordinate Systems

Common Core Standard 5.G.A.2
Represent real-world and mathematical problems by graphing points in the first quadrant of the coordinate plane, and interpret coordinate values of points in the context of the situation.

1. Michael bought a new electric car. He wants to take it on a road trip to see how often he has to charge it. Below is a data table showing his distance traveled and the number of days he traveled.

Days (x)	1	2	3	4
Distance (y)	220 miles	550 miles	658 miles	896 miles

Using the data above and the graph below, answer Part A and Part B.

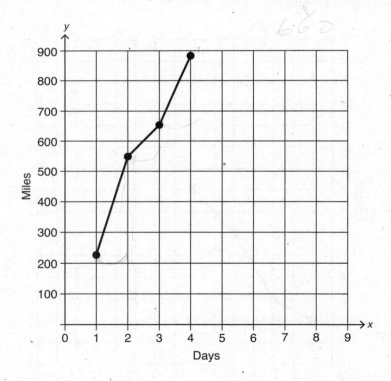

Part A: Between what days did Michael travel the most miles on one charge? Write your answer in the box below.

Part B: About how many miles did he travel between day 3 and day 4? Write your answer in the box below.

(Answers are on page 305.)

Classifying Two-Dimensional Figures

When classifying two-dimensional figures in geometry, you must rely on proving your categorizations. In fourth grade, you focused on identifying two-dimensional figures based on parallel and perpendicular lines and the types of angles. Now, your goal is to classify and categorize based on the figures' properties. In addition, you will need to be able to explain your reasoning for your conclusion.

Practice Exercises—Classifying Two-Dimensional Figures

> **Common Core Standard 5.G.B.3**
> Understand that attributes belonging to a category of two-dimensional figures also belong to all subcategories of that category. For example, all rectangles have four right angles and squares are rectangles, so all squares have four right angles.
>
> **Common Core Standard 5.G.B.4**
> Classify two-dimensional figures in a hierarchy based on properties.

1. Select **all** of the statements that are true.

- ☐ A. All squares are rectangles.
- ☐ B. All squares are rhombuses.
- ☐ C. All rhombuses are quadrilaterals.
- ☐ D. All parallelograms are quadrilaterals.

2. The following table has properties of figures. Select **all** that apply.

Property	This figure always has four sides of equal length.	This figure always has four right angles.	This figure always has two pairs of parallel sides.	This figure has four sides.
Square	☐	☐	☐	☐
Rhombus	☐	☐	☐	☐
Rectangle	☐	☐	☐	☐
Parallelogram	☐	☐	☐	☐
Trapezoid	☐	☐	☐	☐

(Answers are on page 306.)

Measurement and Data

> **Base of a Solid**—the face of a solid that is used to name the solid
> **Capacity**—the volume of a container measured in liquid units
> **Centimeter (cm)**—a metric unit of length. *100 centimeters equals 1 meter.*
> **Cone**—a solid with one circular base. The points on the circle are joined to one point outside the base.
> **Cube**—a solid figure with six flat surfaces called faces. All of the faces are squares.
> **Cubic Unit**—the volume of a cube, 1 unit on each edge
> **Cup**—a customary unit of capacity. *1 cup equals 8 fluid ounces.*
> **Cylinder**—a solid with two circular bases that are congruent and parallel
> **Edge**—a line segment where two faces meet in a solid figure
> **Face**—a flat surface of a polyhedron
> **Fluid Ounces (fl oz)**—the customary unit of capacity, equal to 2 tablespoons
> **Gallon**—a unit for measuring capacity in the customary system. *1 gallon equals 4 quarts.*
> **Gram (g)**—a metric unit of mass, equal to 1,000 milligrams
> **Height**—the length of a segment from one vertex of a polygon perpendicular to the base
> **Kilometer (km)**—a metric unit of length, equal to 1,000 meters
> **Liter (L)**—a metric unit of capacity, equal to 1,000 milliliters
> **Mass**—the measure of the quantity of matter in an object
> **Meter (m)**—a basic unit of length in the metric system
> **Milligram (mg)**—a metric unit of mass. *1,000 milligrams equals 1 gram.*
> **Milliliter (mL)**—a metric unit of capacity, equal to 0.001 L

ACADEMIC VOCABULARY (continued)

> **Millimeter (mm)**—a metric unit of length *1,000 millimeters equals 1 meter*

> **Perimeter**—the distance around the outside of any polygon

> **Plane**—an endless flat surface

> **Point**—an exact location in space

> **Pound (lb)**—a customary unit of weight, equal to 16 ounces

> **Prism**—a solid with two congruent parallel bases and faces that are parallelograms

> **Pyramid**—a solid with a base that is a polygon. The edges of the base are joined to a point outside the base.

> **Quart (qt)**—a customary unit of capacity, equal to 2 pints

> **Solid Figure**—a figure that has three dimensions and volume

> **Sphere**—a solid figure with all points that are the same distance from the center point

> **Surface Area**—the sum of the areas of all faces of a polyhedron

> **Tablespoon (tbsp)**—a customary unit of capacity, equal to 3 teaspoons

> **Teaspoon (tsp)**—a customary unit of capacity, equal to $\frac{1}{3}$ tablespoon

> **Ton (T)**—a customary unit of weight, equal to 2,000 pounds

> **Vertex (in a solid)**—the point when three or more edges meet in a solid figure

> **Volume**—the number of cubic units needed to fill a solid figure

> **Weight**—a measure of how light or how heavy something is

Overview

In fourth grade, you focused on estimating and selecting the correct unit to measure length, weight, or capacity. Now, in fifth grade, you will be asked to find the relationship between these different units. To understand the relationship between units of measurement, you must first convert between the different units. There are two different measurement systems to learn: customary and metric.

In addition, what you know about fractions will be applied to units of measurement. You will have to use fractions of a unit (i.e., $\frac{1}{3}$ of an inch) to solve problems by plotting data on a line graph. Line graphs provide a simple way to organize data so you can solve a problem in an easier way. On the SBAC, you will have to be able to read and interpret a line plot to solve a problem. Lastly, volume is another type of measurement that will be assessed. You will practice a couple of different ways of determining volume.

Converting Customary Units of Length

The term "unit of measurement" refers to anything that can be used to measure something. This could be any object, such as a paper clip or a pencil. A **customary** unit of measurement, however, is an official, agreed-upon unit of measurement. Some customary units of measurement are *inches, feet, yards, and miles*. These are the units of measurement, whether you are measuring length, height, or width.

In this section you will practice converting these units of measurements. Conversion in math means you are finding the numerical equivalent from one unit to another. The number and unit may change, but the size does not. For instance, you may wonder how many feet an object is if it was measured to be 12 inches. Knowing the conversion, or equivalent unit, would help you recognize that 12 inches is equal to 1 foot.

How do you convert one measurement to another? First, you will need to know the basic conversions as a place to start. (Refer to Table 11-1.)

Table 11-1. Conversion of Customary Units

Customary Units		
Length	Weight	Capacity
12 in = 1 ft	16 oz = 1 lb	8 fl oz = 1 cup
3 ft = 1 yd	2,000 lb = 1 ton	2 cups = 1 pint
5,280 ft = 1 mi		2 pt = 1 qt
1,760 yd = 1 mi		8 pt = 1 gal
		4 qt = 1 gal

1 Gallon = ___ fl oz

Let's start with how many inches are in 11 feet. You need to know that there are 12 inches in one foot. Now, notice that you are converting from a larger unit to a smaller unit. When this is the case, you need to multiply: 11 × 12 = 132 inches. There are 132 inches in 11 feet.

Now, let's see what happens when you convert from a smaller unit to a larger unit. How many yards are there in 15 feet? Since feet is a smaller unit than yards, you need to divide this time: 15 ÷ 3 = 5 yards. There are 15 feet in 5 yards.

Practice Exercises—Converting Customary Units of Length

> **Common Core Standard 5.MD.A.1**
> Convert among different-sized standard measurement units within a given measurement system (e.g., convert 5 cm to 0.05 m), and use these conversions in solving multi-step, real-world problems.

1. How many pints are in 3.5 gallons?

   - ○ A. 78
   - ○ B. 38
   - ○ C. 48
   - ◉ D. 28

2. Circle **all** of the measurements that are equal to 24 feet.

   2.4 inches   3 yards   8 yards

   489 inches   288 inches   240 inches

3. Evelyn buys a 2.5 quart container of milk at the store for a recipe.

   Part A: What is the capacity of the container of milk in pints (pt)? Write your answer in the box below.

   5 pts

   Part B: What is the capacity of the container of milk in fluid ounces (fl oz)? Write your answer in the box below.

   80 fl oz

(Answers are on page 306.)

Converting Metric Units of Length

The metric system is another official unit of measurement. This system is based on the powers of 10. This makes it an easier system to do conversions with, since you can depend on your knowledge of place value to make conversions.

   As with the customary units, when you convert from larger units to smaller units, you will have to multiply. When you change from smaller to larger units, you will need to divide. It may help to see the relative sizes from largest to smallest, as outlined in Table 11-2.

Table 11-2. Conversion of Metric Units

Metric Units		
Length	**Weight**	**Volume**
1 km = 1,000 m	1 kg = 1,000 g	1 kL = 1,000 L
1 m = 0.001 km	1 g = 0.001 kg	1 L = 0.001 kL
1 m = 100 cm	1 g = 100 cg	1 L = 100 cL
1 cm = 0.01 m	1 cg = 0.01 g	1 cL = 0.01 L
1 m = 1,000 mm	1 g = 1,000 mg	1 L = 1,000 mL
1 mm = 0.001 m	1 mg = 0.001 g	1 mL = 0.001 L

Practice Exercises—Converting Metric Units of Length

> **Common Core Standard 5.MD.A.1**
> Convert among different-sized standard measurement units within a given measurement system (e.g., convert 5 cm to 0.05 m), and use these conversions in solving multi-step, real-world problems.

1. The mass of Arjuna's new bike is 4.2 kg. Evie's new bike has a mass of 3,200 g.

Part A: What is the mass of Evie's new bike in kilograms? Write your answer in the box below.

3.2 kg ✓

Part B: Which bike has the least amount of mass? How do you know? Explain your answer in the box below.

Evie ✓

1 m = 100 cm

2. Circle **all** of the measurements that are equal to 86 meters.

430 cm	8,600 cm ✓	860 cm
86,000 mm ✓	43,000 mm	43 cm

milli

(Answers are on page 307.)

1 m = 1000 mm

5/10/18

Use of Measurements on Line Plots

Representing measurement data visually can help organize the parts of a problem to be solved. Unlike other graphs, line plots both tally (keep count) and plot at the same time. This makes it easier to see patterns and find answers. On the SBAC, you will need to be able to read and analyze line plots to answer questions about the most common, least common, and outliers.

Remember, an outlier is any number in the data that stands on its own from the rest of the data. Some data has outliers, and some does not. To be an outlier, a number has to be far from the cluster, or group, of most common numbers and must only have one mark.

Practice Exercises—Use of Measurements on Line Plots

Common Core Standard 5.MD.B.2

Make a line plot to display a data set of measurements in fractions of a unit ($\frac{1}{2}$, $\frac{1}{4}$, $\frac{1}{8}$). Use operations on fractions for this grade to solve problems involving information presented in line plots. *For example, given different measurements of liquid in identical beakers, find the amount of liquid each beaker would contain if the total amount in all the beakers were redistributed equally.*

---

1. The line plot below shows the number of video games students have at home. There are 8 students in this class.

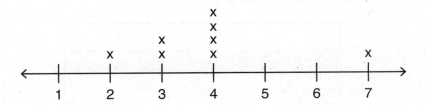

Part A: What is the most common number of video games students have at home in this class? Write your answer in the box below.

4 ✓

Part B: Is the one student who has 7 video games at home an outlier? Why or why not?

Explain your answer in the box below.

2. Liz takes her baby for a walk every morning after his nap. The table below shows the miles she walks the baby each day for one week.

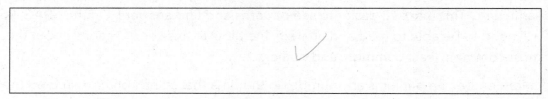

Number of Miles Walked						
1.35	1.75	1.35	1.25	1.25	1.35	1.75

Part A: In the space below, make a line plot of the data from the table above.

Part B: What is the greatest difference in the miles during this one week? Enter your answer in the numerical pad below.

Part C: What was the most common number of miles Liz walked? Enter your answer in the numerical pad below.

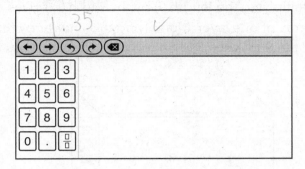

Part D: What was the farthest number of miles Liz walked? Does this number count as an outlier? Why or why not? Explain your answer in the box below.

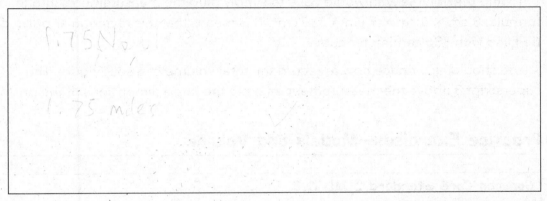

(Answers are on page 307.)

Models and Volume

In this section you will learn to determine the volume of a solid figure. Volume is the amount of space that can fit in a solid figure that is three-dimensional. This means that a solid figure has the measurements of length, width, and height. These units of measurement can be measured using unit cubes. For instance, a rectangular prism that is 5 feet long, 6 feet wide, and 2 feet high can be filled with a bottom layer of 30 cubes and a top layer of 30 cubes, making the prism hold a total of 60 cubes. Each cube represents one unit of measurement, or cubic unit, and each layer of cubes can be seen as an array. These layers are stacked on top of each other to create the total volume of the solid figure.

It is helpful to think of this visually so that you fully understand the concept, but volume of a rectangular prism can also be calculated using a formula. This formula is $V = l \times w \times h$. Multiplying the length (l) by the width (w) gives you the number of cubes inside the array of one layer. Multiplying this answer by the height (h) gives the total number of all the arrays stacked on top of each other. Let's try one example:

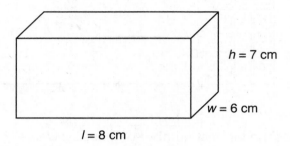

$h = 7$ cm

$w = 6$ cm

$l = 8$ cm

To find the volume, you would have to simply plug the measurements into the formula: 8 cm $\times$ 6 cm $\times$ 7 cm = 336 cm^3. This means that this rectangular prism can be filled with 336 centimeter cubes.

You should also notice how to record the total volume of a solid figure. The superscript 3 above the measurement refers to the three dimensions of the prism.

Practice Exercises—Models and Volume

Common Core Standard 5.MD.C.3
Recognize volume as an attribute of solid figures and understand concepts of volume measurement.

Common Core Standard 5.MD.C.3.A
A cube with side length 1 unit, called a "unit cube," is said to have "one cubic unit" of volume, and can be used to measure volume.

Common Core Standard 5.MD.C.3.B
A solid figure which can be packed without gaps or overlaps using n unit cubes is said to have a volume of n cubic units.

Common Core Standard 5.MD.C.4
Measure volumes by counting unit cubes, using cubic cm, cubic in, cubic ft, and improvised units.

1. Refer to the figure below.

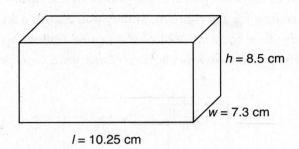

h = 8.5 cm

w = 7.3 cm

l = 10.25 cm

In the box below, write the equation for finding volume. Then, find the total volume.

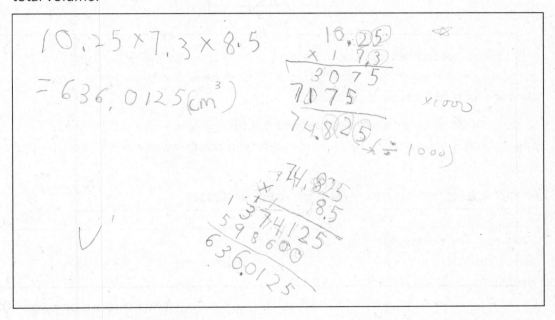

2. In some cases, two rectangular prisms will be joined together to make a figure. You will first need to decide where to mentally cut the figure in half. Then, you would find the volume for each prism. Finally you would add these volumes together to get the final total volume of the figure. Following these steps, what is the total volume of the following figure? Show your work in the box below.

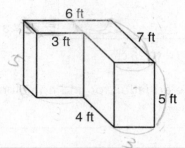

(Answers are on page 308.)

Relating Volume to Real-World Problems

In order to find the volume of a rectangular prism, you would need to multiply the length, width, and height ($V = lwh$).

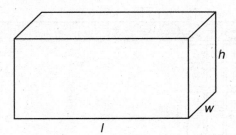

Practice Exercises—Relating Volume to Real-World Problems

Common Core Standard 5.MD.C.5
Relate volume to the operations of multiplication and addition and solve real-world and mathematical problems involving volume.

Common Core Standard 5.MD.C.5.A
Find the volume of a right rectangular prism with whole-number side lengths by packing it with unit cubes, and show that the volume is the same as would be found by multiplying the edge lengths, equivalently by multiplying the height by the area of the base. Represent threefold whole-number products as volumes, e.g., to represent the associative property of multiplication.

Common Core Standard 5.MD.C.5.B
Apply the formulas $V = l \times w \times h$ and $V = b \times h$ for rectangular prisms to find volumes of right rectangular prisms with whole-number edge lengths in the context of solving real-world and mathematical problems.

Common Core Standard 5.MD.C.5.C
Recognize volume as additive. Find volumes of solid figures composed of two non-overlapping right rectangular prisms by adding the volumes of the non-overlapping parts, applying this technique to solve real-world problems.

1. A jewelry box is in the shape of a rectangular prism that is 6 inches long, 4 inches high, and 2 inches wide. What is its volume? Find the volume, in cubic inches, of the rectangular prism. Enter your answer in the numerical pad below.

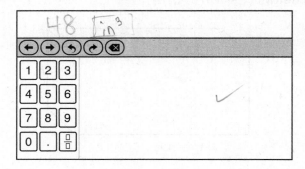

2. The right rectangular prism below has a length of 9 centimeters, a width of 7 centimeters, and a height of 5 centimeters.

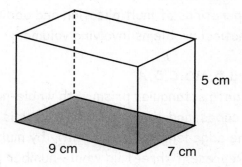

Determine which equation(s) can be used to find the volume. Select Yes or No for each equation.

	Yes	No
$V = 9 \times 7 \times 5$	☑	☐
$V = 63 \times 5$	☑	☐
$V = (9 + 7) \times 5$	☐	☑
$V = 16 \times 5$	☐	☑

(Answers are on page 308.)

Math Performance Task

Overview

What Is the Math Performance Task?

The Math Performance Task portion of the test is a group of questions and tasks focused on applying math thinking to more complex, real-world problems. This set of questions and tasks will be more demanding than the Computer Adaptive portion of the test. In addition to solving multiple-step math problems, you will also be asked to write about math.

What Am I Being Tested On?

The Math Performance Task will test you on how you can apply different math patterns and concepts to everyday problems. The Performance Task will focus on one area, or domain, within the fifth-grade math standards. For instance, it could focus on your ability to work with fractions and mixed numbers, or it could focus solely on finding volume in real-world applications. This does not mean, however, that you will not have to rely on other math skills to successfully complete the tasks.

The SBAC Performance Tasks are designed to test your ability across *multiple* math domains. For instance, let's say that a Math Performance Task focuses on a real-world problem involving the perimeter and area of a school garden being constructed. Instead of whole numbers as measurements, however, decimals (i.e., 4.25 ft) are used. To complete the task now, you must rely on both your knowledge of finding area and perimeter as well as your knowledge of how to add and multiply decimals. Furthermore, the SBAC could ask you to convert these measurements into another unit of measurement, once again covering another math domain. You will need to be prepared to apply any of the math concepts covered in fifth grade.

The Classroom Activity

Prior to the Math Performance Task, you will participate in a classroom activity facilitated by your teacher. The classroom activity is for the whole class and aims to give background information for the theme or topic of the Performance Task. It will not give away any of the concepts being tested in the Math Performance Task. It will, however, help you to better understand the real-world problem presented in the Performance Task. For example, for the Math Performance Task, the task could focus on fractions and the measurement of spaces needed to keep certain pets healthy. The classroom activity would then give background information on the different types of pets and the living spaces they require to be healthy.

Layout and Interface

One aspect of the Performance Task that can be overwhelming for many students is the layout. There is a lot of information to make sense of in a tight space. The problem, data, and testing directions will be on the left, and the tasks with space to answer will be on the right. This setup will require you to scroll back and forth as you check the data for each task.

In some cases, you will have a set of interactive tools for a specific task. For instance, to draw lines on a grid, you will have a point tool and a selector tool. If you are having trouble using these, the teacher or facilitator has permission to help you. These are important for answering the questions correctly, and you should not move on until you are confident that you know how to use them!

Applying Your Strategies

The most important strategy to apply to the Math Performance Task is to **identify the pattern**. The Performance Tasks are designed so that the first task establishes the pattern, or math concept, with the next questions building on top of that pattern. Your goal is to identify this pattern, which you can then apply to the harder questions. Often, the answer to one task will give away the answer to the next task, as long as you can identify the pattern.

Another important strategy is to **use your scratch paper**! Using your scratch paper helps you organize your thoughts and see what works and what doesn't. All too often, students focus more on a straight-ahead way to get to the answer, but math should take up a lot of paper space. Make sure to try different ways of thinking. You can draw things out, try different equations, or guess and check. *It is important to remember that you can get partial credit for showing your work, even if you get the wrong answer, and vice versa.*

Finally, **check your answers**! You want to be confident in your answers. Make sure to check your answers and verify that you did not make a math computation error.

Practice Exercises—Math Performance Task

Math Performance Task: Planning a Garden

You have decided to plant a garden to grow your own vegetables. Your parents have given you permission but leave it up to you to plan it. They have decided to give you a certain amount of space. The total area for you to plant in is a rectangle that is 40 feet long by 25 feet wide. With this amount of area, you have decided to divide the area into 4 different rectangular spaces. Here is how you divided it up:

30 ft long by 20 ft wide

$\frac{1}{3}$ of your garden will be lettuce

$\frac{1}{4}$ of your garden will be beets

$\frac{1}{6}$ of your garden will be sweet potatoes

After analyzing this information, you want to determine a plan to use the space in the most efficient way possible.

1. On the grid below, draw rectangles to represent the four rectangular sections as they will appear in your plan. The grid is divided into 5 by 5 square foot (large square) sections, and each small square represents 1 foot by 1 foot. Label each section of your garden with the labels on the left. Side lengths should only be in whole numbers.

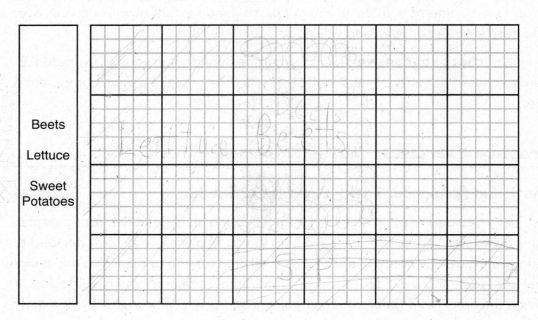

2. Look at your plan from question 1, and enter the fraction of leftover space in your garden plan in the box below.

3. After analyzing your garden plan, you have decided to plant more beets in all of the leftover space of your garden.

Part A: What fraction of your garden will now be planted with beets? Enter the fraction in the numerical pad below.

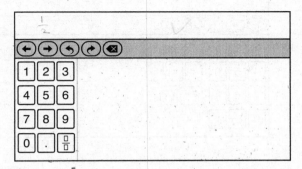

Part B: What is the total square feet of your garden that will be planted with beets? Enter your answer in the numerical pad below.

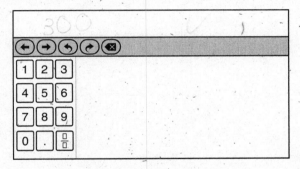

Part C: Explain, in your own words, how you figured out the total square feet in Part B. Write your answer in the box below.

4. Now that you have a new plan for an addition to the Beets section, write an equation that shows the total area of your garden that has food planted in it. Show the equation and the sum in square feet in the numerical pad below.

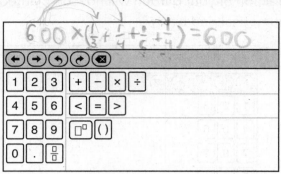

(Answers are on page 309.)

Math Practice Test

Computer Adaptive Test

Directions: On the actual Grade 5 Smarter Balanced exam, the instructions will inform about you about the rules and navigation of the test. These instructions include the fact that you cannot skip questions and all questions on one page must be answered before moving on to the next page. In addition, you will be able to flag, or mark, a question to review later before submitting your test.

1. Enter the quotient to the following problem in the numerical pad below.

$$2,654 \div 4 =$$

2. Which fraction model below represents $3 \times \dfrac{2}{3}$?

○ A.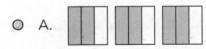

○ B.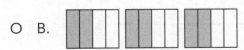

○ C.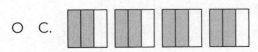

○ D.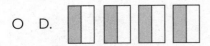

3. What is the perimeter, in **inches**, of the polygon below? Enter your answer in the numerical pad below.

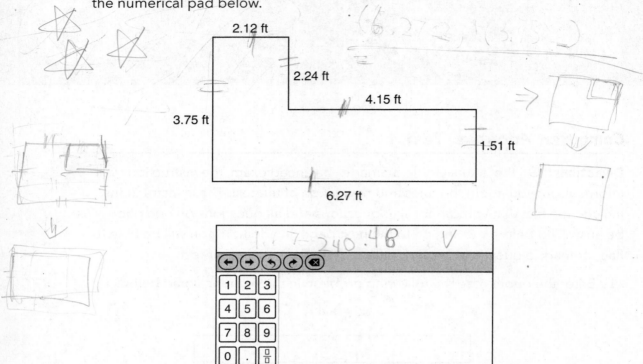

2.12 ft

2.24 ft

4.15 ft

3.75 ft

1.51 ft

6.27 ft

4. Michael is buying tickets to the basketball game for him and his friends. The tickets cost $3.25 each. Michael has $18.00 to spend. What is the greatest number of tickets that Michael can buy?

- ○ A. 8
- ○ B. 7
- ○ C. 6
- ◉ D. 5

5. Enter the product of the following problem in the numerical pad below.

$$158 \times 306 =$$

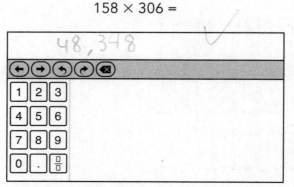

6. Write each expression in the appropriate place in the table.

$\checkmark$ $8 \times \dfrac{2}{3}$ $\qquad$ $\checkmark$ $\dfrac{7}{8} \times 5$ $\qquad$ $\checkmark$ $\dfrac{3}{4} \times 8$

$\checkmark$ $2 \times \dfrac{1}{5}$ $\qquad$ $\checkmark$ $\dfrac{2}{3} \times 3$ $\qquad$ $\checkmark$ $\dfrac{3}{5} \times 5$

$\checkmark$ $5 \times \dfrac{3}{3}$ $\qquad$ $\checkmark$ $5 \times \dfrac{1}{2}$ $\qquad$ $\checkmark$ $\dfrac{4}{5} \times 4$

Less than 5	Equal to 5	Greater than 5
$2 \times \dfrac{1}{5}$ $5 \times \dfrac{1}{2}$ $\dfrac{7}{8} \times 5$ $\dfrac{3}{5} \times 5$ $\dfrac{2}{3} \times 3$ $\dfrac{4}{5} \times 4$	$5 \times \dfrac{3}{3}$ $\checkmark$	$8 \times \dfrac{2}{3}$ $\checkmark$ $\dfrac{3}{4} \times 8$ $\checkmark$

7. The rectangular prism shown below has 3 layers with 18 cubes in each layer.

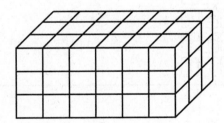

Enter the volume, in cubic centimeters, of the rectangular prism in the numerical pad below.

$54.$ cm^3 $\checkmark$

←	→	↶	↷	⊗

1	2	3
4	5	6
7	8	9
0	.	▢/▢

8. Find the sum of the following mixed numbers. Enter the sum in the numerical pad below.

$$3\frac{1}{6} + 2\frac{3}{4}$$

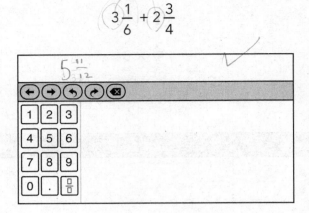

9. Enter the quotient to the following problem in the numerical pad below.

$$6{,}223 \div 38 =$$

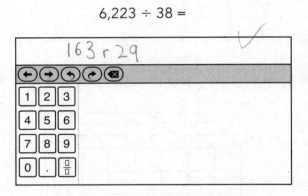

10. Which of the following numbers makes this inequality true?

$$6234.783 > ?$$

○ A. 6234.786
○ B. 6234.784
○ C. 6234.783
◉ D. 6234.782

11. Rectangle *ABCD*, below, is graphed on the coordinate plane.

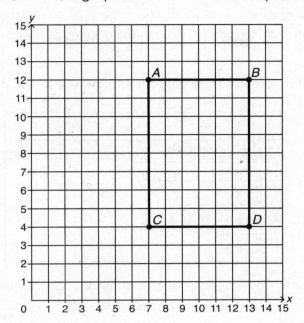

Which set of ordered pairs shows the coordinates of points *A*, *B*, *C*, and *D*?

- ○ A. *A*(7, 7)   *B*(13, 13)   *C*(7, 7)   *D*(13, 13)
- ○ B. *A*(12, 7)   *B*(12, 13)   *C*(4, 7)   *D*(4, 13)
- ◉ C. *A*(7, 12)   *B*(13, 12)   *C*(7, 4)   *D*(13, 4)
- ○ D. *A*(4, 7)   *B*(4, 13)   *C*(7, 7)   *D*(7, 13)

12. Evie is 2 years old. Mekya is 2 years less than 4 times Evie's age.

Enter a numerical expression for Mekya's age in the numerical pad below.

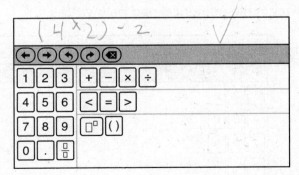

13. Jennifer is running a lemonade stand. She made 1,252 ounces of lemonade that she is dividing evenly into 25 pitchers. Each pitcher contains the same number of ounces of lemonade. How many ounces of lemonade are in each pitcher?

Enter the equation to solve this problem into the numerical pad below.

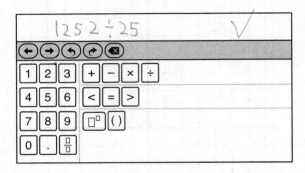

Enter the answer to your equation in the numerical pad below.

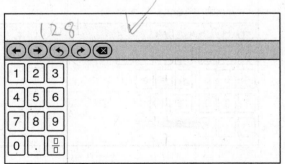

14. Betty, the farmer, has 8 gallons of milk. How many cups of milk does she have? Enter your answer in the numerical pad below.

15. From the numbers on the left, write a number in each box that will create a fraction that correctly completes each statement.

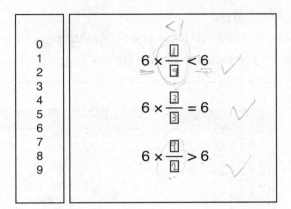

$$6 \times \frac{\boxed{}}{\boxed{9}} < 6$$

$$6 \times \frac{\boxed{3}}{\boxed{3}} = 6$$

$$6 \times \frac{\boxed{4}}{\boxed{2}} > 6$$

Numbers on the left: 0 1 2 3 4 5 6 7 8 9

16. Liz begins running at the start of the trail and runs $8\frac{1}{4}$ miles. The trail is $12\frac{1}{2}$ miles long. In the numerical pad below, enter the distance, in miles, that Liz must run to reach the end of the trail.

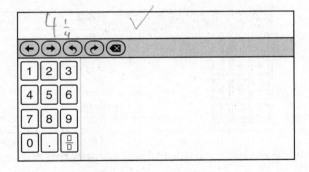

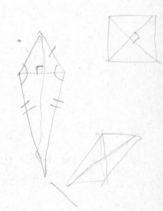

17. Which of the following statements are true? Select **all** that apply.

- ☑ A. Squares, rectangles, and rhombuses have four sides.
- ☐ B. Squares, rectangles, and rhombuses are equal in length.
- ☐ C. Squares, rectangles, and rhombuses have four right angles.
- ☑ D. Squares, rectangles, and rhombuses are quadrilaterals.
- ☑ E. Parallelograms are quadrilaterals.
- ☑ F. Squares, rectangles, and rhombuses are parallelograms.

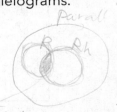

18. Evelyn gets a new paint set and takes 3.2 minutes to paint her first picture. She takes 2.53 minutes to paint her second picture. She then takes 5.63 minutes to paint her third picture.

Part A: How many minutes did she spend painting all three pictures? Enter your answer in the numerical pad below.

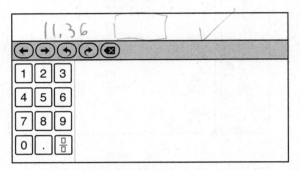

Part B: How much more time did Evelyn spend painting the third picture than she did painting the first picture? Enter your answer in the numerical pad below.

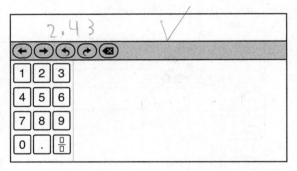

19. Fill in the following division problem by inserting the correct numbers from the left box. Numbers can be used more than once.

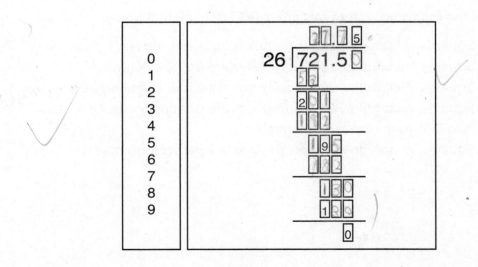

20. The diagram below shows the dimensions, in inches, of two rectangular prisms joined together.

(equal in size)

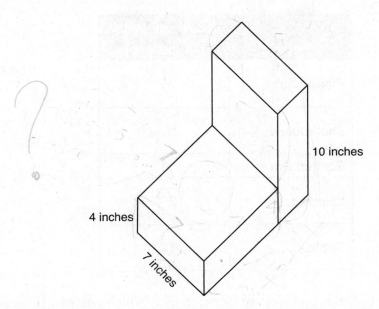

? 10 inches

4 inches

7 inches

What is the combined volume, in cubic inches, of this solid figure? Enter your answer in the numerical pad below.

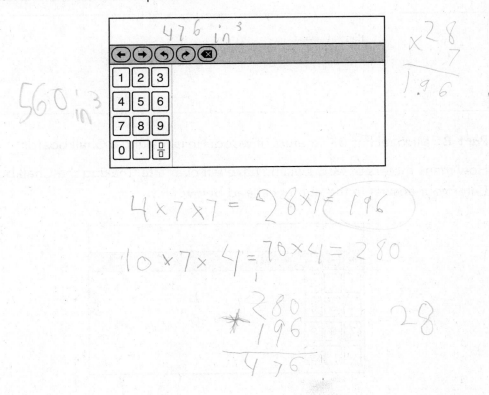

476 in³

560 in³

$x^{2}8$
7
196

$4 \times 7 \times 7 = 28 \times 7 = 196$

$10 \times 7 \times 4 = 70 \times 4 = 280$

$\begin{array}{r} 280 \\ *\ 196 \\ \hline 476 \end{array}$

28

21. The table below shows the length of wood, in meters, needed for different projects.

Project	Length of Wood (in meters)
Flower Pot	$\frac{1}{4}$
Chalkboard	$5\frac{1}{3}$
Garden Gate	3
Counter	$2\frac{3}{4}$
Table	$1\frac{1}{2}$

Part A: Vinod only has 6 meters of wood to use. Which two projects can Vinod make using as much of the 6 meters of wood as possible? Enter your answer in the box below.

Counter, Garden Gate

Part B: Michael has $8\frac{2}{3}$ meters of wood. He is making a Chalkboard.

How many meters of wood will he have left over after making the Chalkboard? Enter your answer in the numerical pad below.

$3\frac{1}{3}$

←	→	↶	↷	⊗

1	2	3
4	5	6
7	8	9
0	.	$\frac{\square}{\square}$

22. Aunt Jennifer plans to create an Easter Egg Hunt for her niece. She wants to buy the Easter eggs for $2.00, 20 stickers at 10 cents (0.10) each, $3.23 for crackers, and a basket for $12.35.

Part A: If Aunt Jennifer has $20.00, does she have enough money to pay for the Easter Egg Hunt? How much is the total? Explain your answer in the box below.

Yes ✓

Part B: If Aunt Jennifer does have enough money with her $20.00, then how much change should Aunt Jennifer get back after paying with her $20.00? Enter your answer in the numerical pad below.

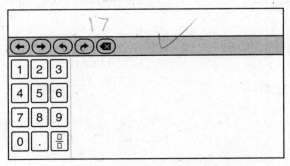

$0.42 ✓

23. Evaluate the following expression. Enter your answer in the numerical pad below.

$$18 - 4 \times 2 + 5 + 2$$

8

17 ✓

P ( )
E
M
D
A
S

24. Julie drinks $5\frac{7}{8}$ cups of tea, and Michael drinks $2\frac{3}{4}$ cups less than Julie.

Part A: How much tea does Michael drink? Enter your answer in the numerical pad below.

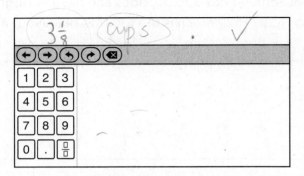

Part B: If Michael then drinks the same amount of tea that Julie drank, how much will he have had in total, including the number of cups that he has already had? Enter your answer in the numerical pad below.

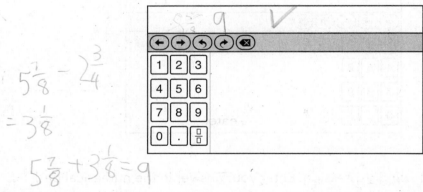

$5\frac{7}{8} - 2\frac{3}{4}$

$= 3\frac{1}{8}$

$5\frac{7}{8} + 3\frac{1}{8} = 9$

25. The number of flowers that Evie has is 4 times the number of flowers that Arjuna has. If the expression 3 + 4 shows how many flowers Arjuna has, which of the following expressions shows how many flowers Evie has?

○ A. 3 + 4 + 4
◉ B. (3 + 4) × 4
○ C. 3 × 4 × 4
○ D. 3 + (4 × 4)

$4(3+4)$

Alomst There!

$$6 ft \times 12 = \cancel{72} \; \boxed{74}$$

26. Michael's height is 2 yards and 2 inches. Jennifer's height is 5 feet and 4 inches. How much taller, in inches, is Michael than Jennifer? Enter your answer in the numerical pad below.

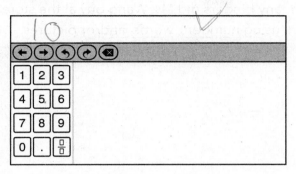

10

1	2	3
4	5	6
7	8	9
0	.	□/□

27. Mrs. Mathew will cut 4 birthday cakes into slices that are $\frac{1}{8}$ each.

Part A: After she cuts the 4 birthday cakes, how many slices does she have? In the box below, show your work using numbers, words, and/or pictures.

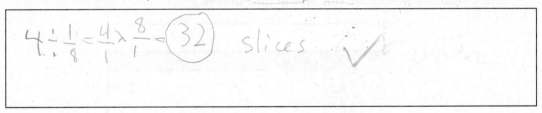

$$4 \div \frac{1}{8} = \frac{4}{1} \times \frac{8}{1} = \boxed{32} \; \text{slices} \; \checkmark$$

Part B: $\frac{3}{4}$ of the slices that were cut were eaten. How many slices were eaten? Enter your answer in the numerical pad below.

24 slices

1	2	3
4	5	6
7	8	9
0	.	□/□

28. Ms. Wang saw a sale at the store. She bought 4 boxes of $1\frac{1}{2}$ inch binders for her students. Each box contains 6 binders.

Part A: How many binders did Ms. Wang buy at the store? In the box below, show your work using numbers, words, and/or pictures.

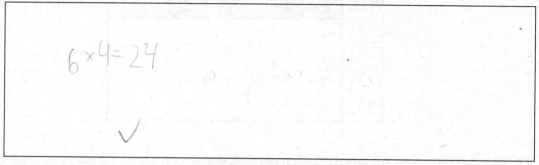

$6 \times 4 = 24$

✓

Part B: Ms. Wang realizes that she needs to buy more binders for her class. Her class has 28 students. How many more binders will she need to purchase? Enter your answer in the numerical pad below.

4 ✓

| ← | → | ↶ | ↷ | ⌫ |

1	2	3
4	5	6
7	8	9
0	.	□/□

Part C: Ms. Wang talks to Mr. Escobar-Ausman about using binders in his classroom. He asks Ms. Wang to purchase a class set of binders for him when she goes to the store next time to buy the rest of the binders for her class. He has 32 students in his class. How many boxes will she need to buy in all (including the number of binders that she still needs to purchase from Part B) on her second trip? In the box below, show your work using numbers, words, and/or pictures.

$32 + 4 = 36$

$36 \div 6 = 6$ ✓

29. Liz is making chocolate cake for a celebratory dinner. She uses $2\frac{1}{5}$ cups of milk for 1 cake. How many cups of milk will she need to create 3 cakes?

   O A. $6\frac{3}{15}$ cups

   ◉ B. $6\frac{3}{5}$ cups

   O C. $6\frac{1}{5}$ cups

   O D. $6\frac{1}{15}$ cups

30. Vinod is creating a bookcase for his daughter's room. He has 6 pieces of wood that are each 8 feet long. He will need 7 pieces of wood that are each 4 feet long to complete this bookcase. Does Vinod have enough pieces of wood to create his daughter's bookcase? Explain your answer in the box below.

   Yes

31. Select Yes or No for whether each fraction can make the inequality true.

   $$\boxed{} < \frac{7}{8}$$

   $\frac{2}{4}$ ◉ Yes   O No

   $\frac{5}{6}$ ◉ Yes   O No

   $\frac{9}{8}$ O Yes   ◉ No

32. $2\frac{1}{5} \times 8\frac{8}{9} =$

- ○ A. $16\frac{8}{45}$
- ● B. $19\frac{5}{9}$
- ○ C. $16\frac{9}{14}$
- ○ D. $19\frac{5}{45}$

33. Select whether each statement below is True or False.

A scalene triangle has no sides that are equal.　　　　● True　　○ False

A right triangle and an isosceles triangle both
always have a right angle.　　　　○ True　　● False

An acute triangle and a right triangle both have
a right angle.　　　　○ True　　● False

An isosceles triangle has no sides that are equal.　　　　○ True　　● False

34. $26.42 \times 2.3 =$

- ● A. 60.766
- ○ B. 6.0766
- ○ C. 60.76
- ○ D. 60.676

35. $4\frac{1}{8} \div 2\frac{1}{6} =$

- ○ A. $2\frac{1}{14}$
- ● B. $1\frac{47}{52}$
- ○ C. $2\frac{1}{48}$
- ○ D. $2\frac{2}{14}$

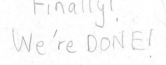

Performance Task

Directions: On the actual Grade 5 Smarter Balanced exam, the instructions will inform about you about the rules and navigation of the test. These instructions include the fact that you cannot skip questions and all questions on one page must be answered before moving on to the next page. In addition, you will be able to flag, or mark, a question to review later before submitting your test.

Part A

Jennifer and her sisters own a bubble tea business called BobaSis Teas. They serve three different sizes. A customer can order a small cup of tea that is 8 fl oz of tea, a medium cup of tea that holds 12 fl oz of tea, or a large cup of tea that holds 16 fl oz of tea. The number of cups of tea that are sold daily for each of these three sizes are displayed in the table below.

Size	Number of Cups of Tea Sold Daily
small	28
medium	36
large	38

1. How many total fluid ounces of the small tea did the sisters sell in one day? Enter your answer in the numerical pad below.

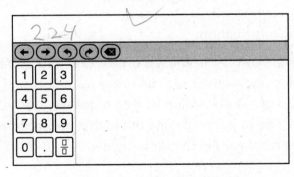

2. If the sisters sell the same amount of medium cups the next day as they did this day, how many total medium cups of tea would the sisters have sold in the two days combined? Enter your answer in the numerical pad below.

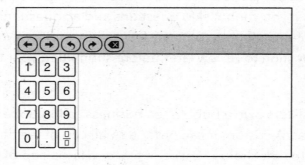

3. How many total fluid ounces did the sisters sell of all three sizes in one day? Enter your answer in the numerical pad below.

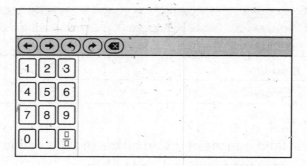

Part B

Reread the following information:

Jennifer and her sisters own a bubble tea business called BobaSis Teas. They serve three different sizes. A customer can order a small cup of tea that is 8 fl oz of tea, a medium cup of tea that holds 12 fl oz of tea, or a large cup of tea that holds 16 fl oz of tea. The number of cups of tea that are sold daily for each of these three sizes are displayed in the table below.

Size	Number of Cups of Tea Sold Daily
small	28
medium	36
large	38

This data is for sales on a weekday. During the weekend, they sell $2\frac{1}{4}$ times that tea on Saturdays and $1\frac{3}{4}$ times that tea on Sundays.

1. How many total cups do they sell on Saturday? How many total cups do they sell on Sunday? Explain your answers in the box below.

> Saturday = 229½ cups
>
> Sunday = 178½ cups

2. If they have to buy 10 gallons of tea for one day during the week, then how many gallons of tea would they need to buy for Saturday, rounded to the nearest gallon? Enter your answer in the numerical pad below.

23

1	2	3
4	5	6
7	8	9
0	.	□/□

3. In the box below, explain how you got your answer for question 2.

(Answers are on page 310.)

Math Answers Explained

Chapter 7: Number and Operations in Base Ten with Decimals

Practice Exercises—Whole Numbers Place Value, pages 170–171

1. **(B)** $70 \times 100 = 7{,}000$

2. **(C)** $50{,}000 \times \dfrac{1}{10} = 5{,}000$

3. **Answers will vary.** Sample answers include:

   Sample Answer 1: The 6 in 5,678 is 100 times greater than the 6 in 24,326. The value of the 6 in 5,678 is 600, and the value of the 6 in 24,326 is 6. I can show this relationship by writing $6 \times 100 = 600$.

   Sample Answer 2: The value of the 6 in 24,326 is $\dfrac{1}{100}$ of the value of the 6 in 5,678. This can also be shown as $600 \div 100 = 6$.

Practice Exercises—Decimal Place Value, pages 173–174

1. **(A)** There are 14 wholes and 548 thousandths. On your scratch paper, make sure to rewrite the problem vertically, lining up the decimals.

2. The correct answer is $(2 \times \dfrac{1}{10}) + (4 \times \dfrac{1}{100}) + (5 \times \dfrac{1}{1{,}000})$.

Practice Exercises—Comparing and Ordering Decimals, page 176

1. The correct order from least to greatest is **8.2, 8.345, 8.37**. I know this because the 4 in the hundredths place of 8.345 is less than the 7 in the hundredths place of 8.37. The 2 in the tenths place of 8.2 is less than the 3 in the tenths place of 8.345 and 8.37.

Practice Exercises—Rounding and Estimating Decimals, pages 177–178

1. **(B)** The 9 to the right of the tenths place is greater than 5, so the 4 should be rounded up. The answer could not be choice A or choice C because the

tenths place does not move up. The answer could not be choice D because the 5 is in the hundredths place when it should be in the tenths place.

2. You should have circled **0.072**, **0.069**, and **0.066**. The 2 in the thousandths place of 0.072 indicates that the 7 in the hundredths place stays the same. The 9 in the thousandths place of 0.069 indicates that the 6 in the hundredths place should be increased to 7. The 6 in the thousandths place of 0.066 indicates that the 6 in the hundredths place should be increased to 7.

3. **(C)** To estimate the answer, round 6.25 pounds to 6 pounds and 0.26 to 0.30. Then divide 6 by 0.30. This equals 20. Although choice D reflects the exact answer that you would get from dividing 6.25 by 0.26, the question asked for *about how many times*, which means that you must estimate to reach the correct answer.

4. There are **4 combinations** that Evelyn can afford to buy with $100. If Evelyn buys all 4 items, she will spend more than $100. This means that she can only buy three of the items. Those possible combinations are:

Combination 1 (book, scarf, tea): $22 + $25 + $45 = $92.00 (YES)

Combination 2 (picture frame, scarf, tea): $12 + $25 + $45 = $82.00 (YES)

Combination 3 (book, picture frame, scarf): $22 + $12 + $25 = $59.00 (YES)

Combination 4 (book, picture frame, tea) = $22 + $12 + $45 = $79.00 (YES)

Practice Exercises—Adding and Subtracting Decimals, pages 179–180

1. **Part A: $34.00** Add the prices for 2 senior citizen tickets and 2 child tickets.

$$
\begin{array}{r}
10.25 \\
10.25 \\
6.75 \\
+\ 6.75 \\
\hline
34.00
\end{array}
$$

Part B: $27.25 Subtract one child ticket, $6.75, from the total from Part A, $34.00.

$$34.00 - 6.75 = 27.25$$

Practice Exercises—Decimals and the Powers of 10, pages 182–183

1. The circled equivalent expressions or numbers are:

8,823,000 $8,823 \times 10^3$ 88.23×10^5 8.823×10^6

2. **0.85 does not have any equivalent expressions. 5.22 is matched with 522 ÷ 10². 8,239 is matched with 8.239 × 10³.**

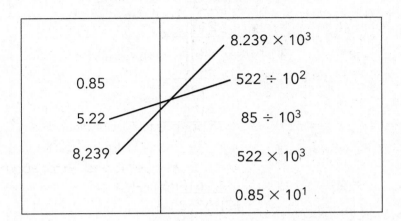

Practice Exercises—Multiplication with Multi-Digit Whole Numbers and Decimals, page 184

1. **Part A: $50.08**

$$12.52 \times 4 = b$$

$$50.08 = b$$

Part B: Yes, Vinod does have enough boxes to resurface the fireplace. He bought 4 boxes of bricks, and each box contains 58 bricks:

$$232 \div 58 = 4 \text{ boxes} \quad or \quad 58 + 58 + 58 + 58 = 232 \text{ bricks}$$
$$or \quad 58 \times 4 = 232 \text{ bricks}$$

Therefore, Vinod has enough boxes to resurface the fireplace.

Practice Exercises—Division with Multi-Digit Whole Numbers, pages 186–187

1. **195R3**

$$
\begin{array}{r}
195\text{R}3 \\
32\overline{)6{,}243} \\
-32 \\
\hline
304 \\
-288 \\
\hline
163 \\
-160 \\
\hline
3
\end{array}
$$

2. **125R20**

$$
\begin{array}{r}
125\text{R}20 \\
21\overline{)\,2{,}645} \\
-21 \\
\hline
54 \\
-42 \\
\hline
125 \\
-105 \\
\hline
20
\end{array}
$$

3. **613R6**

$$
\begin{array}{r}
613\text{R}6 \\
12\overline{)\,7{,}362} \\
-72 \\
\hline
16 \\
-12 \\
\hline
42 \\
-36 \\
\hline
6
\end{array}
$$

Practice Exercises—Division with Multi-Digit Decimals, pages 188–192

1. Part A:

The equation is 256 ÷ 16 = s or 16 × s = 256.

Part B:

$$16\overline{)256} \quad \overset{16}{}$$

The answer is 16 seats per row.

2. **Part A:** Liz ran **6.92 miles each day.**

$$34.6 \div 5 = m$$

$$m = 6.92 \text{ miles each day}$$

Part B: Liz will run **48.44 miles in 7 days.**

$$6.92 \times 7 = d$$

$$d = 48.44 \text{ miles}$$

3. **The developer can build 25 homes.**

$$62.5 \div 2.5 = h$$

$$h = 25 \text{ homes}$$

4. **4.7 × 5.6 = 26.32** and **4.2 × 5.6 = 23.52**

This is a two-part question that requires two correct responses to receive the full 2 points for this question. Partial credit of 1 point will be given if only one answer is correct.

Understanding partial products would help you answer this particular task correctly. You are looking for partial products from the ones place that will equal a number with a 2 in the hundredths place of the product. There is also a 2 in the tens place of the product, which would come from multiplying the tens place of each factor. Knowing this, you can focus on just those two facts to find the correct answers.

Chapter 8: Number and Operations—Fractions and Decimals

Practice Exercises—Adding and Subtracting Fractions with Unlike Denominators, page 196

1.

$\dfrac{3}{6} + \dfrac{4}{8} =$	$\dfrac{1}{8}$
$\dfrac{5}{8} - \dfrac{16}{32} =$	0
$\dfrac{3}{12} - \dfrac{1}{4} =$	1

$\dfrac{3}{6} + \dfrac{4}{8} = 1$ Find the common multiple of 6 and 8 to determine the common denominator.

Multiples of 6: 6, 12, 18, **24**

Multiples of 8: 8, 16, **24**

The common denominator is 24. Now, think of the factors you'll need to get 24. In the first fraction, in order to get a denominator of 24, you need to multiply 6 by 4. Therefore, do the same to the numerator:

$$6 \times 4 = 24$$

$$3 \times 4 = 12$$

In the second fraction, in order to get a denominator of 24, you need to multiply 8 by 3. Therefore, do the same to the numerator:

$$8 \times 3 = 24$$

$$4 \times 3 = 12$$

Now, the denominators are the same, and you can add as normal:

$$\dfrac{12}{24} + \dfrac{12}{24} = 1$$

$\dfrac{5}{8} - \dfrac{16}{32} = \dfrac{1}{8}$ Find the common multiple of 8 and 32 to determine the

common denominator.

Multiples of 8: 8, 16, 24, **32**

Multiples of 32: **32**

The common denominator is 32. Now, think of the factors you'll need to get 32. In the first fraction, in order to get a denominator of 32, you need to multiply 8 by 4. Therefore, do the same to the numerator:

$8 \times 4 = 32$

$5 \times 4 = 20$

In the second fraction, the denominator is already 32, so you can leave this fraction as is.

Now, the denominators are the same, and you can subtract as normal:

$$\frac{20}{32} - \frac{16}{32} = \frac{4}{32}$$

Don't forget to simplify! We can divide each number by 4, resulting in $\dfrac{1}{8}$.

The fraction $\dfrac{1}{8}$ cannot be simplified any further. Therefore, the final answer is $\dfrac{1}{8}$.

$\dfrac{3}{12} - \dfrac{1}{4} = 0$ Find the common multiple of 4 and 12 to determine the common

denominator.

Multiples of 4: 4, 8, **12**

Multiples of 12: **12**

The common denominator is 12. Now, think of the factors you'll need to get 12. In the first fraction, the denominator is already 12, so that fraction can remain as is.

In the second fraction, in order to get a denominator of 12, you need to multiply 4 by 3. Therefore, do the same to the numerator:

$4 \times 3 = 12$

$1 \times 3 = 3$

Now, the denominators are the same, and you can subtract as normal:

$$\frac{3}{12} - \frac{3}{12} = 0$$

Therefore, the final answer is 0.

2. $\frac{3}{4} - \frac{1}{8} = \frac{7}{8}$ The answer is **No** because $\frac{3}{4} - \frac{1}{8} = \frac{6}{8} - \frac{1}{8} = \frac{5}{8}$.

$\frac{8}{12} - \frac{4}{8} = \frac{1}{6}$ The answer is **Yes** because $\frac{8}{12} - \frac{4}{8} = \frac{16}{24} - \frac{12}{24} = \frac{4}{24} = \frac{1}{6}$.

$\frac{3}{5} + \frac{2}{6} = \frac{14}{15}$ The answer is **Yes** because $\frac{3}{5} + \frac{2}{6} = \frac{18}{30} + \frac{10}{30} = \frac{28}{30} = \frac{14}{15}$.

$\frac{8}{12} + \frac{2}{24} = \frac{16}{24}$ The answer is **No** because $\frac{8}{12} + \frac{2}{24} = \frac{16}{24} + \frac{2}{24} = \frac{18}{24}$.

Practice Exercises—Word Problems Involving Adding and Subtracting Fractions with Unlike Denominators, pages 197–198

1. **(D)** First, figure out which math operation to use. Take notice of the words **in all**, which tell you to add. You need to add $\frac{1}{2}$ and $\frac{3}{4}$. Next, find the equivalent fraction for $\frac{1}{2}$ that has a 4 as its denominator. We can multiply the numerator and the denominator by 2, changing $\frac{1}{2}$ to $\frac{2}{4}$. Now, we can add $\frac{2}{4} + \frac{3}{4} = \frac{5}{4}$. $\frac{5}{4}$ is an improper fraction, which we can change into $1\frac{1}{4}$ inches.

2. **Part A:** Your equation should read as follows: $\frac{3}{8} - \frac{3}{16}$. Notice that the problem is asking for the difference, which means you need to subtract.

   Part B: $\frac{3}{16}$ You will need to find an equivalent fraction for $\frac{3}{8}$ with a 16 as the denominator. We can multiply the numerator and the denominator by 2, changing $\frac{3}{8}$ to $\frac{6}{16}$. Now subtract: $\frac{6}{16} - \frac{3}{16} = \frac{3}{16}$, which cannot be simplified.

3. **(C)** First, find the common multiple of 8 and 3 to determine the common denominator.

Multiples of 8: 8, 16, **24**

Multiples of 3: 3, 6, 9, 12, 15, 18, 21, **24**

The common denominator is 24. Now, think of the factors you'll need to get 24. In the first fraction, in order to get a denominator of 24, you will need to multiply 8 by 3. Therefore, do the same to the numerator:

$$8 \times 3 = 24$$

$$1 \times 3 = 3$$

In the second fraction, in order to get a denominator of 24, you need to multiply 3 by 8. Therefore, do the same to the numerator:

$$3 \times 8 = 24$$

$$1 \times 8 = 8$$

Now, the denominators are the same, leaving you with:

$$3\frac{3}{24} - 1\frac{8}{24}$$

But wait! You cannot subtract 8 from 3 in the numerators. You will therefore have to make $\frac{3}{24}$ an improper fraction so that the numerator is a number that is larger than 8. You can do this by adding the whole of the fraction, which is $\frac{24}{24}$. It will look like this:

$$\frac{3}{24} + \frac{24}{24} = \frac{27}{24}$$

Remember, by creating the improper fraction, you are taking a whole away from the whole number (in this case 3), making the new mixed number $2\frac{27}{24}$. Now, you can subtract:

$$2\frac{27}{24} - 1\frac{8}{24} = 1\frac{19}{24}$$

Therefore, Liz spent $1\frac{19}{24}$ hours longer at the Farmer's Market than Taran spent at the supermarket.

Practice Exercises—Interpreting Fractions as Division, page 200

1.

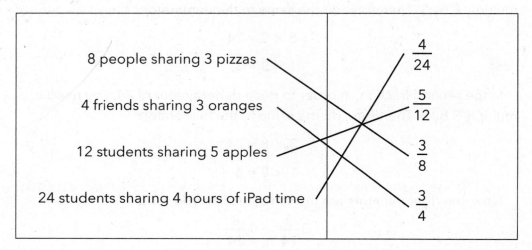

8 people sharing 3 pizzas = $\dfrac{3}{8}$

4 friends sharing 3 oranges = $\dfrac{3}{4}$

12 students sharing 5 apples = $\dfrac{5}{12}$

24 students sharing 4 hours of iPad time = $\dfrac{4}{24}$

Practice Exercises—Multiplication of Fractions and Whole Numbers, pages 202–204

1. **(B)** and **(C)**

   A. $\dfrac{1}{5} \times 3 = \dfrac{3}{5}$ (No)

   B. $11 \times \dfrac{1}{5} = \dfrac{11}{5} = 2\dfrac{1}{5}$ (Yes)

   C. $22 \times \dfrac{1}{10} = \dfrac{22}{10} = 2\dfrac{1}{5}$ (Yes)

   D. $11 \times 5 = 55$ (No)

   E. $\dfrac{1}{5} \times 2 = \dfrac{2}{5}$ (No)

2. **(C)** Choice C is divided into three equal parts, and there are eight shaded parts.

3. **(B)** First, convert the mixed numbers into improper fractions: $6\frac{3}{4}$ becomes

$\frac{27}{4}$ and $4\frac{1}{4}$ becomes $\frac{17}{4}$. Now, your expression reads $\frac{27}{4} \times \frac{17}{4} = ?$ Then,

multiply the numerators and the denominators, resulting in $\frac{459}{16}$. Change the

improper fraction to a mixed number. In other words, divide 459 by 16, which

equals 28 with a remainder of 11. The remainder is the numerator, and the

denominator is the divisor. The final answer is $28\frac{11}{16}$ inches.

Practice Exercises—Division of Fractions with a Whole Number, page 205

1. **(A)**, **(C)**, and **(E)**

A. $3 \div \frac{2}{3} = 3 \times \frac{3}{2} = \frac{9}{2}$ (Yes)

B. $\frac{1}{8} \div 2 = \frac{1}{8} \times \frac{1}{2} = \frac{1}{16}$ (No)

C. $\frac{6}{8} \div 3 = \frac{6}{8} \times \frac{1}{3} = \frac{6}{24} = \frac{1}{4}$ (Yes)

D. $5 \div \frac{2}{5} = 5 \times \frac{5}{2} = \frac{25}{2}$ (No)

E. $2 \div \frac{7}{8} = 2 \times \frac{8}{7} = \frac{16}{7} = 2\frac{2}{7}$ (Yes)

Practice Exercises—Interpreting and Solving Real-World Problems with Fractions Involving Multiplication and Division, pages 206–207

1. **Liz's statement is incorrect.** To solve this problem, set up an equation. You

know that she works out for $3\frac{1}{4}$ hours each day for 3 days of the week. You

also know that she works out for $2\frac{3}{4}$ hours for 2 days of the week.

$$\left(3\frac{1}{4} \times 3\right) + \left(2\frac{3}{4} \times 2\right) = 9\frac{3}{4} + 5\frac{1}{2}$$

All hours will need to be added to figure out if she ran more than 20 hours.

$9\frac{3}{4} + 5\frac{1}{2} = \frac{39}{4} + \frac{11}{2} = \frac{39}{4} + \frac{22}{4} = \frac{61}{4} = 15\frac{1}{4}$ hours. Therefore, Liz's

statement is incorrect.

2. **(D)** $4 \div \frac{1}{8} = 4 \times \frac{8}{1} = 32$ slices of cake

3. **Betty's claim is not correct.** If you find the total amount that Evelyn spilled, by multiplying $\frac{1}{5}$ by 6, that is a total of $1\frac{1}{5}$ gallons spilled. Next, you need to subtract $1\frac{1}{5}$ from the 6 gallons that Betty originally bought:

$$6 - 1\frac{1}{5} = \frac{6}{1} - \frac{6}{5} = \frac{30}{5} - \frac{6}{5} = \frac{24}{5} = 4\frac{4}{5}$$ gallons of milk that was not spilled.

This is less than the 5 gallons of milk that she will need for the party guests. Therefore, Betty does not still have enough milk for all the guests.

Chapter 9: Operations and Algebraic Thinking

Practice Exercises—Interpreting Simple Expressions, pages 219–220

1. **$n + 3$** First, decide what the unknown in the statement is. In this case, you do not know what the *number* is. You can use the letter n as a variable to represent that unknown. Next, you need to identify the operation to use based on key words. The words *more than* should tell you that you need to use addition. The answer is $n + 3$.

2. **$n - 5$** The *number* is the unknown. You can use the letter n as a variable to represent that unknown. Next, you need to identify the operation to use based on key words. The words *less than* should tell you that you need to use subtraction. The answer is $n - 5$.

3. **$8 \times p$ or $8p$ or $8 \bullet p$** First, decide what the unknown in the statement is. In this example, you do not know how many people total there are. You can use the letter p as a variable to represent that unknown. Next, you need to identify the operation to use based on key words. The word *product* should tell you that you need to use multiplication because the product is the answer of a multiplication problem. The answer, therefore, will be $8 \times p$ or $8p$ or $8 \bullet p$.

4. **$\frac{n}{12}$ or $n \div 12$** Again, the *number* is the unknown. You can use the letter n as a variable to represent the unknown. Next, you need to identify the operation to use based on key words. The word *quotient* should tell you that you need to use division because it is an answer to a division problem. The answer, therefore, will be $\frac{n}{12}$ or $n \div 12$.

Practice Exercises—Evaluating Simple Expressions, page 221

1. **8** First, replace the variable, x, with 10, making the expression, $10 - 2$. Then, solve:

$$10 - 2 = 8$$

2. **10** First, replace the variable, x, with 10, making the expression, $100 \div 10$. Then solve:

$$100 \div 10 = 10$$

Practice Exercises—Evaluating Expressions with More Than One Operation, pages 222–223

1. **9 + 5n** If you read the phrase, *nine plus five times a number*, you'll notice that you can separate the phrase into two parts. The first part is *nine plus*, which you can write as $9 +$. The second part is *five times a number*, which you can write as $5n$. You can put these together as

$$9 + 5n$$

2. **10n − 7** If you read the phrase, *ten times a number, minus seven*, you'll notice that you can also separate this phrase into two parts. The first part is *ten times a number*, which you can write as $10n$. The second part is *minus seven*, which is written as -7. You can put this together as $10n - 7$.

3.

Less than 20	Equal to 20	Greater than 20
$(4 \times 5) \div 4$	$(5 \times 4) \times 1$	$10 + (4 \times 5)$
$(4 \times 5) \div 5 \times 4$	$(9 - 8) \times (5 \times 4)$	$(5 \times 4) + 7$
$\frac{1}{4} \times (4 \times 5)$		$4 \times \frac{1}{2} \times (5 \times 4)$

(Note that this is an example of a technology-enhanced question that has more than one answer. On the actual test, you would be asked to drag and drop the correct expressions into the correct boxes in the chart.)

Practice Exercises—Writing Expressions for Real-World Problems, pages 225–226

1. **5s + 20** This expression can be broken down into two parts. The first part is the fact that Mekya earns a $5 commission for each sale, represented by s. Therefore, his commission is 5s, depending upon the number of sales. The second part is the fact that he earns $20 per day, in addition to his commission. This can be represented as + 20. Combine the two parts to write your expression, 5s + 20.

2. **Part A: 150 people** You should have noticed that there is no need for a variable, so this is a numerical expression. Also notice that this is a two-step problem. You will use Step 1 to solve Part A and Step 2 to solve Part B.

   STEP 1 Calculate how many total people are going on the field trip. It should look like this:

   $$(5 \times 29) + 5 = 150 \text{ people}$$

   Part B: (C) Use Step 2.

   STEP 2 Calculate how many people 2 buses will hold. This would look like:

   $$75 \times 2 = 150 \text{ people}$$

   Since the answers from the expressions for Step 1 and Step 2 are the same, this means that there is enough room on 2 buses for the total number of people going on the trip. Therefore, the correct answer is choice C.

Practice Exercises—Evaluating Expressions to Show a Pattern or a Rule, page 227

1. **(B)** Notice that the numbers in the y-output are one-half of the number above them in the x-output. In other words, for every value of x, the value of y is the result of taking half of x, or dividing x by 2. Therefore, the answer is choice B, $y = x \div 2$.

2.

x	y = x + 5
2	7
4	9
6	11
8	13

First, find the missing *y*-values. All you have to do is plug-in the missing *y*-values' corresponding *x*-values in the expression, $y = x + 5$. Therefore, for $x = 4$, the missing *y*-value is $y = 4 + 5 = 9$. For $x = 6$, the missing *y*-value is $y = 6 + 5 = 11$. To find the missing *x*-value, you will need to work backwards. Subtract 5 from 13 to get 8.

Practice Exercises—Distributive Property, page 229

1. **12 + 30*n***

    STEP 1 Multiply the outside number by the two numbers inside the parentheses.

    $$6 \times 2 = 12$$
    $$6 \times 5n = 30n$$

    STEP 2 Add the products.

    $$12 + 30n$$

2. **14*n* − 10**

    STEP 1 Multiply the outside number by the two numbers inside the parentheses.

    $$2 \times 7n = 14n$$
    $$2 \times -5 = -10$$

    STEP 2 Subtract the products.

    $$14n - 10$$

3. **96 + 72*n***

    STEP 1 Multiply the outside number by the two numbers inside the parentheses.

    $$12 \times 8 = 96$$
    $$12 \times 6n = 72n$$

    STEP 2 Add the products.

    $$96 + 72n$$

Practice Exercises—Order of Operations, pages 232–233

1. **(C)**
   A. $5 + 4 \times 3 - 1 = 5 + 12 - 1 = 17 - 1 = 16$ (No)
   B. $(5 + 4) \times 3 - 1 = 9 \times 3 - 1 = 27 - 1 = 26$ (No)
   C. $5 + 4 \times (3 - 1) = 5 + 4 \times 2 = 5 + 8 = 13$ (Yes)
   D. $(5 + 4) \times (3 - 1) = 9 \times 2 = 18$ (No)

2. **(B)**
   A. $8 \times 5 \times 4 = 40 \times 4 = 160$ (No)
   B. $(8 + 4) \times 5 = 12 \times 5 = 60$ (Yes)
   C. $8 + (4 \times 5) = 8 + 20 = 28$ (No)
   D. $(8 + 5) \times 4 = 13 \times 4 = 52$ (No)

3. **(B)** Remember the rules of P.E.M.D.A.S. Always complete the operations within the parentheses first. In this case, the operation inside the parentheses is subtraction.

4. **(A)**
   A. $(5 \times 3) + 3 = 15 + 3 = 18$ (Yes)
   B. $(3 + 5) \times 3 = 8 \times 3 = 24$ (No)
   C. $3 \times (3 \times 5) = 3 \times 15 = 45$ (No)
   D. $5 + 3 \times 3 = 5 + 9 = 14$ (No)

Practice Exercises—Ordered Pairs, pages 236–237

1.

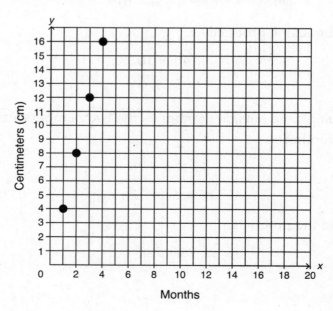

Chapter 10: Geometry and Graphing

Practice Exercises—Graphing Points to Solve Real-World Problems, pages 242–244

1. Your table should read as follows:

Points	x-coordinate	y-coordinate
A	0	0
B	1	2
C	2	4
D	3	6

   Remember, the x-axis is the horizontal line, and the y-axis is the vertical line. They both intersect at the origin (0, 0). When finding a point on a coordinate grid, look at the x-axis first to locate the point. Next, look at the y-axis, and locate that same point. If you look at the coordinate plane, point B is located at 1 on the x-axis, and it is located at 2 on the y-axis. Therefore, the coordinates of point B are (1, 2).

2. Your table should read as follows:

Points	x-coordinate	y-coordinate
School	3	9
Park	12	6
Home	12	2
Library	3	3

   Remember, the x-axis is the horizontal line, and the y-axis is the vertical line. They both intersect at the origin (0, 0). When finding a point on a coordinate grid, look at the x-axis first to locate the point. Next, look at the y-axis, and locate that same point. If you look at the coordinate plane, the Park is located at 12 on the x-axis, and it is located at 6 on the y-axis. Therefore, the coordinates of the Park are (12, 6).

Practice Exercises—Coordinate Systems, pages 246–247

1. **Part A:** Michael traveled the farthest on one charge between day 1 and day 2.

   Part B: Michael traveled about 240 miles between day 3 and day 4.

Practice Exercises—Classifying Two-Dimensional Figures, page 248

1. **All statements should be selected.**

2. Your completed table should read as follows:

Property	This figure always has four sides of equal length.	This figure always has four right angles.	This figure always has two pairs of parallel sides.	This figure has four sides.
Square	■	■	■	■
Rhombus	■	□	■	■
Rectangle	□	■	■	■
Parallelogram	□	□	■	■
Trapezoid	□	□	□	■

Square and rhombuses always have four equal sides. Rectangles, parallelograms, and trapezoids don't always have equal sides, but some do. Squares and rectangles are parallelograms and quadrilaterals.

All squares and rectangles have four right angles. No matter which way you turn the shape, it forms a perfect L that is 90 degrees. Rhombuses, parallelograms, and trapezoids do not always have four right angles.

All squares, rhombuses, rectangles, and parallelograms have at least two pairs of parallel sides. Trapezoids have only one pair of parallel sides.

All squares, rectangles, rhombuses, parallelograms, and trapezoids have four sides.

Chapter 11: Measurement and Data

Practice Exercises—Converting Customary Units of Length, page 252

1. **(D)** Since there are 8 pints in a gallon, then you will want to multiply, $3.5 \times 8 = 28$.

2. The answers that should be circled are **8 yards** and **288 inches**. Since there are 3 feet in one yard, then you divide, 24 ÷ 3 = 8 yards. There are 12 inches in one foot. Therefore, you should have circled 288 inches since 24 × 12 = 288. Of the other choices, 2.4 inches equals 0.2 feet, 3 yards equals 9 feet, 489 inches equals 40.75 feet, and 240 inches equals 20 feet.

3. **Part A: 5 pints** 2.5 × 2 = 5 pints

   Part B: 80 fl oz In order to find the answer, you will have to do 3 conversions. You already know from the previous answer that 2.5 quarts equals 5 pints. Since there are 2 cups for every 1 pint, then you know 5 × 2 = 10 cups. Now, 10 cups × 8 fl oz = 80 fl oz. Therefore, there are 80 fl oz in 2.5 quarts.

Practice Exercises—Converting Metric Units of Length, page 254

1. **Part A:** Evie's new bike is **3.2 kg**. This is because 3,200 g × 0.001 kg = 3.2 kg.

   Part B: Evie's bike has the least amount of mass because 3.2 kg is less than 4.2 kg.

2. The answers that should be circled are **8,600 cm** and **86,000 mm**. Since there are 100 cm for every 1 m: 86 m × 100 cm = 8,600 cm. Also, since there are 1,000 mm for every 1 m: 86 m × 1,000 mm = 86,000 mm. Of the other choices, 430 cm equals 4.3 m, 860 cm equals 8.6 m, 43,000 mm equals 43 m, and 43 cm equals 0.43 m.

Practice Exercises—Use of Measurements on Line Plots, pages 255-257

1. **Part A:** The most common number of video games in the class is **4 video games**.

   Part B: Yes, the student who has 7 video games at home is an outlier because 7 video games is far enough away from the rest of the numbers, and it only has one mark.

2. **Part A:**

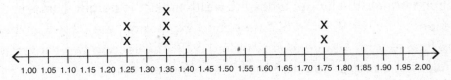

Number of Miles Walked

Part B: $1.75 - 1.25 = \mathbf{0.5}$ **mile (or** $\frac{1}{2}$ **mile) difference.**

Part C: 1.35 miles was the most common distance that Liz walked that week.

Part D: The farthest number of miles that Liz walked was **1.75 miles. This number is not an outlier** because she walked that same distance twice during that week.

Practice Exercises—Models and Volume, pages 258–260

1. The equation for finding volume is: $V = lwh$. To find the total volume:

$$V = lwh$$

$$V = 10.25 \times 7.3 \times 8.5$$

$$\mathbf{V = 636.0125 \ cm^3}$$

2. If you split the figure, you should have two prisms, one with the dimensions $3 \times 5 \times 7$ and another with the dimensions $3 \times 3 \times 5$. These two prisms together equal $105 + 45$, which equals **150 ft³**.

Practice Exercises—Relating Volume to Real-World Problems, pages 261–262

1. In order to find volume, the length, width, and height are multiplied. $6 \times 4 \times 2 = \mathbf{48}$ **cubic inches**.

2. Your completed table should match the one that follows:

	Yes	No
$V = 9 \times 7 \times 5$	■	□
$V = 63 \times 5$	■	□
$V = (9 + 7) \times 5$	□	■
$V = 16 \times 5$	□	■

Volume equals the length times the width times the height. This is represented by $V = 9 \times 7 \times 5$. The second expression, $V = 63 \times 5$, is the same as the first, except 9 is already multiplied by 7. The second two expressions are incorrect because adding 9 and 7 is not necessary.

Chapter 12: Math Performance Task

Practice Exercises—Math Performance Task, pages 265–268

Before we go over how to answer these tasks, let's list the math concepts covered in this Performance Task:

- Identifying fractions
- Adding fractions
- Geometry
- Area (square footage)
- Multiplication

As you can see, the Performance Task covers a wide range of math concepts. Let's look how these skills come together to complete the tasks correctly.

1. When completing this task on the SBAC, you would use an interactive connector tool with which you would drag and make your lines. For this task you should have divided the grid as follows: **The Lettuce section should be a 10 × 20 square foot rectangle, the Beets section should be a 10 × 15 square foot rectangle, and the Sweet Potatoes section should be a 10 × 10 square foot rectangle.** To do this correctly, keep these facts in mind:

   - Remember that fractions represent a whole divided up equally.
   - Each small square on the grid is 1 foot, and each larger square represents 5 feet.
   - You will need to understand how to divide the grid evenly into 3, 4, and 6 parts equally.
   - You now know the measurements for the length and width of each section of plants, which you will need to know for later.

2. **The leftover space where nothing is planted is $\frac{1}{4}$ of the total garden.** You should notice the pattern connecting the fraction of space to the length and width of each rectangle. For instance, $\frac{1}{3}$ of the space is needed for the Lettuce section that is a 10 × 20 rectangle. This means that anywhere you draw out $\frac{1}{3}$ of space in the garden, you will have the same number of larger squares making up the rectangle. Each $\frac{1}{3}$ rectangle will take up 8 large squares. Simply counting the number of large squares where nothing is planted will reveal that you have $\frac{1}{4}$ of leftover space.

3. **Part A:** Remember that you decided to plant more beets, which means that this question is asking for the complete fraction of all beets in your garden. You will need to add the two beets sections, $\frac{1}{4} + \frac{1}{4} = \frac{2}{4}$ or $\frac{1}{2}$. This means that $\frac{1}{2}$ **of the garden is now planted with beets.**

Part B: The best way to approach this question is to remember your answers from questions 1 and 2. Since, according to the pattern, $\frac{1}{4}$ of the garden is a 10×15 rectangle, and you remember that surface area is length × width, then $10 \times 15 = 150$ ft². Now, there are two $\frac{1}{4}$ sections of beets, so you now have to add 150 + 150 to get a total of **300 ft²** of space for beets.

Part C: Answers will vary. This is a task in which you have to explain your thinking using mathematical vocabulary. Much of this was discussed above in the answer for Part B, but another possible correct answer may look like this:

I knew that $\frac{1}{4}$ of the garden was planted with beets. I also knew that the leftover space that will now be used to plant more beets is also $\frac{1}{4}$. This is a total of $\frac{1}{2}$ of the garden space for beets. Since $\frac{1}{2}$ of the garden would be half of the original 20×30 rectangle, I knew that the total square feet for beets is 300 ft².

4. Notice how the sequence of questions sets you up and gives you clues for the next question. Now that you figured out the surface area for the Beets section, you know how to find the area for the rest of the garden. We can now simply multiply to find all the areas of each vegetable section, and then add them together to find the total.

$$300 + 200 + 100 = 600 \text{ ft}^2$$

Note that you must both set up the equation properly and find the correct answer to receive full credit.

Chapter 13: Math Practice Test

Computer Adaptive Test, pages 269–284

1. **663.50** *or* **663R2** *or* **663$\frac{1}{2}$** This problem tests your basic long-division skills.

Many students like to do these problems in their head and enter the answer, but it is easy to make computation mistakes. Make sure you use your scratch paper to rewrite the problem to figure it out vertically.

2. **(A)** For this problem, you should notice that you do not have to solve the multiplication equation to get the correct answer. You are looking for which model represents, or visually shows, the problem. In this case, you have 3 wholes being multiplied by $\frac{2}{3}$. Visually, you would have 3 wholes, each being divided into 3 equal parts. Since the wholes are being multiplied by $\frac{2}{3}$, then each whole would have 2 equal parts shaded.

3. **240.48 inches** Perimeter is found by adding all of the sides of a polygon together. For this task, the SBAC is testing your ability to both add decimals and find the perimeter. Make sure to rewrite the addition problem on your scratch paper. Write the problem vertically, lining up the decimals. You can add all the lengths together at one time or add a few together to make it more manageable.

$$
\begin{array}{r}
6.27 \\
4.15 \\
3.75 \\
2.24 \\
2.12 \\
+\ 1.51 \\
\hline
20.04
\end{array}
$$

You may think that you're finished, and that the answer is 20.04 feet, but wait, there's more! The question asked for the perimeter in *inches*. Therefore, you must convert feet to inches. Remember, there are 12 inches in 1 foot.

$$20.04 \times 12 = 240.48$$

4. **(D)** Michael can buy a total of 5 tickets. For this task, you can use guess and check to eliminate the wrong answers and narrow it down. You can also simply multiply each possible answer by $3.25 to see which one is the closest to $18.00 without going over.

5. **48,348** This task tests your ability to successfully multiply greater numbers. Make sure to use your scratch paper to write out the problem vertically.

6. Your table should read as follows:

Less than 5	Equal to 5	Greater than 5
$2 \times \dfrac{1}{5}$	$5 \times \dfrac{3}{3}$	$8 \times \dfrac{2}{3}$
$\dfrac{2}{3} \times 3$		$\dfrac{3}{4} \times 8$
$5 \times \dfrac{1}{2}$		
$\dfrac{3}{5} \times 5$		
$\dfrac{4}{5} \times 4$		
$\dfrac{7}{8} \times 5$		

This task is testing your ability to multiply a whole number by a fraction and a fraction by a whole number. Remember that to multiply a whole number by a fraction, you simply multiply the whole number by the numerator and then divide by the denominator. For instance, $8 \times \dfrac{2}{4}$ would be $8 \times 2 = 16 \div 4 = 4$, which is less than 5.

7. **54 cm^3** First, you need to understand that each single cube in the rectangular prism is 1 cm $\times$ 1 cm $\times$ 1 cm. Putting them together creates an array. To make a prism, these arrays are stacked on each other. To find the total of all the arrays together, you should have followed the formula $l \times w \times h$. You should have counted the cubes to find out the length, width, and height, which would be $6 \times 3 \times 3 = 54$ cm^3.

8. **$5\dfrac{11}{12}$** This task is testing you on your ability to add mixed numbers. You will need to find the common denominator for both mixed numbers. $3\dfrac{1}{6} + 2\dfrac{3}{4} = 3\dfrac{2}{12} + 2\dfrac{9}{12}$. Once added, the answer becomes $5\dfrac{11}{12}$.

9. **163R29**

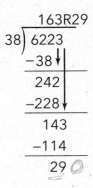

```
        163R29
   38) 6223
      −38↓
       242
      −228↓
       143
      −114
        29 ◯
```

10. **(D)** This task tests your ability to compare decimals based on their place value. You can see that that all place values are equal except the thousandths place after the decimal where the 2 is less than the 3 in the thousandths place of the original number, making 6234.783 greater than (>) 6234.782.

11. **(C)** To complete this task correctly, you will need to test each point to make sure that the ordered pairs are shown.

12. **M = (4 × 2) − 2** Mekya's age is 6 years old. This task is testing your ability to write numerical expressions in order to solve a real-world problem. In this case, you would want to pay attention to two key words, *less* and *times*. Since Mekya's age is 2 years less than 4 times Evie's age, we can figure out the multiplication first, 4 × 2 = 8. Then we can subtract the fact that Mekya is 2 less than that amount, 8 − 2 = 6.

13. The correct equation is **1,252 ÷ 25**. The correct answer to the equation is **50.08 ounces of lemonade per pitcher**. In this question, you are being tested on setting up an equation and dividing large numbers with decimals. This problem will require you to add a decimal to add more zeros to the dividend to finish the problem.

```
          50.08
   25) 1252.00
      −125↓
        02
       −0↓
        20
       −0↓
        200
       −200
          0
```

14. **128 cups of milk** 16 cups = 1 gallon. Therefore, 16 cups per gallon × 8 gallons = 128 cups. This is a measurement task that tests you on converting between capacity measurements. On the SBAC, the test makers will not remind you of the unit conversion. You will need to memorize these. In this case, there are 16 cups in each gallon. Since this conversion is going from something bigger to something smaller, you will need to multiply.

15. **Answers will vary.** Below is a sample response.

$6 \times \dfrac{1}{3}$ (or any fraction less than 1 would apply) < 6

$6 \times \dfrac{6}{6}$ (or any fraction equal to 1 would apply) = 6

$6 \times \dfrac{3}{2}$ (or any fraction greater than 1 would apply) > 6

This task is testing two things: your ability to multiply a whole number by a fraction and your ability to compare numbers. This will take some guess and check. There are different possibilities for answers, which can make it tricky if you are unsure of your calculations. Remember that you have to simply multiply the whole number by the numerator, and then divide that answer by the denominator.

16. **$4\dfrac{1}{4}$ miles** $12\dfrac{1}{2} - 8\dfrac{1}{4} = 12\dfrac{2}{4} - 8\dfrac{1}{4} = 4\dfrac{1}{4}$ miles. In this task, you are being tested on subtracting mixed numbers with unlike denominators, which will require you to also be able to find equivalent fractions. Following the clues in the word problem, you should be able to guess that you need to subtract to find the difference between the miles run and the total miles of the trail. Before subtracting the two mixed numbers, you will need to change $12\dfrac{1}{2}$ to $12\dfrac{2}{4}$ by multiplying $\dfrac{1}{2}$ by $\dfrac{2}{2}$. When subtracting, the denominators stay the same.

17. **(A), (D), (E)**, and **(F)** For this task, you will need to know how to classify geometric shapes based on their properties. You should use your scratch paper to draw these shapes out to verify their properties.

18. **Part A: 11.36 minutes** Add up all the times it took to paint the three pictures:

$$\begin{array}{r} 3.2 \\ 2.53 \\ +\ 5.63 \\ \hline 11.36 \end{array}$$

Part B: 2.43 minutes Subtract the amount of time it took to paint the first picture from the amount of time it took to paint the third picture:

$$\begin{array}{r} 5.63 \\ -\ 3.2 \\ \hline 2.43 \end{array}$$

In this task, you are being tested on adding and subtracting decimals. On your scratch paper, make sure to line up the decimals before adding or subtracting.

19. This task requires you to understand how to perform long-division with two-digit divisors and decimals. The completed answer should read as follows:

$$\begin{array}{r}
27.75 \\
26\overline{)721.50} \\
-52 \\
\hline
201 \\
-182 \\
\hline
195 \\
-182 \\
\hline
130 \\
-130 \\
\hline
0
\end{array}$$

20. **560 inches³** To find the volume of the solid:

- Find the volume of one rectangular prism first. Look for parallel and congruent lines to help you.
- If the length of the front prism is 7 inches, and you can see that that line is equal to the base of the back prism, then you know that the length for the back prism is also 7 inches.
- You should also see that if the height of the front prism is 4 inches, then the width of the back prism, which is equal to the height of the front prism, is also 4 inches.
- The height of the back prism is equal to the width of the front prism. Both are 10 inches.
- The formula for volume is length × width × height (*lwh*): 4 × 7 × 10 = 280.
- Since there are two rectangular prisms that are equal in size, you can multiply the answer by 2, or add 280 + 280 to get 560 inches³.

21. **Part A:** The **Garden Gate** and the **Counter** For this part, you have two options: either the Garden Gate and the Counter, or the Chalkboard and the Flower Pot. After adding these options together, using equivalent fractions, you

will need to compare each answer to see which one is closest to 6. In this case, $5\frac{7}{12}$ (the Chalkboard and the Flower Pot) vs. $5\frac{9}{12}$ (the Garden Gate and the Counter). Clearly, $5\frac{9}{12}$ is greater than $5\frac{7}{12}$. Therefore, making the Garden Gate and the Counter uses as much of the 6 meters of wood as possible.

Part B: $3\frac{1}{3}$ meters of wood In order to solve this part of the problem, you will need to find the difference by subtracting the meters of wood it takes to make the Chalkboard from how much wood Michael actually has: $8\frac{2}{3} - 5\frac{1}{3} = 3\frac{1}{3}$.

22. **Part A: Yes, Aunt Jennifer has enough money to pay for the Easter Egg Hunt with her $20.00.** This part of the question requires you to both add and multiply decimals. First, you should multiply 20 stickers by 0.10 (10 cents each), which comes out to $2.00. Then you can add all the costs together. The total comes out to $19.58.

    Part B: 0.42 (42 cents) For this part of the question, you must take the total cost of all of these items for the Easter Egg Hunt, and subtract it from the $20.00 she paid with to find the amount of change she should get back, which is 0.42 or 42 cents.

23. **17** This task requires you to use the order of operations. The process should be as follows:

    STEP 1 $4 \times 2 = 8$

    STEP 2 $18 - 8 = 10$

    STEP 3 $10 + 5 = 15$

    STEP 4 $15 + 2 = 17$

24. **Part A: $3\frac{1}{8}$ cups of tea** You must first find equivalent fractions to make both denominators the same. 4 is a factor of 8. Therefore, you only need to change $\frac{3}{4}$ to $\frac{6}{8}$. Then you can subtract: $5\frac{7}{8} - 2\frac{6}{8} = 3\frac{1}{8}$. Michael drinks $3\frac{1}{8}$ cups of tea.

    Part B: 9 cups of tea You will need to add $5\frac{7}{8}$ (the number of cups that Julie drank) + $3\frac{1}{8}$ (the number of cups that Michael drank), which equals 9 cups.

25. **(B)** This task is testing translating words into a math expression and your knowledge of the order of operations. Since knowing how many flowers Evie has depends on how many flowers Arjuna has, you must find Arjuna's amount first. This amount, 3 + 4, must be in parentheses so it is done first. Once this is calculated, multiply that amount by 4 to get Evie's amount. If you were to

solve the expression, you would find that Arjuna has 7 flowers and Evie has 28 flowers, which is 4 times as many as Arjuna.

26. **10 inches** First, you would need to convert yards to feet for Michael's height. 3 feet = 1 yard. So, Michael is 6 feet and 2 inches, while Jennifer is 5 feet and 4 inches. Second, you will need to convert the feet into inches. 1 foot = 12 inches. Therefore, Michael's height is 12 × 6 = 72 + 2 = 74 inches. Jennifer's height is 12 × 5 = 60 + 4 = 64 inches. Finally, you will have to subtract 74 − 64 = 10 inches.

27. **Part A: 32 slices** You could use numbers, words, or pictures to illustrate the answer. Using numbers: $4 \div \frac{1}{8} = 32$ slices. Using words: four cakes divided by one-eighths equals thirty-two slices. Using pictures:

= 32 slices

Part B: 24 slices To find out how many of the cut slices were eaten, multiply the total number of slices by $\frac{3}{4}$. $32 \times \frac{3}{4} = 24$ slices.

28. **Part A: 24 binders** Using numbers: 4 × 6 = 24 or 6 + 6 + 6 + 6 = 24. Using words: There are 6 binders in each box. If there are 4 boxes, then I will have to add all the binders, or multiply the number of binders per box (six) by four. Using pictures:

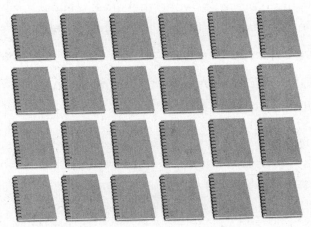

= 24 binders

Part B: 4 more binders To find the answer, subtract the number of binders she purchased (your answer to Part A) from the number of students in her class. 28 − 24 = 4 more binders that are needed.

Part C: 6 more boxes 4 boxes equals 24 binders, and 5 boxes equals 30 binders. In order to buy binders for Mr. Escobar-Ausman's class with 32 students and the additional 4 binders, which added together equals 36 binders total, Ms. Wang will have to buy 6 more boxes on her second trip. She will have exactly the right amount.

29. **(B)** $2\frac{1}{5} \times 3 = \frac{11}{5} \times 3 = \frac{33}{5} = 6.6 = 6\frac{3}{5}$ cups

30. **Yes, Vinod has enough pieces of wood to create his daughter's bookcase.** For the bookcase, Vinod needs 7 pieces of wood that are 4 feet each. 7 × 4 = 28 feet of wood. He has 6 pieces of wood that are 8 feet each, which is 6 × 8 = 48 feet of wood. Vinod has enough wood to create his daughter's bookcase.

31. **You should have selected Yes for $\frac{2}{4}$, Yes for $\frac{5}{6}$, and No for $\frac{9}{8}$.**

    This task is asking you to compare fractions. You will need to find equivalent fractions for some of them to be able to compare and answer correctly.

    $\frac{2}{4} = \frac{4}{8}$. Is $\frac{4}{8} < \frac{7}{8}$? Yes

    $\frac{5}{6} = \frac{40}{48}$, $\frac{7}{8} = \frac{42}{48}$. Is $\frac{40}{48} < \frac{42}{48}$? Yes

    Is $\frac{9}{8} < \frac{7}{8}$? No

32. **(B)** First, you will have to change the mixed numbers to improper fractions. $2\frac{1}{5} = \frac{11}{5}$ and $8\frac{8}{9} = \frac{80}{9}$. Then, multiply across the numerator: $11 \times 80 = 880$. Next, multiply across the denominator: $5 \times 9 = 45$. Therefore, $\frac{11}{5} \times \frac{80}{9} = \frac{880}{45}$. To convert the improper fraction to a mixed number, divide 880 by 45, which equals $19\frac{25}{45}$, which can be simplified to $19\frac{5}{9}$.

33. **You should have selected True for "A scalene triangle has no sides that are equal," False for "A right triangle and an isosceles triangle both always have a right angle," False for "An acute triangle and a right triangle both have a right angle," and False for "An isosceles triangle has no sides that are equal."**

34. **(A)** Make sure to line up the decimals correctly when multiplying. Your multiplication should look like this:

$$
\begin{array}{r}
11 \\
26.42 \\
\times \quad 2.3 \\
\hline
7926 \\
52840 \\
\hline
60.766
\end{array}
$$

35. **(B)** First, change the mixed numbers to improper fractions. $4\frac{1}{8} = \frac{33}{8}$ and $2\frac{1}{6} = \frac{13}{6}$. Since this is a division problem with fractions, you will need to find the reciprocal of $\frac{13}{6}$, which is $\frac{6}{13}$. Next, multiply $\frac{6}{13}$ by $\frac{33}{8}$, which equals $\frac{198}{104}$. Then, divide 198 by 104, which equals $1\frac{94}{104}$. This can be simplified even further, becoming $1\frac{47}{52}$.

Performance Task, pages 285–288

Part A

1. **224 fluid ounces** According to the question, one small cup of tea contains 8 fl oz of tea. Therefore, if the sisters sold 28 cups of the small tea, and each cup holds 8 fl oz, multiply the two amounts together to get your answer: $28 \times 8 = 224$ fluid ounces.

2. **72 medium cups of tea** Based on the table, you can see that, in one day, the sisters sold 36 medium cups of tea. Therefore, if they sold the same amount the

next day, they would have sold 36 + 36 or 36 × 2 = 72 medium cups of tea in 2 days.

3. **1,264 fluid ounces** This problem requires a few steps. First, you need to figure out how many fluid ounces of each size were sold that day. Then, you need to add all the sizes together to get the total number of fluid ounces sold that day.

   STEP 1 28 small cups of tea × 8 fluid ounces per small cup = 224 fluid ounces

   STEP 2 36 medium cups of tea × 12 fluid ounces per medium cup = 432 fluid ounces

   STEP 3 38 large cups of tea × 16 fluid ounces per large cup = 608 fluid ounces

   STEP 4 224 + 432 + 608 = 1,264 fluid ounces sold in that one day

Part B

1. **229.50 cups or $229\frac{1}{2}$ cups sold on Saturday. 178.50 cups or $178\frac{1}{2}$ cups sold on Sunday.** First, add up the total number of cups sold on a weekday: 28 + 36 + 38 = 102 cups sold on a weekday. Next, to find the total number of cups sold on Saturday, multiply 102 by $2\frac{1}{4}$. Note that $2\frac{1}{4}$ can be changed to the improper fraction $\frac{9}{4}$. Therefore 102 × 9 = 918, which divided by 4 equals 229.5 or $229\frac{1}{2}$ cups sold on Saturday. Then, to find the total number of cups sold on Sunday, multiply 102 by $1\frac{3}{4}$. Note that $1\frac{3}{4}$ can be changed to the improper fraction $\frac{7}{4}$. Therefore, 102 × 7 = 714, which divided by 4 equals 178.5 or $178\frac{1}{2}$ cups sold on Sunday.

2. **23 gallons of tea** If they need to buy 10 gallons of tea for one weekday, then, based on the information in the question, they need to buy $2\frac{1}{4}$ times as much for Saturday. Therefore, multiply 10 by $2\frac{1}{4}$. Note that $2\frac{1}{4}$ can be changed to the improper fraction $\frac{9}{4}$. Therefore, 10 × 9 = 90 which divided by 4 equals 22.5 gallons. Remember, the question asked you to round to the nearest gallon. Therefore, the answer is 23 gallons.

3. **Answers will vary.** Refer to the explanation for question 2 in order to see exactly what steps you should have mentioned in your answer.

Smarter Balanced Performance Task Scoring Rubrics

How to Use the Smarter Balanced Performance Task Scoring Rubrics

When the SBAC scores your writing, there are certain skills and elements that they look for. A rubric organizes these elements by level of mastery. Each level of mastery is given a score. It is helpful for you to understand these different levels so you can write with these expectations in mind. Actually, it is encouraged to treat the rubrics as a checklist. When you are done with your writing, check it against each element in the rubric.

There are three different rubrics: Informative Writing, Opinion Writing, and Narrative Writing. The Informative and Opinion rubrics are divided into three areas (Purpose/Organization, Evidence/Elaboration, and Conventions). The Purpose/Organization and Evidence/Elaboration sections range in scores from 1 to 4, with 4 being the highest. The Conventions section ranges from 0 to 2, with 2 being the highest. When you read each section to assess your own writing, pay attention to the progression of adjectives to describe each element of writing. For instance, in the Purpose/Organization section, the element of transitional strategies (i.e., *then*, *furthermore*, *in conclusion*, etc.) progresses from a 1 score with "no" strategies used to a 2 score with an "inconsistent use" of strategies to a 3 score with an "adequate use" of strategies to a 4 score with a "consistent use" of strategies. This pattern is the same for each writing element in the rubrics. Knowing these for each element will help you assess, or score, your own writing.

Each of these areas can have their own score. For example, a student could receive a 4 for Purpose/Organization, but only receive a 2 for Evidence/Elaboration. Let's say the student also receives a score of 1 for Conventions. The total for all three areas is 10. This student, then, scored a 7 out of 10.

Let's look at the specific areas to get a better understanding of SBAC writing expectations.

Purpose/Organization

The Purpose/Organization section of the rubric refers to how well your writing is structured from beginning to end. Does your writing have a clear purpose? Did you include a main idea that is supported throughout the rest of your essay?

You may have a good main idea stated, but if you don't have the appropriate ideas to support it, then the response is not "fully sustained." This simply means that if you state that your essay is about the benefits of owning a dog, then the rest of the essay should only be about that topic.

Evidence/Elaboration

The Evidence/Elaboration section focuses solely on the skill of using evidence to support your ideas and claims. This can refer to direct quotes, indirect paraphrasing, or relating facts to an expert or source.

There are two things that are being examined here: (1) Whether or not the evidence being used is appropriate and relevant. Did you use the right evidence to support your idea? (2) Did you elaborate, or explain, effectively why and how that evidence supported your idea?

Conventions

The Conventions section assesses your command over grammar, punctuation, and spelling. It is a golden rule to always read over your writing after you are done to edit any convention mistakes.

Narrative Rubric

The Narrative rubric is also divided into three areas. The first area, Purpose/Organization, also focuses on the structure of your writing, but, instead of following a main idea to a conclusion, a narrative will follow a developed plot with a "logical sequence of events."

Instead of an Evidence/Elaboration area, the Narrative rubric has a Development/Elaboration area. This area looks for elaboration in your story using sensory details, dialogue, and descriptions that help develop setting, character, and plot.

The Narrative rubric also requires that the Conventions areas be addressed.

Smarter Balanced Performance Task Scoring Rubrics

	4-Point Informative-Explanatory Performance Task Writing Rubric (Grades 3–5)
Score	**Purpose/Organization**
4	The response has a clear and effective organizational structure, creating a sense of unity and completeness. The response is fully sustained, and consistently and purposefully focused: > controlling or main idea of a topic is clearly communicated, and the focus is strongly maintained for the purpose, audience, and task > consistent use of a variety of transitional strategies to clarify the relationships between and among ideas > effective introduction and conclusion > logical progression of ideas from beginning to end; strong connections between and among ideas with some syntactic variety
3	The response has an evident organizational structure and a sense of completeness, though there may be minor flaws and some ideas may be loosely connected. The response is adequately sustained and generally focused: > controlling or main idea of a topic is clear, and the focus is mostly maintained for the purpose, audience, and task > adequate use of transitional strategies with some variety to clarify the relationships between and among ideas > adequate introduction and conclusion > adequate progression of ideas from beginning to end; adequate connections between and among ideas
2	The response has an inconsistent organizational structure, and flaws are evident. The response is somewhat sustained and may have a minor drift in focus: > controlling or main idea of a topic may be somewhat unclear, or the focus may be insufficiently sustained for the purpose, audience, and task > inconsistent use of transitional strategies and/or little variety > introduction or conclusion, if present, may be weak > uneven progression of ideas from beginning to end; and/or formulaic; inconsistent or unclear connections between and among ideas

1	The response has little or no discernible organizational structure. The response may be related to the topic but may provide little or no focus:
	> controlling or main idea may be confusing or ambiguous; response may be too brief or the focus may drift from the purpose, audience, or task
	> few or no transitional strategies are evident
	> introduction and/or conclusion may be missing
	> frequent extraneous ideas may be evident; ideas may be randomly ordered or have an unclear progression
NS	> Unintelligible > In a language other than English > Off-topic > Copied text > Off-purpose

Score	Evidence/Elaboration
4	The response provides thorough and convincing support/evidence for the controlling idea and supporting idea(s) that includes the effective use of sources, facts, and details. The response clearly and effectively elaborates ideas, using precise language: > comprehensive evidence from sources is integrated; references are relevant and specific > effective use of a variety of elaborative techniques* > vocabulary is clearly appropriate for the audience and purpose > effective, appropriate style enhances content
3	The response provides adequate support/evidence for the controlling idea and supporting idea(s) that includes the use of sources, facts, and details. The response adequately elaborates ideas, employing a mix of precise and more general language: > adequate evidence from sources is integrated; some references may be general > adequate use of some elaborative techniques > vocabulary is generally appropriate for the audience and purpose > generally appropriate style is evident

2	The response provides uneven, cursory support/evidence for the controlling idea and supporting idea(s) that includes uneven or limited use of sources, facts, and details. The response elaborates ideas unevenly, using simplistic language: > some evidence from sources may be weakly integrated, imprecise, or repetitive; references may be vague > weak or uneven use of elaborative techniques; development may consist primarily of source summary > vocabulary use is uneven or somewhat ineffective for the audience and purpose > inconsistent or weak attempt to create appropriate style
1	The response provides minimal support/evidence for the controlling idea and supporting idea(s) that includes little or no use of sources, facts, and details. The response is vague, lacks clarity, or is confusing: > evidence from the source material is minimal or irrelevant; references may be absent or incorrectly used > minimal, if any, use of elaborative techniques > vocabulary is limited or ineffective for the audience and purpose > little or no evidence of appropriate style
NS	> Unintelligible > In a language other than English > Off-topic > Copied text > Off-purpose

*Elaborative techniques may include the use of personal experiences that support the controlling idea.

Score	2-Point Informative-Explanatory Performance Task Writing Rubric (Grades 3–5)
	Conventions
2	**The response demonstrates an adequate command of conventions:** > adequate use of correct sentence formation, punctuation, capitalization, grammar usage, and spelling
1	**The response demonstrates a partial command of conventions:** > limited use of correct sentence formation, punctuation, capitalization, grammar usage, and spelling
0	**The response demonstrates little or no command of conventions:** > infrequent use of correct sentence formation, punctuation, capitalization, grammar usage, and spelling
NS	> Unintelligible > In a language other than English > Off-topic > Copied text (Off-purpose responses will still receive a score in Conventions.)

Holistic Scoring:

> **Variety:** A range of errors includes formation, punctuation, capitalization, grammar usage, and spelling.
> **Severity:** Basic errors are more heavily weighted than higher-level errors.
> **Density:** The proportion of errors to the amount of writing done well. This includes the ratio of errors to the length of the piece.

	4-Point Opinion Performance Task Writing Rubric (Grades 3–5)
Score	Purpose/Organization
4	The response has a clear and effective organizational structure, creating a sense of unity and completeness. The response is fully sustained and consistently and purposefully focused: > opinion is introduced, clearly communicated, and the focus is strongly maintained for the purpose, audience, and task > consistent use of a variety of transitional strategies to clarify the relationships between and among ideas > effective introduction and conclusion > logical progression of ideas from beginning to end; strong connections between and among ideas with some syntactic variety
3	The response has an evident organizational structure and a sense of completeness, though there may be minor flaws and some ideas may be loosely connected. The response is adequately sustained and generally focused: > opinion is clear, and the focus is mostly maintained for the purpose, audience, and task > adequate use of transitional strategies with some variety to clarify relationships between and among ideas > adequate introduction and conclusion > adequate progression of ideas from beginning to end; adequate connections between and among ideas
2	The response has an inconsistent organizational structure, and flaws are evident. The response is somewhat sustained and may have a minor drift in focus: > opinion may be somewhat unclear, or the focus may be insufficiently sustained for the purpose, audience, and task > inconsistent use of transitional strategies and/or little variety > introduction or conclusion, if present, may be weak > uneven progression of ideas from beginning to end; and/or formulaic; inconsistent or unclear connections between and among ideas

1	The response has little or no discernible organizational structure. The response may be related to the opinion but may provide little or no focus:
	> opinion may be confusing or ambiguous; response may be too brief or the focus may drift from the purpose, audience, or task
	> few or no transitional strategies are evident
	> introduction and/or conclusion may be missing
	> frequent extraneous ideas may be evident; ideas may be randomly ordered or have an unclear progression
NS	> Unintelligible
	> In a language other than English
	> Off-topic
	> Copied text
	> Off-purpose
Score	**Evidence/Elaboration**
4	The response provides thorough and convincing support/evidence for the opinion and supporting idea(s) that includes the effective use of sources, facts, and details. The response clearly and effectively expresses ideas, using precise language:
	> comprehensive evidence from sources is integrated; references are relevant and specific
	> effective use of a variety of elaborative techniques*
	> vocabulary is clearly appropriate for the audience and purpose
	> effective, appropriate style enhances content
3	The response provides adequate support/evidence for the opinion and supporting idea(s) that includes the use of sources, facts, and details. The response adequately expresses ideas, employing a mix of precise with more general language:
	> adequate evidence from sources is integrated; some references may be general
	> adequate use of some elaborative techniques
	> vocabulary is generally appropriate for the audience and purpose
	> generally appropriate style is evident

2	The response provides uneven, cursory support/evidence for the opinion and supporting idea(s) that includes partial or uneven use of sources, facts, and details. The response expresses ideas unevenly, using simplistic language:
	> some evidence from sources may be weakly integrated, imprecise, or repetitive; references may be vague
	> weak or uneven use of elaborative techniques; development may consist primarily of source summary
	> vocabulary use is uneven or somewhat ineffective for the audience and purpose
	> inconsistent or weak attempt to create appropriate style
1	The response provides minimal support/evidence for the opinion and supporting idea(s) that includes little or no use of sources, facts, and details. The response's expression of ideas is vague, lacks clarity, or is confusing:
	> evidence from the source material is minimal or irrelevant; references may be absent or incorrectly used
	> minimal, if any, use of elaborative techniques
	> vocabulary is limited or ineffective for the audience and purpose
	> little or no evidence of appropriate style
NS	> Unintelligible
	> In a language other than English
	> Off-topic
	> Copied text
	> Off-purpose

*Elaborative techniques may include the use of personal experiences that support the opinion.

	2-Point Opinion Performance Task Writing Rubric (Grades 3–5)
Score	**Conventions**
2	**The response demonstrates an adequate command of conventions:** > adequate use of correct sentence formation, punctuation, capitalization, grammar usage, and spelling
1	**The response demonstrates a partial command of conventions:** > limited use of correct sentence formation, punctuation, capitalization, grammar usage, and spelling
0	**The response demonstrates little or no command of conventions:** > infrequent use of correct sentence formation, punctuation, capitalization, grammar usage, and spelling
NS	> Unintelligible > In a language other than English > Off-topic > Copied text (Off-purpose responses will still receive a score in Conventions.)

Holistic Scoring:
> **Variety:** A range of errors includes formation, punctuation, capitalization, grammar usage, and spelling.
> **Severity:** Basic errors are more heavily weighted than higher-level errors.
> **Density:** The proportion of errors to the amount of writing done well. This includes the ratio of errors to the length of the piece.

	4-Point Narrative Performance Task Writing Rubric (Grades 3–8)
Score	**Purpose/Organization**
4	**The organization of the narrative, real or imagined, is fully sustained and the focus is clear and maintained throughout:** > an effective plot helps to create a sense of unity and completeness > effectively establishes and maintains setting, develops narrator/characters, and maintains point of view* > consistent use of a variety of transitional strategies to clarify the relationships between and among ideas; strong connection between and among ideas > natural, logical sequence of events from beginning to end > effective opening and closure for audience and purpose
3	**The organization of the narrative, real or imagined, is adequately sustained, and the focus is adequate and generally maintained:** > an evident plot helps to create a sense of unity and completeness, though there may be minor flaws and some ideas may be loosely connected > adequately maintains a setting, develops narrator/characters, and/or maintains point of view* > adequate use of a variety of transitional strategies to clarify the relationships between and among ideas > adequate sequence of events from beginning to end > adequate opening and closure for audience and purpose
2	**The organization of the narrative, real or imagined, is somewhat sustained and may have an uneven focus:** > there may be an inconsistent plot, and/or flaws may be evident > unevenly or minimally maintains a setting, develops narrator and/or characters, and/or maintains point of view* > uneven use of appropriate transitional strategies and/or little variety > weak or uneven sequence of events > opening and closure, if present, are weak

1	The organization of the narrative, real or imagined, may be maintained but may provide little or no focus:
	> there is little or no discernible plot or there may just be a series of events
	> may be brief or there is little to no attempt to establish a setting, narrator and/or characters, and/or point of view*
	> few or no appropriate transitional strategies may be evident
	> little or no organization of an event sequence; frequent extraneous ideas and/or a major drift may be evident
	> opening and/or closure may be missing
NS	> Unintelligible
	> In a language other than English
	> Off-topic
	> Copied text
	> Off-purpose
Score	**Development/Elaboration**
4	The narrative, real or imagined, provides thorough, effective elaboration using relevant details, dialogue, and description:
	> experiences, characters, setting, and events are clearly developed
	> connections to source materials may enhance the narrative
	> effective use of a variety of narrative techniques that advance the story or illustrate the experience
	> effective use of sensory, concrete, and figurative language that clearly advances the purpose
	> effective, appropriate style enhances the narration
3	The narrative, real or imagined, provides adequate elaboration using details, dialogue, and description:
	> experiences, characters, setting, and events are adequately developed
	> connections to source materials may contribute to the narrative
	> adequate use of a variety of narrative techniques that generally advance the story or illustrate the experience
	> adequate use of sensory, concrete, and figurative language that generally advances the purpose
	> generally appropriate style is evident

2	The narrative, real or imagined, provides uneven, cursory elaboration using partial and uneven details, dialogue, and description: > experiences, characters, setting, and events are unevenly developed > connections to source materials may be ineffective, awkward or vague but do not interfere with the narrative > narrative techniques are uneven and inconsistent > partial or weak use of sensory, concrete, and figurative language that may not advance the purpose > inconsistent or weak attempt to create appropriate style
1	The narrative, real or imagined, provides minimal elaboration using few or no details, dialogue, and/or description: > experiences, characters, setting, and events may be vague, lack clarity, or confusing > connections to source materials, if evident, may detract from the narrative > use of narrative techniques may be minimal, absent, incorrect, or irrelevant > may have little or no use of sensory, concrete, or figurative language; language does not advance and may interfere with the purpose > little or no evidence of appropriate style
NS	> Unintelligible > In a language other than English > Off-topic > Copied text > Off-purpose

*Point of view begins at grade 7.

	2-Point Narrative Performance Task Writing Rubric (Grades 3–11)
Score	**Conventions**
2	**The response demonstrates an adequate command of conventions:** > adequate use of correct sentence formation, punctuation, capitalization, grammar usage, and spelling
1	**The response demonstrates a partial command of conventions:** > limited use of correct sentence formation, punctuation, capitalization, grammar usage, and spelling
0	**The response demonstrates little or no command of conventions:** > infrequent use of correct sentence formation, punctuation, capitalization, grammar usage, and spelling
NS	> Unintelligible > In a language other than English > Off-topic > Copied text (Off-purpose responses will still receive a score in Conventions.)

Holistic Scoring:
> **Variety:** A range of errors includes formation, punctuation, capitalization, grammar usage, and spelling.
> **Severity:** Basic errors are more heavily weighted than higher-level errors.
> **Density:** The proportion of errors to the amount of writing done well. This includes the ratio of errors to the length of the piece.

Common Core Standards

English Language Arts Standards

Reading: Literature
Key Ideas and Details
CCSS.ELA-LITERACY.RL.5.1 Quote accurately from a text when explaining what the text says explicitly and when drawing inferences from the text.
CCSS.ELA-LITERACY.RL.5.2 Determine a theme of a story, drama, or poem from details in the text, including how characters in a story or drama respond to challenges or how the speaker in a poem reflects upon a topic; summarize the text.
CCSS.ELA-LITERACY.RL.5.3 Compare and contrast two or more characters, settings, or events in a story or drama, drawing on specific details in the text (e.g., how characters interact).
Craft and Structure
CCSS.ELA-LITERACY.RL.5.4 Determine the meaning of words and phrases as they are used in a text, including figurative language such as metaphors and similes.
CCSS.ELA-LITERACY.RL.5.5 Explain how a series of chapters, scenes, or stanzas fits together to provide the overall structure of a particular story, drama, or poem.
CCSS.ELA-LITERACY.RL.5.6 Describe how a narrator's or speaker's point of view influences how events are described.

Integration of Knowledge and Ideas

CCSS.ELA-LITERACY.RL.5.7 Analyze how visual and multimedia elements contribute to the meaning, tone, or beauty of a text (e.g., graphic novel, multimedia presentation of fiction, folktale, myth, poem).

CCSS.ELA-LITERACY.RL.5.8 (RL.5.8 not applicable to literature)

CCSS.ELA-LITERACY.RL.5.9 Compare and contrast stories in the same genre (e.g., mysteries and adventure stories) on their approaches to similar themes and topics.

Range of Reading and Level of Text Complexity

CCSS.ELA-LITERACY.RL.5.10 By the end of the year, read and comprehend literature, including stories, dramas, and poetry, at the high end of the grades 4–5 text complexity band independently and proficiently.

Reading: Informational Text

Key Ideas and Details

CCSS.ELA-LITERACY.RI.5.1 Quote accurately from a text when explaining what the text says explicitly and when drawing inferences from the text.

CCSS.ELA-LITERACY.RI.5.2 Determine two or more main ideas of a text and explain how they are supported by key details; summarize the text.

CCSS.ELA-LITERACY.RI.5.3 Explain the relationships or interactions between two or more individuals, events, ideas, or concepts in a historical, scientific, or technical text based on specific information in the text.

Craft and Structure

CCSS.ELA-LITERACY.RI.5.4 Determine the meaning of general academic and domain-specific words and phrases in a text relevant to a *grade 5 topic or subject area*.

CCSS.ELA-LITERACY.RI.5.5 Compare and contrast the overall structure (e.g., chronology, comparison, cause/effect, problem/solution) of events, ideas, concepts, or information in two or more texts.

CCSS.ELA-LITERACY.RI.5.6 Analyze multiple accounts of the same event or topic, noting important similarities and differences in the point of view they represent.

Integration of Knowledge and Ideas

CCSS.ELA-LITERACY.RI.5.7 Draw on information from multiple print or digital sources, demonstrating the ability to locate an answer to a question quickly or to solve a problem efficiently.

CCSS.ELA-LITERACY.RI.5.8 Explain how an author uses reasons and evidence to support particular points in a text, identifying which reasons and evidence support which point(s).

CCSS.ELA-LITERACY.RI.5.9 Integrate information from several texts on the same topic in order to write or speak about the subject knowledgeably.

Range of Reading and Level of Text Complexity

CCSS.ELA-LITERACY.RI.5.10 By the end of the year, read and comprehend informational texts, including history/social studies, science, and technical texts, at the high end of the grades 4–5 text complexity band independently and proficiently.

Reading: Foundational Skills

Phonics and Word Recognition

CCSS.ELA-LITERACY.RF.5.3 Know and apply grade-level phonics and word analysis skills in decoding words.

CCSS.ELA-LITERACY.RF.5.3.A

Use combined knowledge of all letter-sound correspondences, syllabication patterns, and morphology (e.g., roots and affixes) to read accurately unfamiliar multisyllabic words in context and out of context.

Fluency

CCSS.ELA-LITERACY.RF.5.4 Read with sufficient accuracy and fluency to support comprehension.

CCSS.ELA-LITERACY.RF.5.4.A

Read grade-level text with purpose and understanding.

CCSS.ELA-LITERACY.RF.5.4.B

Read grade-level prose and poetry orally with accuracy, appropriate rate, and expression on successive readings.

CCSS.ELA-LITERACY.RF.5.4.C

Use context to confirm or self-correct word recognition and understanding, rereading as necessary.

Writing

Text Types and Purposes

CCSS.ELA-LITERACY.W.5.1 Write opinion pieces on topics or texts, supporting a point of view with reasons and information.

CCSS.ELA-LITERACY.W.5.1.A

Introduce a topic or text clearly, state an opinion, and create an organizational structure in which ideas are logically grouped to support the writer's purpose.

CCSS.ELA-LITERACY.W.5.1.B

Provide logically ordered reasons that are supported by facts and details.

CCSS.ELA-LITERACY.W.5.1.C

Link opinion and reasons using words, phrases, and clauses (e.g., *consequently*, *specifically*).

CCSS.ELA-LITERACY.W.5.1.D

Provide a concluding statement or section related to the opinion presented.

CCSS.ELA-LITERACY.W.5.2 Write informative/explanatory texts to examine a topic and convey ideas and information clearly.

CCSS.ELA-LITERACY.W.5.2.A

Introduce a topic clearly, provide a general observation and focus, and group related information logically; include formatting (e.g., headings), illustrations, and multimedia when useful to aiding comprehension.

CCSS.ELA-LITERACY.W.5.2.B

Develop the topic with facts, definitions, concrete details, quotations, or other information and examples related to the topic.

CCSS.ELA-LITERACY.W.5.2.C

Link ideas within and across categories of information using words, phrases, and clauses (e.g., *in contrast*, *especially*).

CCSS.ELA-LITERACY.W.5.2.D

Use precise language and domain-specific vocabulary to inform about or explain the topic.

CCSS.ELA-LITERACY.W.5.2.E

Provide a concluding statement or section related to the information or explanation presented.

CCSS.ELA-LITERACY.W.5.3 Write narratives to develop real or imagined experiences or events using effective technique, descriptive details, and clear event sequences.

> **CCSS.ELA-LITERACY.W.5.3.A**
>
> Orient the reader by establishing a situation and introducing a narrator and/or characters; organize an event sequence that unfolds naturally.
>
> **CCSS.ELA-LITERACY.W.5.3.B**
>
> Use narrative techniques, such as dialogue, description, and pacing, to develop experiences and events or show the responses of characters to situations.
>
> **CCSS.ELA-LITERACY.W.5.3.C**
>
> Use a variety of transitional words, phrases, and clauses to manage the sequence of events.
>
> **CCSS.ELA-LITERACY.W.5.3.D**
>
> Use concrete words and phrases and sensory details to convey experiences and events precisely.
>
> **CCSS.ELA-LITERACY.W.5.3.E**
>
> Provide a conclusion that follows from the narrated experiences or events.

Production and Distribution of Writing

CCSS.ELA-LITERACY.W.5.4 Produce clear and coherent writing in which the development and organization are appropriate to task, purpose, and audience. (Grade-specific expectations for writing types are defined in standards 1–3 above.)

CCSS.ELA-LITERACY.W.5.5 With guidance and support from peers and adults, develop and strengthen writing as needed by planning, revising, editing, rewriting, or trying a new approach. (Editing for conventions should demonstrate command of Language standards 1–3, up to and including grade 5.)

CCSS.ELA-LITERACY.W.5.6 With some guidance and support from adults, use technology, including the Internet, to produce and publish writing as well as to interact and collaborate with others; demonstrate sufficient command of keyboarding skills to type a minimum of two pages in a single sitting.

Research to Build and Present Knowledge

CCSS.ELA-LITERACY.W.5.7 Conduct short research projects that use several sources to build knowledge through investigation of different aspects of a topic.

CCSS.ELA-LITERACY.W.5.8 Recall relevant information from experiences or gather relevant information from print and digital sources; summarize or paraphrase information in notes and finished work, and provide a list of sources.

CCSS.ELA-LITERACY.W.5.9 Draw evidence from literary or informational texts to support analysis, reflection, and research.

CCSS.ELA-LITERACY.W.5.9.A

Apply *grade 5 Reading standards* to literature (e.g., "Compare and contrast two or more characters, settings, or events in a story or a drama, drawing on specific details in the text [e.g., how characters interact]").

CCSS.ELA-LITERACY.W.5.9.B

Apply *grade 5 Reading standards* to informational texts (e.g., "Explain how an author uses reasons and evidence to support particular points in a text, identifying which reasons and evidence support which point[s]").

Range of Writing

CCSS.ELA-LITERACY.W.5.10 Write routinely over extended time frames (time for research, reflection, and revision) and shorter time frames (a single sitting or a day or two) for a range of discipline-specific tasks, purposes, and audiences.

Speaking & Listening

Comprehension and Collaboration

CCSS.ELA-LITERACY.SL.5.1 Engage effectively in a range of collaborative discussions (one-on-one, in groups, and teacher-led) with diverse partners on *grade 5 topics and texts*, building on others' ideas and expressing their own clearly.

CCSS.ELA-LITERACY.SL.5.1.A

Come to discussions prepared, having read or studied required material; explicitly draw on that preparation and other information known about the topic to explore ideas under discussion.

CCSS.ELA-LITERACY.SL.5.1.B

Follow agreed-upon rules for discussions and carry out assigned roles.

CCSS.ELA-LITERACY.SL.5.1.C

Pose and respond to specific questions by making comments that contribute to the discussion and elaborate on the remarks of others.

CCSS.ELA-LITERACY.SL.5.1.D

Review the key ideas expressed and draw conclusions in light of information and knowledge gained from the discussions.

CCSS.ELA-LITERACY.SL.5.2 Summarize a written text read aloud or information presented in diverse media and formats, including visually, quantitatively, and orally.

CCSS.ELA-LITERACY.SL.5.3 Summarize the points a speaker makes and explain how each claim is supported by reasons and evidence.

Presentation of Knowledge and Ideas

CCSS.ELA-LITERACY.SL.5.4 Report on a topic or text or present an opinion, sequencing ideas logically and using appropriate facts and relevant, descriptive details to support main ideas or themes; speak clearly at an understandable pace.

CCSS.ELA-LITERACY.SL.5.5 Include multimedia components (e.g., graphics, sound) and visual displays in presentations when appropriate to enhance the development of main ideas or themes.

CCSS.ELA-LITERACY.SL.5.6 Adapt speech to a variety of contexts and tasks, using formal English when appropriate to task and situation. (See grade 5 Language standards 1 and 3 for specific expectations.)

Language

Conventions of Standard English

CCSS.ELA-LITERACY.L.5.1 Demonstrate command of the conventions of standard English grammar and usage when writing or speaking.

CCSS.ELA-LITERACY.L.5.1.A

Explain the function of conjunctions, prepositions, and interjections in general and their function in particular sentences.

CCSS.ELA-LITERACY.L.5.1.B

Form and use the perfect (e.g., *I had walked; I have walked; I will have walked*) verb tenses.

CCSS.ELA-LITERACY.L.5.1.C

Use verb tense to convey various times, sequences, states, and conditions.

CCSS.ELA-LITERACY.L.5.1.D

Recognize and correct inappropriate shifts in verb tense.

CCSS.ELA-LITERACY.L.5.1.E

Use correlative conjunctions (e.g., *either/or, neither/nor*).

CCSS.ELA-LITERACY.L.5.2 Demonstrate command of the conventions of standard English capitalization, punctuation, and spelling when writing.

CCSS.ELA-LITERACY.L.5.2.A

Use punctuation to separate items in a series.

CCSS.ELA-LITERACY.L.5.2.B

Use a comma to separate an introductory element from the rest of the sentence.

CCSS.ELA-LITERACY.L.5.2.C

Use a comma to set off the words *yes* and *no* (e.g., *Yes, thank you*), to set off a tag question from the rest of the sentence (e.g., *It's true, isn't it?*), and to indicate direct address (e.g., *Is that you, Steve?*).

CCSS.ELA-LITERACY.L.5.2.D

Use underlining, quotation marks, or italics to indicate titles of works.

CCSS.ELA-LITERACY.L.5.2.E

Spell grade-appropriate words correctly, consulting references as needed.

Knowledge of Language

CCSS.ELA-LITERACY.L.5.3 Use knowledge of language and its conventions when writing, speaking, reading, or listening.

CCSS.ELA-LITERACY.L.5.3.A

Expand, combine, and reduce sentences for meaning, reader/listener interest, and style.

CCSS.ELA-LITERACY.L.5.3.B

Compare and contrast the varieties of English (e.g., *dialects, registers*) used in stories, dramas, or poems.

Vocabulary Acquisition and Use

CCSS.ELA-LITERACY.L.5.4 Determine or clarify the meaning of unknown and multiple-meaning words and phrases based on grade 5 reading and content, choosing flexibly from a range of strategies.

CCSS.ELA-LITERACY.L.5.4.A

Use context (e.g., cause/effect relationships and comparisons in text) as a clue to the meaning of a word or phrase.

CCSS.ELA-LITERACY.L.5.4.B

Use common, grade-appropriate Greek and Latin affixes and roots as clues to the meaning of a word (e.g., *photograph, photosynthesis*).

CCSS.ELA-LITERACY.L.5.4.C

Consult reference materials (e.g., dictionaries, glossaries, thesauruses), both print and digital, to find the pronunciation and determine or clarify the precise meaning of key words and phrases.

CCSS.ELA-LITERACY.L.5.5 Demonstrate understanding of figurative language, word relationships, and nuances in word meanings.

CCSS.ELA-LITERACY.L.5.5.A

Interpret figurative language, including similes and metaphors, in context.

CCSS.ELA-LITERACY.L.5.5.B

Recognize and explain the meaning of common idioms, adages, and proverbs.

CCSS.ELA-LITERACY.L.5.5.C

Use the relationship between particular words (e.g., synonyms, antonyms, homographs) to better understand each of the words.

CCSS.ELA-LITERACY.L.5.6 Acquire and use accurately grade-appropriate general academic and domain-specific words and phrases, including those that signal contrast, addition, and other logical relationships (e.g., *however, although, nevertheless, similarly, moreover, in addition*).

Math Standards

Operations and Algebraic Thinking

Write and Interpret Numerical Expressions

CCSS.MATH.CONTENT.5.OA.A.1 Use parentheses, brackets, or braces in numerical expressions, and evaluate expressions with these symbols.

CCSS.MATH.CONTENT.5.OA.A.2 Write simple expressions that record calculations with numbers, and interpret numerical expressions without evaluating them. *For example, express the calculation "add 8 and 7, then multiply by 2" as 2 × (8 + 7). Recognize that 3 × (18932 + 921) is three times as large as 18932 + 921, without having to calculate the indicated sum or product.*

Analyze Patterns and Relationships

CCSS.MATH.CONTENT.5.OA.B.3 Generate two numerical patterns using two given rules. Identify apparent relationships between corresponding terms. Form ordered pairs consisting of corresponding terms from the two patterns, and graph the ordered pairs on a coordinate plane. *For example, given the rule "Add 3" and the starting number 0, and given the rule "Add 6" and the starting number 0, generate terms in the resulting sequences, and observe that the terms in one sequence are twice the corresponding terms in the other sequence. Explain informally why this is so.*

Number and Operations in Base Ten

Understand the Place Value System

CCSS.MATH.CONTENT.5.NBT.A.1 Recognize that in a multi-digit number, a digit in one place represents 10 times as much as it represents in the place to its right and 1/10 of what it represents in the place to its left.

CCSS.MATH.CONTENT.5.NBT.A.2 Explain patterns in the number of zeros of the product when multiplying a number by powers of 10, and explain patterns in the placement of the decimal point when a decimal is multiplied or divided by a power of 10. Use whole-number exponents to denote powers of 10.

CCSS.MATH.CONTENT.5.NBT.A.3 Read, write, and compare decimals to thousandths.

CCSS.MATH.CONTENT.5.NBT.A.3.A
Read and write decimals to thousandths using base-ten numerals, number names, and expanded form, e.g., $347.392 = 3 × 100 + 4 × 10 + 7 × 1 + 3 × (1/10) + 9 × (1/100) + 2 × (1/1000)$.

CCSS.MATH.CONTENT.5.NBT.A.3.B
Compare two decimals to thousandths based on meanings of the digits in each place, using >, =, and < symbols to record the results of comparisons.

CCSS.MATH.CONTENT.5.NBT.A.4 Use place value understanding to round decimals to any place.

Perform Operations with Multi-digit Whole Numbers and with Decimals to Hundredths

CCSS.MATH.CONTENT.5.NBT.B.5 Fluently multiply multi-digit whole numbers using the standard algorithm.

CCSS.MATH.CONTENT.5.NBT.B.6 Find whole-number quotients of whole numbers with up to four-digit dividends and two-digit divisors, using strategies based on place value, the properties of operations, and/or the relationship between multiplication and division. Illustrate and explain the calculation by using equations, rectangular arrays, and/or area models.

CCSS.MATH.CONTENT.5.NBT.B.7 Add, subtract, multiply, and divide decimals to hundredths, using concrete models or drawings and strategies based on place value, properties of operations, and/or the relationship between addition and subtraction; relate the strategy to a written method and explain the reasoning used.

Number and Operations—Fractions

Use Equivalent Fractions as a Strategy to Add and Subtract Fractions

CCSS.MATH.CONTENT.5.NF.A.1 Add and subtract fractions with unlike denominators (including mixed numbers) by replacing given fractions with equivalent fractions in such a way as to produce an equivalent sum or difference of fractions with like denominators. *For example, 2/3 + 5/4 = 8/12 + 15/12 = 23/12. (In general, a/b + c/d = (ad + bc)/bd.)*

CCSS.MATH.CONTENT.5.NF.A.2 Solve word problems involving addition and subtraction of fractions referring to the same whole, including cases of unlike denominators, e.g., by using visual fraction models or equations to represent the problem. Use benchmark fractions and number sense of fractions to estimate mentally and assess the reasonableness of answers. *For example, recognize an incorrect result 2/5 + 1/2 = 3/7, by observing that 3/7 < 1/2.*

Apply and Extend Previous Understandings of Multiplication and Division

CCSS.MATH.CONTENT.5.NF.B.3 Interpret a fraction as division of the numerator by the denominator ($a/b = a \div b$). Solve word problems involving division of whole numbers leading to answers in the form of fractions or mixed numbers, e.g., by using visual fraction models or equations to represent the problem. *For example, interpret 3/4 as the result of dividing 3 by 4, noting that 3/4 multiplied by 4 equals 3, and that when 3 wholes are shared equally among 4 people each person has a share of size 3/4. If 9 people want to share a 50-pound sack of rice equally by weight, how many pounds of rice should each person get? Between what two whole numbers does your answer lie?*

CCSS.MATH.CONTENT.5.NF.B.4 Apply and extend previous understandings of multiplication to multiply a fraction or whole number by a fraction.

CCSS.MATH.CONTENT.5.NF.B.4.A

Interpret the product (a/b) × q as a parts of a partition of q into b equal parts; equivalently, as the result of a sequence of operations $a \times q \div b$. *For example, use a visual fraction model to show (2/3) × 4 = 8/3, and create a story context for this equation. Do the same with (2/3) × (4/5) = 8/15. (In general, (a/b) × (c/d) = ac/bd.)*

CCSS.MATH.CONTENT.5.NF.B.4.B

Find the area of a rectangle with fractional side lengths by tiling it with unit squares of the appropriate unit fraction side lengths, and show that the area is the same as would be found by multiplying the side lengths. Multiply fractional side lengths to find areas of rectangles, and represent fraction products as rectangular areas.

CCSS.MATH.CONTENT.5.NF.B.5 Interpret multiplication as scaling (resizing), by:

CCSS.MATH.CONTENT.5.NF.B.5.A

Comparing the size of a product to the size of one factor on the basis of the size of the other factor, without performing the indicated multiplication.

CCSS.MATH.CONTENT.5.NF.B.5.B

Explaining why multiplying a given number by a fraction greater than 1 results in a product greater than the given number (recognizing multiplication by whole numbers greater than 1 as a familiar case); explaining why multiplying a given number by a fraction less than 1 results in a product smaller than the given number; and relating the principle of fraction equivalence $a/b = (n \times a)/(n \times b)$ to the effect of multiplying a/b by 1.

CCSS.MATH.CONTENT.5.NF.B.6 Solve real-world problems involving multiplication of fractions and mixed numbers, e.g., by using visual fraction models or equations to represent the problem.

CCSS.MATH.CONTENT.5.NF.B.7 Apply and extend previous understandings of division to divide unit fractions by whole numbers and whole numbers by unit fractions.[1]

[1]Students able to multiply fractions in general can develop strategies to divide fractions in general, by reasoning about the relationship between multiplication and division. But division of a fraction by a fraction is not a requirement at this grade.

CCSS.MATH.CONTENT.5.NF.B.7.A

Interpret division of a unit fraction by a non-zero whole number, and compute such quotients. *For example, create a story context for (1/3) ÷ 4, and use a visual fraction model to show the quotient. Use the relationship between multiplication and division to explain that (1/3) ÷ 4 = 1/12 because (1/12) × 4 = 1/3.*

CCSS.MATH.CONTENT.5.NF.B.7.B

Interpret division of a whole number by a unit fraction, and compute such quotients. *For example, create a story context for 4 ÷ (1/5), and use a visual fraction model to show the quotient. Use the relationship between multiplication and division to explain that 4 ÷ (1/5) = 20 because 20 × (1/5) = 4.*

CCSS.MATH.CONTENT.5.NF.B.7.C

Solve real-world problems involving division of unit fractions by non-zero whole numbers and division of whole numbers by unit fractions, e.g., by using visual fraction models and equations to represent the problem. *For example, how much chocolate will each person get if 3 people share 1/2 lb of chocolate equally? How many 1/3-cup servings are in 2 cups of raisins?*

Measurement and Data

Convert Like Measurement Units within a Given Measurement System

CCSS.MATH.CONTENT.5.MD.A.1 Convert among different-sized standard measurement units within a given measurement system (e.g., convert 5 cm to 0.05 m), and use these conversions in solving multi-step, real-world problems.

Represent and Interpret Data

CCSS.MATH.CONTENT.5.MD.B.2 Make a line plot to display a data set of measurements in fractions of a unit (1/2, 1/4, 1/8). Use operations on fractions for this grade to solve problems involving information presented in line plots. *For example, given different measurements of liquid in identical beakers, find the amount of liquid each beaker would contain if the total amount in all the beakers were redistributed equally.*

Geometric Measurement: Understand Concepts of Volume

CCSS.MATH.CONTENT.5.MD.C.3 Recognize volume as an attribute of solid figures and understand concepts of volume measurement.

CCSS.MATH.CONTENT.5.MD.C.3.A
A cube with side length 1 unit, called a "unit cube," is said to have "one cubic unit" of volume, and can be used to measure volume.

CCSS.MATH.CONTENT.5.MD.C.3.B
A solid figure which can be packed without gaps or overlaps using n unit cubes is said to have a volume of n cubic units.

CCSS.MATH.CONTENT.5.MD.C.4 Measure volumes by counting unit cubes, using cubic cm, cubic in, cubic ft, and improvised units.

CCSS.MATH.CONTENT.5.MD.C.5 Relate volume to the operations of multiplication and addition and solve real-world and mathematical problems involving volume.

CCSS.MATH.CONTENT.5.MD.C.5.A
Find the volume of a right rectangular prism with whole-number side lengths by packing it with unit cubes, and show that the volume is the same as would be found by multiplying the edge lengths, equivalently by multiplying the height by the area of the base. Represent threefold whole-number products as volumes, e.g., to represent the associative property of multiplication.

CCSS.MATH.CONTENT.5.MD.C.5.B
Apply the formulas $V = l \times w \times h$ and $V = b \times h$ for rectangular prisms to find volumes of right rectangular prisms with whole-number edge lengths in the context of solving real-world and mathematical problems.

CCSS.MATH.CONTENT.5.MD.C.5.C
Recognize volume as additive. Find volumes of solid figures composed of two non-overlapping right rectangular prisms by adding the volumes of the non-overlapping parts, applying this technique to solve real-world problems.

Geometry

Graph Points on the Coordinate Plane to Solve Real-World and Mathematical Problems

CCSS.MATH.CONTENT.5.G.A.1 Use a pair of perpendicular number lines, called axes, to define a coordinate system, with the intersection of the lines (the origin) arranged to coincide with the 0 on each line and a given point in the plane located by using an ordered pair of numbers, called its coordinates. Understand that the first number indicates how far to travel from the origin in the direction of one axis, and the second number indicates how far to travel in the direction of the second axis, with the convention that the names of the two axes and the coordinates correspond (e.g., x-axis and x-coordinate, y-axis and y-coordinate).

CCSS.MATH.CONTENT.5.G.A.2 Represent real-world and mathematical problems by graphing points in the first quadrant of the coordinate plane, and interpret coordinate values of points in the context of the situation.

Classify Two-Dimensional Figures into Categories Based on Their Properties

CCSS.MATH.CONTENT.5.G.B.3 Understand that attributes belonging to a category of two-dimensional figures also belong to all subcategories of that category. For example, all rectangles have four right angles and squares are rectangles, so all squares have four right angles.

CCSS.MATH.CONTENT.5.G.B.4 Classify two-dimensional figures in a hierarchy based on properties.

Index